Managing **People** in the
New Economy

Managing **People** in the **New Economy**

Targeted HR Practices that Persuade People to Unlock their Knowledge Power

Mohan Thite

Response Books
A division of Sage Publications
New Delhi ◆ Thousand Oaks ◆ London

First published in 2004 by

Response Books
A division of Sage Publications India Pvt Ltd
B–42, Panchsheel Enclave
New Delhi – 110 017

Sage Publications Inc	**Sage Publications Ltd**
2455 Teller Road	1 Oliver's Yard
Thousand Oaks	55 City Road
California 91320	London EC1Y 1SP

Published by Tejeshwar Singh for Response Books, typeset in 10.5 pt. Palatino by InoSoft Systems and printed at Chaman Enterprises, New Delhi.

Library of Congress Cataloging-in-Publication Data

Thite, Mohan.
    Managing people in the new economy: targeted HR practices that persuade people to unlock their knowledge power / Mohan Thite.
      p. cm.
    Includes bibliographical references and index.
    1. Knowledge management. 2. Personnel management. I. Title.

HD30.2.T493   658.4'038—dc22   2004   2003020113

ISBN: 0–7619–9836–5 (US-PB)   81–7829–329–3 (INDIA-PB)

Production Team: Roshni Basu, R.A.M. Brown, Shyama Warner and Santosh Rawat

To
my parents
Suman and Ranganath Thite

Contents

Preface

People management is central to the thinking and practice of management today. Gone are the days when management paid only lip service to the importance of people and employed ad hoc ways to manage them. While human relations have always been and will always be largely governed by the basic philosophy of trust and fairness, the application and operationalization of Human Resource Management (HRM) principles and practices need to be more relevant to the emerging knowledge economy.

For example, recruitment practices need to incorporate global and multi-cultural perspectives and performance management needs to be embedded in the changing nature of work. Similarly, reward management needs to be viewed in a team context and career management needs to focus more explicitly on the changing employment profile and psychological contracts. Finally, all the HR practice areas need to revolve around the creation, sharing and utilization of knowledge, which is central to a sustainable competitive advantage. Thus, when knowledge management becomes the core of organizational strategy, the significance, structure and process of HRM are radically transformed.

While many current textbooks on HRM do refer to these aspects, they still subscribe to traditional concepts and theories that have questionable relevance to the global, knowledge-based economy and the changing world of work. They also tend to prescribe universal solutions which often overlook cultural, organizational and demographic diversity and the changing employment profile that characterize the core, contract and casual employees.

Thus, the focus of this book is to strategically link the practice of HRM to knowledge management in a global environment. It attempts to fill the void left by the knowledge management body of literature which has undervalued HR issues and the HR body of literature which has under-emphasized knowledge economy. Today, HR is every manager's responsibility. This book addresses the broad HR issues and challenges in the 21st-century economy. The purpose of this book is to assist managers in any functional area, be it finance, marketing, information technology or manufacturing, to understand why and how HRM plays a key role in managing knowledge and competition.

There are no universally applicable HR principles and practices as HRM is highly localized and even within the same country or organization, people are different and motivated for different reasons. While commonalities could be found in the occupational characteristics of knowledge workers, no set of standard solutions could be offered as universally applicable. The rapid pace of globalization of markets is compelling management researchers to explore solutions to economic problems with universal applicability. However, despite global production, global markets and global communications, the 'global culture' is still an elusive concept. Therefore, the ideas and concepts discussed in this book need to be examined in one's own context.

There are no 'radically new' ideas in this book. It merely brings together those HR concepts and practices that are more relevant to the knowledge economy. Most of these concepts have been around for a long time, even though some have now acquired new names. One may argue that most of the concepts discussed here are already present in the best practice HRM and organizational learning literature. The objective of this book is to simply reinforce the relevance of those concepts to the knowledge economy and deepen the commitment to their practice. Even where such practices exist, they may still require some modification. For example, best practice HRM literature does not often sit comfortably with management ethics as it is mainly business-case driven. But ethical management practice is a prerequisite to knowledge management as discussed in chapter 3.

This book is the result of a combination of influences: the author's experience as an HR professional, academic and consultant in a multi-industry, multinational and multi-cultural environment; interviews with various business leaders and HR professionals over the years; deliberations in international conferences; and a review of the contemporary best practices in HRM and knowledge management in high-performing learning organizations. It is a compilation of a set of HR practices that hold promise to be of relevance to successful management of people in the knowledge economy. It attempts to add value to the literature on knowledge management by keeping people and their employment-related issues at the centre, something that the author believes has not been sufficiently addressed despite the obvious importance of people in the knowledge economy.

Organization of the Book

The book begins with a brief introduction of knowledge economy and management. It explores the complexities in defining and measuring knowledge, knowledge work and knowledge worker and the challenges in tapping the tacit knowledge.

Chapter 2 explores the strategic linkage between HRM and knowledge management. It deals with the danger of over-emphasizing information technologies in harnessing knowledge at the cost of people issues, the chequered history of HRM as a profession, the increasing strategic focus of HRM concepts and practices and the difficulties in measuring HRM effectiveness. It also identifies some of the macro HR issues and trends in the knowledge economy and the characteristics of knowledge workers.

Chapter 3 emphasizes the importance of building a trustworthy and sound management philosophy in creating a people-centric culture to be able to unlock knowledge power. It describes how trust and fairness have been a casualty of endless reengineering exercises, alienating management from employees. It identifies key elements of ethical people management philosophy to restore the balance.

Chapter 4 is devoted to understanding the design, philosophy and characteristics of learning organizations that aim to deploy 'learning to learn' as a key competitive weapon in leveraging intellectual capital. It describes how a free flow of thinking and action stimulates innovation and creativity. It cautions that risks are inherent in such an endeavour, and unless managers take those risks, defensive postures will hinder the learning process and adoption of best practices. It explores how to encourage people to share their knowledge instead of hoarding it; how to help employees learn on the job through mentoring and job rotation and how measures, such as a corporate university, can assist in institutionalizing learning to learn competency.

Chapter 5 deals with how to attract scarce talent in a competitive marketplace. It underscores the importance of holistic competencies in performing beyond expectations and the methods to identify them in potential employees. It also describes how to design recruitment strategies to suit the changing complexion of employment profile and maintain high standards in people outside of traditional employment boundaries.

Chapter 6 covers retention issues that encompass a wide gamut of the employment relationship. It highlights the critical role of frontline managers in influencing morale and the need to nurture the community aspect of employment as glue for retention.

Chapter 7 explores why performance appraisal is much disliked and what can be done to improve its acceptance. It identifies perception of fairness, minimizing the fallout of negative emotions, management by coaching, inclusiveness and multisource feedback as some of the key success factors in improving the effectiveness of performance management.

Chapter 8 describes the evolution of New Pay concepts and the ways to embed recognition measures that cost little but go to the heart of employee motivation.

Chapter 9 is devoted to cross-cultural and international aspects of managing people and the ways to balance the conflicting demand of convergence and divergence in HR practices.

Finally, Chapter 10 brings together the key themes of the preceding chapters and provides a roadmap that can help people managers successfully cope with the inherent paradoxes and conflicts in HRM concepts and practices.

Throughout the book, ideas and practices conducive to a learning environment are identified and explored. Each chapter concludes with an agenda for managerial action that reinforces key points and provides a checklist of action steps for the management practitioner. Further, each chapter features a case study, representing a wide variety of organizations, to stimulate further thinking and debate.

Acknowledgements

In the process of writing my first book, I have gone through a lot of anxiety mixed with excitement. It is not an easy task to put together the essence of one's professional experience of more than 15 years in a way that catches and retains the attention of readers and appeals to both academics and practitioners alike. The initial drafts of the manuscript had many rough edges, which were smoothened under the watchful eye of my friend, Anant Bellary, who enthusiastically accepted my request to be a reviewer and did a commendable job. I am thankful to the School of Management of Griffith University for funding my sabbatical that enabled me to visit many scholars from around the world, interview HR practitioners in successful enterprises, attend international conferences and above all, provided a breather from my routine to pause and introspect.

I am grateful to all the people and companies that opened their doors to me and helped me gain an insight into how they manage and motivate their people. They include N.M. Agrawal and Kalyani Gandhi of Indian Institute of Management, Bangalore, India, Hema Ravichandar of Infosys, Ranjan Acharya of Wipro, Santrupt Misra of Birla Group of Companies, Hari Iyer of Sasken, A.S. Murty of Satyam, Avinash Agrawal of Sun Microsystems, Athar Siddiqee of Cisco, and Bruce Highfield of Virgin Blue. Thanks to my postgraduate students for their positive reception to the initial draft of the manuscript and to all the individuals who have endorsed the book. This book would not have been a reality but for the enthusiastic support and personal commitment of Chapal Mehra, Managing Editor of Sage India.

On a personal note, I am grateful to my late parents for encouraging me to be an optimist and turn failure into an opportunity and treat success as a blessing of God. Finally, I wish to thank my wife, Anjana and children, Pallavi and Parag, my staunch critics, admirers and the centre of my life.

Overview of Knowledge Economy and Management

It is not what we know we don't know that hurts, it is what we don't know we don't know

—**George Bernard Shaw**

Management—A Balancing Act

Management science, as we understand and practice today, is barely hundred years old. Considering that documented human history is a few thousand years old, the so-called scientific management is still in its infancy. Obviously, our ancestors practised some form of management and their achievements testify their success. Any traveller to countries which have had ancient civilizations, such as India, China or Greece, will marvel at how human beings scaled great heights of success in politics, science, commerce, religion, etc. only to fall later and then start all over again. The very concept of management is understood and practised differently in different countries. From that perspective, contemporary management concepts and practices are just another wave of thought in the vast ocean of human history and are bound to change with the passage of time and culture.

Having a rich past is an asset as well as a liability. At times of crises, the past can guide us out of the tunnel of darkness but if the present is radically different from the past, then the past can stifle new, innovative and creative solutions by rusting the brains of the leaders and their followers. Past glories can lull people into thinking that they can somehow overcome the emerging problems by relying on the so-called time-tested techniques. This presents a new challenge to the decision-makers: How, and how much to break from the past and how to chart a new future?

It is obvious that the 21st-century economy and its surrounding political and social environment are considerably different from the past. Since the advent of the scientific management theories, we have not faced the breadth and depth of uncertainty that we are facing today due to a host of factors, such as widespread globalization, technological revolution, political realignments and more recently, religious fanaticism. Faced with these new and difficult challenges, the organizational decision-makers are taking different routes. Some have panicked into thinking that the past has to be abandoned altogether. Consider the reaction of some of the corporations to e-commerce. For some time, many thought that the days of the so-called old brick and mortar companies were numbered and believers of this prediction concentrated on radical reengineering of their strategy, structure, staff and management style. Others have concentrated on continuing to do what they do best and at the same time, initiated the change process to adapt to the emerging future, be it in e-commerce, international business, or the empowerment of their people.

Management is a balancing act. It is about balancing the seemingly contradictory concepts and approaches as illustrated in Table 1.1.

Management is also highly contextual. When a management consultant says, 'it depends . . .' in response to a management

Table 1.1: Management as a Balancing Act

Management Concept	Approach
Management strategy and philosophy	Short term vs. Long term
Decision-making	Reason vs. Intuition
International business	Standardization vs. Customization
Structure	Centralization vs. Decentralization
People management	Autonomy vs. Control
People skilling	Specialization vs. Generalization
Culture	Assimilation vs. Diversity
Leadership	Task focused vs. People focused
Corporate citizenship	Private good vs. Public good

issue, he/she may not necessarily be avoiding the issue; it indeed could be a more holistic realization of the problem and hence, the hesitation to commit to a narrow description. Any management solution depends on a host of contingency factors, such as the external and internal environment, organizational size, life cycle, culture, and management philosophy.

Knowledge Management: A Passing Fad?

As with any new management concept, knowledge management is seen with scepticism by many as another fad, fashion or fantasy in modern management. While most management trends such as scientific management theory, human relations' movement, strategic planning, quality circles and business process reengineering are relevant for their time and have made their own contribution, they have had limited influence. This is mainly due to their process- and culture-specific issues. Knowledge management is more than a trend. It is a defining movement in world commerce associated with knowledge economy after the agricultural and industrial revolution. As the economic foundation moved from agriculture to industry and then to knowledge, the source of wealth has moved from land to machinery and now to intellectual capital. Neef makes the case for knowledge management by illustrating that in the US, the total output in tonnes has not changed significantly in a hundred years, despite a twenty-fold increase in GNP, thus, making the economy 'weightless'.[1]

It is true that knowledge has always been important to organizations but it has never been so 'explicitly' important. Today's economy is more global, hyper-competitive, technology intensive and networked as never before. Each of these changes has a profound impact on the way organizations and people think, organize and act throughout the world.

For example, take the case of India. In 1998, the author addressed a meeting of the chamber of commerce on globalization in a medium-sized town in India, consisting mainly of farmers and small businessmen. It was the time when India was about to liberalize most products and services under its obligation as a member of the World Trade Organization. He cautioned the audience that India would be flooded with Chinese goods and would face stiff competition in the farm sector from large, well-organized farmers around the world. A year later, the Indian press reported how innovatively designed and yet cheap goods produced in Chinese factories were causing havoc in the market, forcing the closure of many small-scale businesses. Some of these Chinese factories could single-handedly produce more than the entire output of those products in India. Today, vegetable shops in India offer the choice between Indian and Australian apples, the latter slightly more expensive but far superior.

While India is facing an uphill task in some markets, it is scoring impressive victories in an unlikely field: computer software services. Its 2.5 million-strong technical workforce helped the Indian IT companies notch up a staggering compounded annual growth rate of 62.3 per cent in software exports from 1995 to 2000.[2] The effects of India's success in IT are felt in several countries where Indian IT organizations have become the preferred supplier of software consultancy services replacing the local IT professionals. Similarly, Indian doctors, engineers, nurses and teachers are being recruited around the world to fill critical skill shortages.

Thus, today no country or company is immune from the effects of globalization. Traditional competitive advantages such as capital, market share and superior technology are no longer sustainable. The performance of computing equipment is expected to double every 18 months with almost no change in price. Similarly, communication capabilities double every nine months and data storage capacity, every 12 months.[3] Even mega mergers and acquisitions cannot guarantee an assured future. Microsoft Corporation controls 90 per cent of the world's PC market but its founder, Bill Gates, says he is constantly worried about competition. If Microsoft could dislodge the once-powerful IBM, somebody else could repeat the unthinkable. Under these circumstances, Peter Drucker, the most enduring management guru of our times, believes that 'the most important contribution management needs to make in the 21st century is to increase the productivity of knowledge work and knowledge workers'.[4]

In this discontinuous and hyper-competitive age, the past can no longer guide the future and the only sustainable competitive advantage is the ability of organizations and individuals to continuously innovate and successfully and swiftly convert knowledge into commercial products and services. This requires organizations to become learning entities where knowledge about the company's products and ser-vices, markets and processes is continuously updated, distri-buted and utilized. In an uncertain environment, knowledge is the only torch to find our way out of the tunnel of darkness.

Knowledge management embodies several distinct no-tions—that it involves continuous cycles of creativity and innovation, that it is experiential and primarily driven by knowledge workers facilitated by organizational vision and support.

Many mistakenly believe that knowledge management mainly applies to high technology and sunrise industries where knowledge flow is fast and thick. Many of the success-ful organizations known for their innovative knowledge management practices operate in traditional industries, such as health care, shipbuilding and civic services. In an environment where even a roadside milk bar owner or a farmer in a remote area is affected by global trends, knowledge about new products, services and markets becomes paramount for survival and sustenance. Knowledge generation is not just limited to managers and employees in an organization. It could come from suppliers, customers and even collaborative competitors. It could come from somebody and somewhere in an underdeveloped country. Thus, knowledge economy and management operate without boundaries between tasks, departments, organizations and markets.

Unlike previous management trends which were essentially owned, initiated and scripted by senior management, knowledge offers only limited and management opportunities for control or direction. It is a mental not physical asset and can flourish even under extremely low environmental conditions and support. Thus, knowledge economy and management are distinct from any other management trend in that they are more pervasive, unique and global.

What is Knowledge?

Let us turn to history and see how knowledge has been perceived and practised over the ages. Ancient Greeks thought of knowledge in four different dimensions:

- ◻ Episteme—basis and essence of sciences through scientific laws and principles
- ◻ Techne—technical know-how through manuals and communities of practice
- ◻ Phronesis—practical wisdom, and
- ◻ Metis—an embodied, incarnate, substantial form of knowledge with no quest of ideal, but a search for a practical end.[5]

Ancient Indians thought of knowledge as one of the keys to fulfilment of life and called it *jnana marga*, path of knowledge or wisdom. It requires the individual to seek and acquire insight into the ultimate truth of the universe. This necessitates a long period of spiritual and physical discipline, the renunciation of all worldly attachments, and the following of a rigorous course of ascetic and mystical practices, such as yoga. The Hindu philosophy postulates that proper utilization of *manas* (sense perception) and *buddhi* (making meaning of experience) leads to the knowledge of truth and wisdom.[6]

The Japanese philosopher Kitaro Nishida proposed the concept of 'ba' (place) that can be thought of as a shared space (whether physical, mental or virtual) where knowledge is created through one's own experience or reflections on others' experience.[7]

In the modern period of Western philosophy (1650–1770), the focus has been on internal workings of the brain and mind of the individual. This period has been characterized by movements based on rationalism (reason), empiricism (senses), and pragmatism (practical consequence) and focused on scientific truth as the basis of knowledge.[6]

There seems to be an East–West cultural dimension to the concept of knowledge and human existence in general. While the West seems to focus on explicit knowledge with a view to exploit knowledge for short-term gains through management and measurement, the East seems to focus on tacit knowledge with a view to create knowledge for long-term advantage through nurturing knowledge cultures and communities.[8]

Thus, what is knowledge and how to manage it depends on who is looking at it and for what purpose. There is no common definition that captures its essence. However, in the context of this book, knowledge is defined as 'actionable wisdom' or, in other words, 'experience in action'.

An overview of the current literature on knowledge management reveals that, generally, it is about

- □ Creation, distribution, validation and utilization of
- □ explicit and tacit knowledge at
- □ the individual, group, organizational and community
  level through
- □ harnessing of people, process and technology for
- □ the benefit of those involved and affected by it.

Knowledge by itself has little value. It needs to be applied for social or commercial benefit. Knowledge grows only when it is shared with others. Thus, knowledge management encompasses creation, sharing and utilization of knowledge in a group, organizational or wider community setting.

Knowledge is different from data and information. The latter are the means and the former the goal. While information is data that has been given structure, knowledge is information that has been given meaning.[9]

$$\text{Data} \xrightarrow[\text{(Structure)}]{\text{IT}} \text{Information} \xrightarrow[\text{(Meaning)}]{\text{People}} \text{Knowledge}$$

For example, in Human Resource Information Systems (HRIS), statistics on age, gender, qualifications, etc. are the data. When they are analysed in terms of, say, average age, gender ratio and number and types of graduates at the unit level, they become information. Such information helps to plan recruitment, launch affirmative action programmes, schedule training programmes to bridge skill gaps, etc. but 'how' one can do that is what constitutes knowledge. More than what and why, knowledge is about how. It is procedural and mostly hidden in the minds of individuals and groups in the organization.

One could distinguish between different kinds of knowledge. For instance, Whitehill lists 'encoded knowledge' (know what), 'habitual knowledge' (know how), 'scientific knowledge' (know why), 'collaboration knowledge' (know who), 'process knowledge' (know when and where), and 'communal knowledge' (care why).[10] Similarly, Blackler categorizes knowledge that is 'embrained' (conceptual skills and cognitive abilities), 'embodied' (action oriented), 'encultured' (shared understandings), 'embedded' (systemic routines), and 'encoded' (signs and symbols transmitted through information technologies).[11] These distinctions help us identify the concept as well as the context of knowledge.

However, as Blackler points out, the concept of knowledge is problematic as it is 'multi-faceted and complex, being both situated and abstract, implicit and explicit, distributed and individual, physical and mental, developing and static, verbal and encoded'. Instead of studying knowledge as something that people have, Blackler prefers to study 'knowing' as something people do. He suggests that knowing is mediated (through systems of language, technology, collaboration and control), situated (specific to time, space and context), provisional (constantly developing), pragmatic (purposeful), and contested (subject to power struggle).[11]

Tapping the Tacit Knowledge

Individuals and groups can possess both explicit and tacit knowledge. It is natural that explicit knowledge follows tacit knowledge. While explicit knowledge that is embedded in policies, procedures, organizational routines and roles can be relatively easily harnessed through information technologies and other knowledge management mechanisms, the challenge is the tapping of tacit knowledge. Lew Platt, chairman of Hewlett-Packard, highlighted the challenge by saying 'I wish we knew what we know at HP.' It is personal (mental models), practical, context specific and difficult to formalize. This fits into Blackler's prediction that 'a shift is occurring away from dependence on the embodied and embedded knowledge towards embrained and encultured knowledge'. As Polanyi, an early proponent of tacit knowledge said, human beings 'know more than they can tell or have a power to know more than they can tell'. When artists, such as painters or singers, are asked how they do their work so well, they may say 'I don't know, it just happens' as very few would be able to exactly identify the secrets of their success.

In the command and control regime of the past, management hardly noticed or bothered to tap this hidden knowledge. Those who volunteered to share this knowledge were either brushed aside or not given credit which made them just do their job as directed by the management and go home. In many cases, managers would look to an inexperienced industrial engineer to improve productivity rather than asking the operator who worked on the machine all his life. Employee trade unions effectively blocked workers from contributing to productivity improvement as there was nothing in it for workers. The thinking process was deliberately confined to senior management, which was far away from the front line where all the action happened. Similarly, no attempt was made to recognize, document or share the social and contextual knowledge accumulated by teams. As a result, one team would work on the same problem or issue, which was resolved long ago by another team in the same organization. The silos between jobs, departments, roles and responsibilities prevented knowledge sharing within organizational boundaries.

Today, with increasing competitive pressures, organizations are realizing the importance of tacit knowledge hidden in the minds of individuals and groups and try to tap it through delayering of jobs, empowerment and team structures. However, their HR philosophy has not altered enough to generate trust and openness necessary to persuade knowledge workers to share their knowledge.

When organizations try to convert tacit knowledge into explicit knowledge, they need to realize that the heart and soul of the experience that is being converted can only be transferred when individuals and groups 'volunteer' to take it and exert the necessary energy and enthusiasm to internal-ize it. According to Japanese organizational theorist Ikujiro Nonaka, most Western managers hold a too-narrow view of what knowledge is and believe that 'the only useful know-ledge is hard (read: quantifiable) data' and they see the company as a kind of machine for 'information processing'.[12] However, successful Japanese companies depend on tapping the tacit and often highly subjective insights, intuitions, and ideals of employees for continuous innovation. While every-one knows the legendary success of Toyota's production systems, it is difficult to copy it because it is hidden in the cultural DNA of Toyota.

Can we operationalize tacit knowledge, an intangible phe-nomenon? Nonaka suggests four basic patterns for creating knowledge in any organization: From tacit to tacit (through socialization); from tacit to explicit (through articulation); from explicit to tacit (through internalization); and from explicit to explicit.[12] According to Nonaka, 'All four of these patterns exist in dynamic interaction, a kind of spiral know-ledge.' However, articulation and internalization play a criti-cal role in the process and require 'the active involvement of the self—that is, personal commitment'—and therefore, know-ledge management should go beyond know-how and influ-ence mental models and beliefs.

If inter-firm transfer of tacit knowledge is difficult, so is intra-firm transfer. Tacit knowledge or skills can have a varying degree of becoming explicit. Ambrosini and Bowman propose 'causal mapping' as a technique to help organizations and researchers in surfacing tacit skills.[13] Cause maps focus on action that is context specific by ordering and analysing something that is fuzzy. The tacit skill elicitation process can include focus groups, semi-structured interviews, self-Q, storytelling, and metaphors to peel layer after layer of hidden knowledge. This could be further complemented with partici-pant observation. It needs to be noted that any attempt in converting tacit to explicit will be successful only when the knower and the receiver are skilled in how to articulate and the knower is motivated enough to share the knowledge without reservations. This is where organizational intervention is necessary to instil necessary skills and create a conducive and motivating atmosphere.

Knowledge Work and Knowledge Worker

When we shift our attention from knowledge to knowledge work, new dimensions emerge. If knowledge workers give us the sustainable competitive advantage, we need to understand who they are and if and how they are different from the other so-called non-knowledge workers.

There is a lot of hype about knowledge workers. Many regard that only highly educated people working in high-profile jobs, such as IT professionals, scientists, academics, and doctors qualify to be called knowledge workers. The fact is that most of the jobs in the 21st-century economy are generated in the low-value service jobs. The central feature of knowledge economy is the services industry which is experiencing phenomenal growth. The share of employment in services in the OECD countries accounted for nearly two-thirds of all jobs in the 1990s.[14] While part of this growth occurred in the high-value knowledge work, most of the growth occurred in low-value service jobs, such as cleaning, fast food, retail and hospitality.

If we define knowledge as innovation and creativity applied to create new or improve existing products, services, processes and markets, then by that definition, every worker becomes a knowledge worker—that is to say, an entrepreneur.[15] In many instances, people with no educational qualifications have shown high levels of practical intelligence. Recorded cases include a garbage collector who made a difference to his employer's bottomline by suggesting a new method of collecting garbage and a hospital attendant who came out with a new way of making beds and increased productivity manifold. The famous dabbawalas in Mumbai (formerly, Bombay), India are uneducated workers who have developed a simple but effective system of collecting thousands of lunch boxes meant for office workers from homes all over Mumbai, transporting them in crowded trains and return the same by evening. The boxes are marked with different colours to identify different suburbs in Mumbai, and despite the volume and chaotic transport system, hardly any box is misplaced. Similarly, a women's co-operative, also based in Mumbai, employs over 40,000 uneducated women who make Lijjat Papad by hand for domestic and export markets. The co-operative runs on simple yet effective principles: All employees are co-owners; only an employee who has worked on the shop floor can be elected as a member of the management committee or the president; all accounts are squared off on a daily basis; no supplier is asked for credit and none is extended; every unit works as a profit centre, and in case of a loss, workers receive less daily wages till the profitability improves.[16]

One can, therefore, argue that there is no such thing as non-knowledge worker. The entire participative management theory is based on this tenet. Most of the process-related improvement in Japanese industry was realized from the understanding and motivation that everyone who comes in contact with a business process is intellectually involved in it.

Knowledge work is also defined as one where 'the nature of work may be physical or mental, output is mainly intangible, inputs are not clearly definable and the task involves high levels of discretion, uncertainty and unstructured decisions requiring tactical and strategic endeavours'.[17] It is thus clear that knowledge work lacks any occupational identity and cannot be classified under the traditional occupational categories.

However, as Drucker states, knowledge may be subordinate in low-value jobs, such as that of a file clerk, and predominant in high-value jobs, such as that of a surgeon, but it forms the foundation and is absolutely crucial to both. He emphasizes the importance of technologists, combining both manual and knowledge work, in providing the defining competitive advantage in the knowledge economy. When a car salesman realizes that he is in the business of providing transportation service and not just selling cars, his attitude is transformed and his work becomes more knowledgeable and aligned to business.

Recognizing the difficulty in distinguishing between knowledge and non-knowledge workers, some management researchers, such as Thompson emphasize more on the *knowledge-ability in work* than *knowledge work*.[18] Thompson cites the example of customer service representatives (CSRs) in call centres and retail shops to highlight the importance of tacit knowledge even in low-value, routine service jobs. It is not the technical knowledge about the products and services but the life experience of CSRs that sets them apart with the right attitude, personality, energy and enthusiasm required to do their job. However, he cautions that the development and deployment of such knowledge is still a matter of negotiation between workers and management.

Incidentally, even in the high-value information technology-related jobs, managements are realizing that technical skills play a smaller role compared to soft skills. The findings of recent research on IT professionals and interviews with their HR managers suggest that managerial and leadership competencies are most wanted by software professionals followed by competencies relating to business domain, self/role/organizational issues, knowledge management, customers and project and process management.[19] Soft skills are generally tacit in nature as they are the result of a personal and social experience. Training can only provide the framework but soft skills need to be internalized.

The importance of tacit knowledge in all jobs in the knowledge economy has implications for HR management in selecting and placing the right person for the right job and institutionalizing the matching process through appropriate training, performance and reward management.

Finally, Scarbrough draws attention to the inherent conflict between 'knowing' as part of the work experience and 'knowledge' as an economic commodity.[20] One tends to generate knowledge while the other secures its appropriation. At the institutional level, the conflict is between commercial enterprises and knowledge producing institutions; at the organizational level, it is between corporate culture of managers and professional culture of knowledge workers; and at the individual level, it is between the employer and the employee in terms of employment security and responsibility for career development. Scarbrough believes that the management of knowledge workers centres on the quasi-resolution of such conflict. He points out 'the ability to combine technical autonomy with managerial control or to develop open cultures yet retain a tight grasp of intellectual property' as examples of quasi-resolution of conflict leading to competitive advantage.

Measuring Knowledge

If knowledge is the key capital asset in the knowledge economy, we need to develop appropriate measures that are reliable and valid. To a scientific mind, particularly grounded in Western culture, anything that is not measurable is not valuable. The argument is that anything that cannot be measured cannot be examined and hence, cannot be understood.

Before we proceed to examine some of the attempts in measuring knowledge, we need to understand that there are many things in life that cannot be accurately measured, at least in the short term, and the measures themselves may be subject to controversy. For example, we generally use financial and tangible measures, such as per capita income, to judge how developed a country is. However, it is difficult to argue against the futility of measuring the development of a country without taking into account aspects that are fundamental to human happiness, such as stability of marriage and family.

Similarly, the two main areas of focus in this book, knowledge and human resources, fall into the same category. No accounting method can accurately capture the value of both of them. Particularly, tacit knowledge has a cognitive dimension and includes our intuitions, gut feelings, values, beliefs and mental models that we ourselves may not be aware of. In a social context, how can we accurately measure the culture, mindset, heart, soul and spirit of the people within whom knowledge is embedded? It does not have any of the characteristics of a physical asset. Knowledge workers own the asset and the 'knowledge between their ears is totally portable' making its owners mobile and free from physical control.[4]

Glazer illustrates the point in his article, 'Measuring the knower: Towards a theory of knowledge equity', quite powerfully, thus:

> (Knowledge) as a commodity differs from the typical good in that it is not easily divisible or appropriable (i.e., 'either I have it or you have it'); it is not inherently scarce (although it is often perishable); and it may not exhibit decreasing returns to use, but often in fact *increases in value the more it is used*. Furthermore, unlike other commodities, which are (with few exceptions) non-renewable and depletable (knowledge), is essentially 'self-regenerative' and 'feeds on itself', such that the identification of a new 'piece' of knowledge immediately creates both the demand and conditions for the production of subsequent pieces.[21]

Once we understand the difficulties in measuring knowledge with traditional standards, it is possible to look for holistic ways of measuring knowledge, which is predominantly tacit. Glazer points out that 'measuring the knower involves incorporating notions such as "context" and "subjective interpretation"—traditionally the domain of psychology and other "softer" disciplines—into our formal investigations'.

After analysing how information is acquired, stored, distributed and interpreted, Glazer gives a few examples of successful evaluation of knowledge assets that implicitly involve measuring the knower. One such example given is Aaker's work on valuating brand equity using trade-off analysis.[22]

Glazer concludes by quoting psychologist Herbert Simon, 'what information consumes is rather obvious; it consumes the attention of its recipients. Hence, a wealth of information creates a poverty of attention, and a need to allocate that attention efficiently among the overabundance of information sources that might consume it.' One radical way of reducing attention impoverishment in the face of information overdose is to replace information with knowledge. Since knowledge is more agenda neutral than information, its acceptability is higher.[23]

Finally, knowledge creation is a never-ending process. It keeps accumulating (but discarding the obsolete), changing and regenerating to suit the times. As such, learning and knowledge management are always 'work in progress'.

Agenda for Managerial Action

Points to Ponder . . .	. . . Steps to Consider
The source of wealth has moved from land to machinery and now to intellectual capital. However, there is considerable scepticism about the relevance and durability of knowledge management (KM) as a managerial concept. It requires a fundamental change in management thinking on strategy, structure, staffing and style accompanied by commitment of resources in terms of time, effort and money.	Consider establishing a dedicated knowledge management function with the responsibility to create and sustain awareness about KM throughout the organization. Make the position report directly to the CEO to underscore its importance. Consider filling the position with a committed senior person with a holistic, rather than IT dominated, approach KM. It is not the creation of a KM position but the way it operates that

is more important. Otherwise, it will end up as another support function with no genuine commitment, as happened to safety and quality movements.

The most important managerial challenge today is tapping the tacit knowledge hidden in people.

The nature and importance of tacit knowledge has implications for HRM, in terms of recruitment, training, performance management and remuneration as detailed in subsequent chapters.

Knowledge is fundamental to any task or occupation; only its importance varies. Knowledge work lacks any occupational identity and cannot be classified under the traditional occupational categories.

Organizations have to be careful in defining a knowledge worker so as not to create an elitist class and demoralize the rest. There is already a growing resentment among the temporary and casual labour for being treated as a wandering underclass.

The quest to acquire knowledge is deeper than the desire to appropriate it as a commercial commodity. It is personal, portable and free from any physical control. Therefore, it cannot be accurately 'measured' by traditional accounting methods nor 'controlled' by commercial contracts. Knowledge is self-generative and can grow with little or no environmental support.

As knowledge and knowledge workers are different from any other physical asset, managing them through traditional methods will be futile. Organizations no longer own them and, therefore, management can no longer control them. This reality calls for revamping management processes through tools such as empowerment, respect, self-management and equitable sharing of wealth.

Case Scenario: Setting the Scene—Funky Business

Brainpower dominates modern corporations. It is their essence. We are increasingly competing on competence. People can make your organization, your products and your service solutions unique. How you manage and lead people, and how you organize your operations, determines whether you succeed.

Organizing is the art of achieving extraordinary things with ordinary people. In our times, organizational innovation means creating conditions that enable a constant flow of creativity, not churning out yet another standardized product or service. The funky firm needs to be different, look different, and work in new ways. The future cannot be predicted—it has to be created. Funky business means there will be many more questions with fewer universal answers. Either you see things happen or you make them happen.

Leadership and management are more important than ever. How a company is managed and how a company is led are vital differentiators. They can create sustainable uniqueness.

The boss is dead. No longer can we believe in a leader who claims to know more about everything and who is always right. Management by numbers is history. Management by fear won't work. If management is people, management must become humanagement.

The job is dead. No longer can we believe in having a piece of paper with 'job description' at the top. The new realities call for far greater flexibility. The days of the long-serving corporate man, safe and sound in the dusty recess of the corporation are long gone. Soon the emphasis will be on getting a life instead of a career, and work will be viewed as a series of gigs or projects. Inevitably new roles demand new skills.

Technology is reshaping our world. It is the rhythm section of funky business. The central contribution of technology to funky business is in creating information systems.

Chaotic times are here again. (However) . . . avoiding uncertainty is human nature. Uncertainty reduction is a ritualistic part of corporate life. Uncertainty gives leaders anywhere in organizations a new job. They must produce uncertainty. Real leaders challenge people. They do not control them. True leaders set people free.

The problem with most organizations is not that they know too little but that they do not know what they know. To thrive we must create a learning organization. Learning does not happen automatically. Enabling learning is one of the key tasks for any leader. Leaders must ensure the continuous transfer of knowledge across organizational boundaries. The individual parts must be able to reflect the whole.

Of course, working faster is not a question of trying harder but working smarter. Even though the new economy comes without speed limits, creativity cannot be forced upon people. To be creative, we need time and resources. We need time to sit down and reflect.

Funky Inc. applies organizational solutions capable of combining and recombining knowledge across any type of border at the speed of light. So forget organizational pyramids with the CEO sitting atop them. Who wants to work in pyramids, the greatest tombs ever created by man? Playgrounds must gradually replace the pyramids.

The most intensive learning experiences tend to occur when we fail rather than when we succeed. Failure happens. Give people trust and it will happen more productively. It is not about promoting risk taking per se but about making it less risky to take risks. Give people freedom and they will pursue their own creative byways. Give people time and creative results will emerge.

Human beings are not bulk goods. They come in different shapes and forms. To attract and retain people, we have to treat them as individuals. Today's employees are more questioning and demanding. They are confident enough to air their concerns, grievances and aspirations.

Funky business is like playing the lottery. If you participate, there is a 99 per cent chance that you will lose. On the other hand, if you do not take part, your chances of losing are 100 per cent. To succeed we have to go for that single per cent. The future belongs to those who seize the opportunity to create it— those who dare to take risks, break rules and make new ones.

Source: Excerpts reprinted with permission from the interview with Kjell Nordstrom by Les Pickett in *HR Monthly*, March 2003. Copyright © 2003 by the Australian Human Resources Institute, Melbourne, Australia. All rights reserved.

References

1. **Neef, D.** (1999) 'Making the case for knowledge management: The bigger picture'. *Management Decision*, Vol 37 No 1, pp. 72–79.
2. National Association of Software and Services Companies (2001) 'The Indian software industry in India: A strategic review'. New Delhi, India.
3. **Brown J.S.** (2002) An epistemological perspective on organisations and innovation. Keynote address to the 3rd Organisational Knowledge and Learning Conference (OKLC).
4. **Drucker, P.** (1999) 'Knowledge-worker productivity: The biggest challenge'. *California Management Review*, Vol 41 No 2, pp. 79–94.
5. **Prusak, L.** (2000) Knowledge—Can it be managed? Presented at the IBM Academy of Technology conference on knowledge management, Fishkill, NY, 27–29 June 2000.
6. **Rinder, H.** (1995) Quest for Truth and Fulfilment http://members.aol.com/rhrrr/phileast.htm (13 May 2002).
7. **Nonaka, I.** and **Konno, N.** (1998) 'The concept of "Ba": Building a foundation for knowledge creation'. *California Management Review*, Vol 40 No 3.
8. **Cohen, D.** (1998) 'Toward a knowledge context: Report on the first annual U.C. Berkely forum on knowledge and the firm'. *California Management Review*, Vol 40 No 3.
9. **Whitehill, M.** (1997) 'Knowledge-based strategy to deliver sustained competitive advantage'. *Long Range Planning*, Vol 30 No 4, pp. 621–27.
10. **Whitehill** (1998) Quoted in Glazer, R., 'Measuring the knower: Towards a theory of knowledge equity'. *California Management Review*, Vol 40 No 3.
11. **Blackler, F.** (1995) 'Knowledge, knowledge work and organisations: An overview and interpretation'. *Organisation Studies*, Vol 16 No 6.
12. **Nonaka, I.** (1991) 'The knowledge-creating company'. *Harvard Business Review*, November–December 1991.
13. **Ambrosini, V.** and **Bowman, C.** (2001) 'Tacit knowledge: Some suggestions for operationalisation'. *Journal of Management Studies*, Vol 38 No 6.
14. OECD Employment Outlook, 2001 http://www.oecd.org/pdf/M00028000/M00028052.pdf

15. **Blackler, F., Crump, N.** and **McDonald, S.** (1998) 'Knowledge, organisations and competition'. In von Krogh, G., Roos, J. and Kleine, D. (Eds.), *Knowing in Firms*, London, Sage, pp. 67–86.

16. **Jayaraman, M.** (2003) 'Feet on the ground'. *Businessworld*, India, 6 January.

17. **Beruvides, M.G.** and **Koelling, C.P.** (2001) 'An investigation of the work characteristic composition in blue-collar, white-collar, and knowledge work'. *International Journal of Human Resources Development and Management*, Vol 1 No 2/3/4, pp. 283–303.

18. **Thompson, P., Warhurst, C.** and **Callaghan, G.** (2001) 'Ignorant theory and knowledgeable workers: Interrogating the connections between knowledge, skills and services'. *Journal of Management Studies*, Vol 38 No 7.

19. **Agrawal, N.M.** and **Thite, M.** (2003) Nature and importance of soft skills in software project leaders. Working Paper 2/4, Indian Institute of Management, Bangalore, India, September.

20. **Scarbrough, H.** (1999) 'Knowledge as work: Conflicts in the management of knowledge workers'. *Technology Analysis and Strategic Management*, Vol 11 No 1, pp. 5–16.

21. **Glazer, R.** (1998) 'Measuring the knower: Towards a theory of knowledge equity'. *California Management Review*, Vol 40 No 3.

22. **Aaker, D.A.** (1991) *Managing Brand Equity*, New York, Free Press.

23. **Bellary, A.** Personal observations while reviewing the manuscript.

Human Resources and Knowledge Management: People-centric Partnership

The literature on knowledge management is clearly divided into two camps. One camp is in favour of people as the central theme and people management as the key managerial intervention. The other camp is in favour of Information Technology (IT) as the central theme and IT applications as the key facilitating mechanism to harness knowledge. It is not that both the camps deny the existence or importance of the other. They mention each other in passing but invariably focus their attention on one. According to Gloet and Berrell,

> The dual paradigm nature of KM suggests that strategies driven by IT exhibit quite different characteristics to those driven by organisational learning, the former being driven by technology (with its focus on collection, manipulation and application of data and information), while the latter is dominated more by a focus on people (and is concerned with nature of learning, organisational processes and harnessing tacit forms of knowledge). (It is necessary to develop and sustain) more integration between approaches to KM. This involves recognising the important role of technology and the tools of IT, but recognising the fundamental role played by human and intellectual resources'.[1]

It is clear that knowledge resides between the ears of the people. The most important challenge to knowledge management is how to 'persuade' people to share it and let it be part of the organizational knowledge repository. It is only after we successfully unlock knowledge that we can think about documenting, sharing, growing and institutionalizing it, and that is where IT plays a pivotal role. Those who believe that IT is knowledge management clearly have got their priorities wrong.

If innovation and entrepreneurship are the key to the knowledge economy, knowledge workers hold the key. This radically alters the bargaining power in employment relationship. In the new environment, employees are no longer costs but assets. However, unlike capital, these assets cannot be controlled within physical boundaries and confined to commercial contracts of the organization. They walk out from the gates of the organization every day and to make them come back and share their intellectual capital, organizations must find ways to engage their hearts, minds and souls in fulfilling the organizational goals.

Leading management thinkers such as Drucker, Handy and Senge suggest that 'it is not technology, but the art of human- and humane-management' that is the continuing challenge for executives.[2] The challenge includes 'how to lead the organizations that create and nurture knowledge, how to know when to set our machines aside and rely on instinct and judgement, and how to maintain, as individuals and organizations, our ability to learn'.

IT—Mistaking the Messenger for the Message

Organizations have fairly elaborate information infrastructure, such as intranet, data warehouse and data mining to distribute explicit knowledge. In fact, there is no doubt that IT has inspired the growth of knowledge management. It is inconceivable to think of managing knowledge without deploying information technologies. Technology makes people comfortable because it provides precision and structure.[1] However, the messenger has been mistaken for the message and many organizations spend considerable time, effort and money in developing information technologies to manage knowledge at the cost of investment in people. Information technology can only be a tool, not a source of knowledge. Technology cannot replace people and social interactions in generating, distributing and utilizing knowledge. This debate is important not because it provides a platform for a political turf war between the HR & IT disciplines at the strategy table but because of the need for optimum utilization of scarce organizational resources. This issue has important implications for knowledge management strategy, structure, staffing, styles, competency building and reward management.

The limitations of IT are all the more prominent in dealing with tacit knowledge. It is argued that USA focuses more on exploiting existing explicit knowledge through information technologies whereas Japan pays more attention to creating new knowledge and sharing tacit knowledge through social processes.[3] Excessive emphasis on technology to the detriment or neglect of people issues could be counter-productive in the long run, even though it may produce some short-term results, such as dazzling the market on a high-tech platform.

If organizations believe that technology alone gives them an edge over their competitors, they are ignoring the importance of the mindset of the people who use it. Wherever technology is used, ultimately, it is the attitude of the people manning it that determines the quality of customer service and satisfaction. Technology is great in handling matters that are standard and routine. But when it comes to interpretation of rules using discretion, people have to step in and use their judgement and experience. Post-September 11, many analysts have alleged that the lack of human intelligence, as a result of funding cuts and overreliance and overconfidence on technology contributed to FBI's failure to see what was coming.

Research shows that success in knowledge management is primarily defined by the culture of people in the organization.[4,5] If knowledge management were to be the core competency and strategic intent of an organization, it needs to be defined primarily in terms of its people and their social context—their cultural values, attitudes, competencies and commitment. Only then it becomes a difficult-to-imitate competitive advantage. Successful learning organizations are able to attract best talent and retain them in an atmosphere of trust and openness. They have a psychological contract with their employees that motivates them to generate and share knowledge in return for nurturing and nourishing their professional skills. Their HR philosophy develops trust and encourages organizational citizenship behaviours. They deploy appropriate HR systems that identify, assess, reward and develop competencies that form the core of organizational success.

Smith and Kelly believe that 'future economic and strategic advantage will rest with the organizations that can most effectively attract, develop and retain a diverse group of the best and the brightest human talent in the marketplace'.[6] Obviously, this puts HR at the forefront of the knowledge economy. But is the HR profession ready to take the mantle?

Human Resource's Elusive Search for Status and Respect

The Human Resources profession has been facing an identity crisis throughout its evolution.[7] Peter Drucker observed, as far back as 1954 that 'the constant worry of all personnel administrators is their inability to prove that they are making a contribution to the enterprise. Their preoccupation is with the search for a "gimmick" that will impress their management associates. Their persistent complaint is that they lack status.'

Nothing much has changed since then. While HR has been able to gain the professional recognition it has craved for, its credibility is still in doubt. Today the HR department is an integral part of any professional organization and increasingly, the heads of HR sit on the Board of Directors. However, the unfortunate reality is that everyone loves to hate HR.

Recently, a Personnel Manager made a desperate plea in an electronic discussion forum for HR professionals seeking help to justify his position in the company. He wrote that his General Manager believes that the HR function serves no business purpose and he was at a loss to prove otherwise.

A recent survey of 25,000 leaders in different functional areas by the Management Research Group had this to say about HR leaders:

> Typical HR leaders present themselves as nice people and enthusiastic cheerleaders. While they excel themselves in their traditional role of employee advocates, they are not seen as particularly visionary, innovative, risk taking, hard driving, or results oriented. They are not inclined to challenge the status quo or stand up for unpopular causes.

To be fair to HR professionals, there are in-built difficulties in their profession which cast a natural doubt on their credibility. Compared to all other management functions, people management is more 'sensitive, personalized, context-dependent and cannot be managed through a set of predefined techniques'. The slippery nature of people issues makes it difficult to measure HR's contribution to the bottomline. From the beginning, HR has been driven by top management and HR professionals have had little exposure and opportunity to contribute to strategy formulation and implementation. At the operational level, HR is administered by line personnel who have historically disliked people management roles. However, one of the major weaknesses of HR professionals is their inability to understand and adapt to the business environment they operate in. In their enthusiasm to be policy police, HR people are perceived as a stumbling block to line personnel in quickly and effectively responding to a fast-changing business environment.

Despite the inability of the HR profession in resolving its credibility problem, the situation has never been as favourable to HR professionals as it is now in making their mark at the strategy table.[8] Knowledge management offers the much-needed window of opportunity that the profession so desperately needs. According to Watkins and Marsick,

> HR professionals have long sought to define who they are in order to clarify what is that they do that is unique . . . the concept of knowledge management or learning organisation is one such niche for HR as it brings together the two primary foci for this field: learning and the workplace context in which it takes place.[9]

However, there appears to be little realization amongst many HR professionals on the importance of knowledge management and the critical role they are required to play. In a recent conference, when the author asked a gathering of HR people how many of them believed that knowledge management was here to stay, only a few responded in the affirmative. But when he asked if knowledge management were to stay, how many of them believed that HR had a critical role to play, nearly all of them agreed! It is precisely this lack of critical understanding of key success factors in business and the inability to link HR with strategy formulation and implementation that have deprived the HR profession of its rightful place in management. The writing on the wall is clear: If HR functionaries waste the opportunity provided by the knowledge economy, they will be pushed back to routine tasks and stripped of important responsibilities. As people management is no longer just a support function but a strategic tool for competitive advantage, other people will take over key HR responsibilities.

Strategic Human Resource Management

Thanks to the knowledge economy, today human resource management is seen to be a key competitive advantage by the senior management and taken seriously in strategic decision-making. In fact it is difficult to practise customer-centric strategic management without first achieving employee satisfaction. Quoting Thomas Stewart, Horibe points out that a customer's decision to be loyal or to defect is the sum of many small encounters with a company and it is the company employees who control these small encounters.[10] Thus, employee satisfaction is a prerequisite to customer satisfaction. There is growing evidence that HR practices influence organizational performance and competitive advantage and those organizations which deploy good people management practices reap the benefits.[11]

The literature on strategic human resource management (SHRM) indicates that successful organizations follow certain common high performance work practices (Refer Appendix 1):

- Their HR philosophy and practices are intricately linked to the strategic objectives of the organization and are based on trust, transparency and fairness.
- The HR function in these organizations establishes business partnership with line managers who have a direct interest and involvement in delivering HR. The HR functionaries become an integral part of the strategic business units (SBUs) and customize HR solutions to provide fast and efficient service. It is their attitude to internal and external customer service that distinguishes their work from traditional HR delivery. Rather than being policy police, they are interested in moulding the policies to suit customer requirements.
- They identify, operationalize and implement the competencies and characters that they believe are at the core of their organizational culture.
- They believe in leadership by example.
- They leverage intellectual capital in and around the organization by institutionalizing learning to learn.
- They aim to recruit the best talent available in the market by carefully cultivating the image of a preferred employer reinforced through employee referral.
- Performance management is based on the person rather

than the job. Assessment is done frequently and relies on multi-rater feedback.

□ Their remuneration system is timely, performance based and profit sharing. It rewards and reinforces the competencies and characters valued by organizational members.

□ Their career management practices recognize the importance of employment security through employable skills. Their commitment to employees is demonstrated in several ways, such as continuous training, opportunity to work on challenging tasks, job rotation, and flexi time.

□ They develop organizational structures that revolve around autonomy, self-leadership and team-based learning and problem-solving.

□ They deploy human resource information systems (HRIS) to disseminate accurate and real-time information on HR policies and procedures through intranet.

□ They establish enduring partnerships with external consultants and service providers to deliver state-of-the-art, best-in-class HR services in recruitment, performance management, training and development, remuneration and career management.

□ They believe in constructive engagement with the trade union movement based on trust and openness in managing change and adapting or adopting best practices in productivity, quality and service improvement that match global standards.

While some of these best practices will be discussed in detail in subsequent chapters, we need to remind ourselves that in a global economy, such practices are not universally applicable or relevant. Their success is contingent upon national and organizational culture, size, industry type, occupational category, etc. Further, these practices need to be considered in total, not in isolation. They are interrelated elements in an internally consistent human resource 'bundle' or system.[12] An organization that follows a coercive approach to one part of the HRM system cannot succeed in adopting a collaborative approach to another part.

The success of strategic HRM in the knowledge economy also depends on its ability to harness the potential hidden in the informal social architecture, including tacit knowledge, co-operation, informal learning, that emerges over a long period of time and is largely unplanned.[13] Sometimes, the informal culture may override the formal HR policy and therefore, both need to work together to produce the desired results. For example, Truss observes that in Hewlett-Packard, despite the formal policy on performance-based promotion, a strong internal network with influential people played a crucial role in promotions.[14]

Measuring Human Resource Effectiveness

One of the difficulties of the HR discipline is with the measurement of its effectiveness. The same HR concept can be either good or bad depending on how it is used. For example, internal promotion can be a good practice if merit is not sacrificed. Similarly, recruiting like-minded people can become a bad practice if it leads to organizational behaviour where diversity is resented. Such an organization could end up with clones. Therefore, an organization cannot claim that it employs best practices in HR unless it is able to demonstrate that its practice matches the rhetoric.

We also need to note that change takes place relatively slowly in the HRM area.[15] Truss, using a longitudinal study of Hewlett-Packard, points that 'even a highly successful company with a strong record of excellence in people management practices cannot achieve all-round success'.[14] People's expectations and motivation swing during economic ups and downs and HR policies may be viewed differently in different times. Therefore, any short-term assessment of HR effectiveness is fraught with danger and open to misrepresentation. Motorola does not believe in strict measures of evaluating training effectiveness and treats training as part and parcel of an overall management process.[16]

Particularly, the HR's efforts in tapping tacit knowledge in informal social networks is an ongoing and delicate process and 'managing strictly by formal measurement' is only going to backfire. Pfeffer cautions that 'there is politics involved in the measurement process, and that entering a game where winning is unlikely and playing by rules set by others exposes human resource professionals to the possibility of at best short-term victories and long-term problems'.[17] As long as data from measures such as voluntary turnover, employee survey feedback, internal customer satisfaction with HR services, occupational health and safety, and productivity per employee look good in the medium to long term, and comparable to the best in class, one can safely assume that HR is being well handled.

As more and more people work outside the traditional boundaries of full-time employment, we also need to consider ways and means of extending the reach and influence of HRM to cover most, if not all, types of employees. Referring to the growing trend in outsourcing HR activities and contracting, Drucker warns that organizations may forget that 'developing talent is business's most important task—the sine qua non of competition in a knowledge economy. If by offloading employee relations, organizations also lose their capacity to develop people, they will have made a devil's bargain indeed.'[18]

Thus, it is clear that HR has a critical role to play in the knowledge economy in creating people-centric partnership. The question is not whether but how HR is able to play the role. Here, HR needs unreserved support from the senior management and active co-operation from non-HR managers who need to embrace the HR agenda with equal enthusiasm. The contribution of HR to knowledge management is at the high end of the value chain as it is primarily to create and sustain a culture that fosters innovation, creativity and learning. In this respect, HR needs to position itself at the high end of being 'strategically proactive' as against the low end of being operationally reactive.[19] This requires that we treat the HR department neither as cost centre nor as profit centre but as 'investment centre'.

Before we proceed to examine the operational details of the role to be played by HRM in the knowledge economy, we need to look at the big picture and understand the macro issues and challenges in the knowledge economy, particularly the social and workplace trends. While some of these trends are clearly visible on the horizon, some are in the making and may change their shape and character as they develop. Further, as William Gibson said, 'future is already here, it is just unevenly distributed' highlighting the uneven distribution of development. It needs to be emphasized that the identification and analysis of the change process is more of crystal gazing than empirical as the transformation of industrial economy into knowledge economy is still under way and shows mixed patterns of the old and the new era.

Macro Human Resource Issues and Trends in the Knowledge Economy

Demographic Changes

With the rapid decline in the birth and death rates, the developed countries will face a shortage in the working age population combined with an increasing responsibility for taking care of its older generation. By 2010, the baby boomers will start to retire, creating an 'agequake'. By 2020, over half the population will be over 50 years of age. As most of the population growth takes place in the developing countries, immigration will be the principal means of addressing the population imbalance in developed countries.

By 2030, more than 60 per cent of people will live in cities creating many more megalopolises of 10 million people and above. In most countries, the proportion and status of women in the workplace is increasing rapidly. By 2015, women are expected to outnumber and outqualify men in the knowledge economy. Like businesses, people are increasingly outsourcing personal services, creating the fastest growth in the household services sector.

The workplace implications of the above changes are enormous:

- With life expectancy expected to reach 80 years for men and 85 years for women by 2025, the developed countries will have to increase the retirement age and explore new ways of harnessing the productivity of older people, often in part-time and consulting capacities. As lifestyle issues of older people are quite different from those of younger people, organizations will have to tailor their workplace motivation measures accordingly. The Organization for Economic Cooperation and Development (OECD) states that, 'One of the most striking paradoxes of today's OECD societies is that, although people live longer, they also tend to retire earlier, a situation which is clearly unsustainable from both the economic and social points of view. This is why expanding the range and quality of labour market opportunities open to older workers has become increasingly important'.

- With increased migration of people from developing to developed countries, the governments, education institutes and businesses will have to train the new migrants, mainly in jobs that demand manual as well as knowledge skills (technologists, as Peter Drucker calls them), to suit the needs of the knowledge economy. Increased cultural diversity at the workplace will bring its own issues and challenges. Businesses that harness the positive effects of diversity will prosper. Silicon Valley is already reaping the benefits of employing Indian and Chinese professionals.

- With the increased pressure on urbanization, organizations will have to explore new ways of working away from the office.

- Gender issues, such as equality, dual-career couples, work–family balance, maternity and childcare provisions will become more prominent creating more pressure on organizations to address.
- In many developed countries, single people constitute one-third of the working population. Their work expectations will be quite different from those of married people. For example, they may want to spend more time in office for socialization beyond office hours. Thus, organizations will have to cater to contrasting aspirations of single and married employees.
- There are remarkable differences in the expectations and motivations of baby boomers (those born between 1943 and 1960) and Generation Xers (those born between 1961 and 1981).[20] The baby boomers have grown up with highly individualistic characteristics, such as challenging authority. While the Generation Xers continue the trend, it is 'balanced by the desire to place boundaries on the infringement of work on their personal lives'. Being the children of dual-career couples and victims of soaring divorce rates, Xers are well aware of the havoc overwork can cause on the quality of life. Thus, Xers are less attached to the organization they work for and are keen to develop an independent personality.

Employment Profile

Organizations are increasingly outsourcing their activities by reducing the number of their full-time staff and relying on contract and casual or part-time employees. The workforce is becoming more 'externalized' or 'contractualized'. This reflects the trend towards make-or-buy decisions in human capital. While the rationale behind the trend is debatable and perceived benefits questionable, the fact is that the employment market will continue to have different types of employees requiring different ways of managing them.

Charles Handy classified employees as core, contract and temporary. The core employees are central to the organizational human core and act as DNAs of organizational knowledge and culture. They have extensive experience in the organization and possess core skills that differentiates the organization from its competitors. They provide 'greater stability and predictability of a firm's stock of skills and capabilities'. And yet, the irony is that they are paid less, are largely taken for granted and it is assumed that they are staying because they cannot go elsewhere.[21]

However, the internalization of a workforce constrains a firm's ability to respond to environmental changes. Therefore, firms resort to externalization of labour by employing contractors and part-time employees to be more flexible and competitive. Contractors provide cutting-edge expertise gained through working in different organizational settings and even though they cost more, their contribution is immediate and situation specific.

Part-time and casual employees constitute the third layer of employment and are hired on a need basis to cater to generic but cyclical skill demands. All three sets of employees offer exclusive benefits and cater to different needs of the organization. Thus, staffing becomes more of a make-and-buy rather than make-or-buy decision.

Accordingly, Lepak and Snell develop a human resource architecture that caters to different employment nodes based on the value and uniqueness of human capital.[22] They propose

- 'Internal development' of those employees who possess skills and competencies that are firm specific and are 'both unique and valuable' to the organization. The employment relationship with these core employees is based on long-term involvement, investment and commitment by both the parties.
- 'Acquiring' or buying human capital that is 'valuable but generic', as it is widely available in the open market and

is not firm specific. These are skilled employees, such as IT professionals, with specialized and readymade skills developed elsewhere. The employment relationship with them is 'symbiotic' based on mutual benefit and market forces. Both employee and the employer remain committed to each other as long as the mutual need exists with no expectation of a long-term relationship.

□ 'Contracting' human capital that is 'generic and of limited value'. As the skills are neither highly valuable nor unique, such as clerical and maintenance jobs, organizations prefer to contract them on a temporary basis. The employment relationship with this category is transactional, based on short-term economic exchanges.

□ 'Alliance' with human capital that is 'somewhat unique but of limited value, at least in the short run'. The employment relationship becomes a hybrid form of internal and external employment. Many high-technology firms today form an alliance with external parties to conduct basic research enabling creation and sharing of knowledge without incurring all the costs. However, the partnership poses unique challenges of creating trust and reciprocity.[22]

What is clear is that today, there are different types of employment to cater to changing business needs and HR has to employ different strategies in recruiting, training, assessing and remunerating them. For example, firms making successful use of temporary employees ensure that they do not become a 'wandering underclass in the labour pool" by carefully developing HR practices to attract, retain and motivate temps.[23]

However, the 'valuation' of human capital is going to be highly contentious and will greatly impact on organizational commitment and morale. For example, how valuable are call centre staff or receptionists? They are the most visible and direct ambassadors of the company to customers and can contribute greatly to competitive advantage. People who are acquired or contracted can develop firm-specific skills over a period of time, and letting go of them only to recruit afresh and train new people all over again is a waste of investment. Further, the demand and supply of labour can impact the valuation too. In a booming economy, the value and uniqueness of skills increase and those organizations that apply pure economic rationalization to recruitment of human capital will be more disadvantaged.

The bottomline is that while in today's business environment, we can no longer afford lifelong employment and paternalistic HR policies, the organization has to demonstrate basic respect and commitment to all employees, not in vision statements but in action through commitment to training, opportunities for growth, fair play and openness.

Characteristics of Knowledge Workers

Even though there is lack of research on the characteristics of knowledge workers in general, we can see some limited research on technical and scientific professionals in high-technology companies. These studies show that knowledge workers tend to have certain unique personality and occupational characteristics.[24] Similarly, studies on high-performing and learning organizations throw light on the likely personality profile of knowledge workers. Some of them are described below:

Autonomy

It is clear that innovation and creativity cannot flourish under tightly controlled conditions. The command and control type of managerial styles that dominated much of the 20th century stifled creativity and encouraged compliance, sycophancy, single-loop learning and politicization of the workforce. When there is a lack of decentralized decision-making, open communication, facilitative leadership and debeauracratized structures, the environment is not conducive for the free flow of knowledge. Knowledge workers need enough breathing space to express themselves openly and experiment boldly. Managerial mentality plays a key role in the process. Unless front-line managers give up their obsession on command and control, no amount of rhetoric by senior management can empower people.

Challenging Tasks

Knowledge workers thrive on creative chaos. Studies of IT professionals reveal that they need challenging stretch assignments which require working on latest technology or practice.[25] While this may appear as a very desirable characteristic, it may also pose practical problems. Even global organizations cannot always provide opportunities to work on latest technology or practice as they also need people for work that is routine and maintenance oriented. This gives rise to equity issues as people carefully watch how the organization allocates human resources. Knowledge workers realize that their professional standing and career prospects with the present and prospective employers depend on how current and critical their knowledge base is. They want to have a say in the allocation of their work to ensure that they do not lose out on plum knowledge postings.

Immediate and Frequent Feedback and Rewards

Knowledge workers engaged in non-routine work are eager to get frequent feedback from their peers, team members and leaders. When they think of a breakthrough idea, they want somebody around to talk about it. Initial reaction to creative work is crucial in maintaining the motivation and momentum of a knowledge worker. Any hint of cynicism, lack of enthusiasm and support has the potential to sap the creative flow. Thus, performance management of knowledge workers is quite non-traditional. Similarly, knowledge workers require and expect immediate and frequent rewards in recognition of their good work. A pat on the back in front of the team or a congratulatory email from a manager is sometimes more powerful than financial rewards.

Ownership of Ideas and Enterprise

Ownership of intellectual property rights is of serious concern to knowledge workers. If people see their employer failing in properly acknowledging their creative ownership and contribution, they will certainly keep their tacit knowledge to themselves. Increasing interest in owning company stocks shows that they also expect a fair share of rewards. Many high-technology companies prefer to promote intrapreneurship by seed funding new ventures of their employees rather than losing them altogether. Today organizations aim to tap creative ideas of all levels of employees as they realize that small ideas create a multiplier effect. However, the success of such efforts depends on how knowledge workers perceive the fairness of the recognition and reward that their creative contribution receives.

Commitment to Profession More than Organization

A knowledge economy imposes a heavy burden on individuals to constantly update their knowledge and align their skills and competencies to fast-changing business requirements. They are largely left alone to manage their career and learning. In their quest for employability, knowledge workers constantly seek positions that facilitate lifelong learning and in the process, they are more committed to their profession than the organization they are working for, whether as full-time or fractional employees or contractors. In the absence of trusting relationships and rewards, they prefer to hoard their tacit knowledge and create a niche for themselves.

Teamwork/Community of Practices

Knowledge workers typically deal with issues that are uncertain, ambiguous and complex. By working as a team, they pool their intellectual capabilities and cross-functional skills to 'make sense' of a complex task environment.[26] Their informal learning often takes the form of a 'community of practice' where 'a group of people, with diverse viewpoints, roles, etc. are engaged in joint work over a significant period of time, in which they build things, solve problems, learn, invent, nego-tiate meaning, and evolve a way of talking and reading each other'.[27] These communities often cut across organizational boundaries and extend to global networks of people with similar interests and passion. While knowledge workers prefer to work in teams, they would like to be given suffi-cient autonomy and operational freedom with minimal bureaucracy.

Lifestyle

Today, more and more people are conscious of the quality of their lifestyle and prefer those employers whose employment practices promote work-life balance through measures such as flexi-time, tele-commuting, job sharing, hot-desking, on-the-job childcare and health promotion. They also tend to judge the ethical standards of their employers in areas such as corporate citizenship, environmental responsibility, and dealings with third world countries. The growing popularity of 'ethical funds' with investors and successful public cam-paigns against companies that indirectly encourage child labour in third world countries is an indication of how seriously people take their social responsibilities.

Organizations such as Hewlett-Packard (HP) have long recognized and respected the characteristics of knowledge workers and have built their strategies, structures, systems, staff and shared values around those characteristics. The HP Way, developed way back in 1957, reflected the HP philoso-phy and emphasized belief in and respect for people, oppor-tunity for meaningful participation, shared work, responsibilities and rewards, informal and open working environment, inter-nal promotion, decentralized work groups, and individual freedom. The rhetoric was made into reality as the HP Way was embedded in all people management practices.[14]

From the above we can see a clear connection between the typical characteristics of knowledge workers and high-performance work practices that have been discussed earlier.

Agenda for Managerial Action

Points to Ponder . . .	. . . Steps to Consider
While IT has certainly fuelled the knowledge revolution, it cannot be the driving engine without proper people management processes in place. Knowledge management has to be people centric with support from IT and not the other way round.	Organizations need to avoid the temptation of investing heavily in IT at the cost of HRM. Even though managing people is a long-term and uncertain investment, it is still worth the effort because without bright and motivated people, there is no future in a knowledge economy.
HR professionals have always craved for due recognition of their role in management. The knowledge economy has provided them the perfect platform.	The HR function needs the right kind of professionals to act as change agents, facilitators of learning, employee champions, and catalysts for creativity and innovation. It is possible to attract such people only when the function is given its due importance and respect.
Today, HR is at the core of business strategy.	The best way to elevate HR to a strategic level is to integrate HR responsibility into every manager's function, starting from the top, and make it a key performance indicator. HR should be located as close to business units as possible.
The best practices literature within the domain of strategic human resource management is an excellent starting point in the drive for a learning organization. However, apart from the organization-driven HR	Organizations need to identify, develop and reward such learning champions.

interventions, the informal social architecture is equally important to create communities of practices to be managed by volunteers.	
Falling birth rates and ageing population will dramatically alter the composition of the workforce in developed nations.	To address the looming shortfall in working age people, organizations need to globalize their recruitment to attract qualified immigrants, harness the potential of women and minorities at all levels of employment and address the training needs of older workers to extend their working life. This calls for efficient management of diversity in the workplace.
Organizations are increasingly using flexible and competitive types of workforce, such as core, contract and casual. Each type of workforce will need to be managed differently.	The changing employment profile has implications for management of recruitment, training, performance, reward and careers. However, every type of employee is important to the bottomline of the organization and deserves basic respect, dignity, fair wages, and opportunities for training and advancement.
The characteristics of knowledge workers are quite different, in context and content, from those of industrial workers.	Work practices need to revolve around the characteristics of knowledge workers. For example, Generation Xers expect work-life balance to enhance quality of life, necessitating flexible and innovative work practices.

Case Scenario: Hewlett-Packard—A Model of Consistency

Hewlett-Packard (H-P), a US multinational producer of electronic equipment, provides an excellent illustration of strong consistency and alignment among a firm's HR practices. H-P is widely regarded as a pioneer in high-commitment work systems. Their progressive employment policies are designed to cultivate and convey trust in the workforce, provide a superior quality of work life, and 'create an

environment in which employees can fulfil their natural de-
sires to do good, creative work.' This approach fits their
business strategy of designing, manufacturing, and then servicing top-quality, leading-edge, and somewhat premium-
priced products. Among the policies H-P has employed toward
these ends are: Long-term employment and efforts to minimize layoffs; above-market compensation; extensive discretion for employees; extremely liberal benefits; intensive (and
continual) training; and programs aimed at providing flexibility to workers in balancing work and family responsibilities.
Not surprisingly, these 'investments' are supported by careful
screening of initial hires, promotion from within, reliance on
peer pressure and peer review, and programs aimed at
minimizing turnover, which all interact to ensure that H-P
reaps a good return from these investments in its workforce.

The benefits to H-P from such a consistent and tightly
aligned set of HR policies seem clear. In an industry characterized by intense competition for technical and marketing
talent, H-P is able to attract and retain highly gifted and
motivated personnel. H-P's system of promotion from within,
the expectations of long-term employment, and the intensive
training and professional development provided have historically reinforced the basic message that workers at H-P can
have a gratifying career there. Those practices also help the
firm ensure that employees internalize and embody the
company's values, which is particularly important in so far as
H-P cannot closely supervise some work activities (especially
the creative work) and has chosen instead to cultivate a
relationship of trust and rely on peer pressure. Its compensation and evaluation procedures reinforce the message of
trust and of being part of a family; for instance, there are no
individualized bonus systems anywhere within H-P, even for
the CEO, only generally awarded rewards based on H-P
stock. Of course, these practices leave H-P open to opportu-
nistic behaviour by some of its employees; for example,
because it would muddy the message of trust to rely on

methods such as surveillance of the workplace or lie detector tests, H-P does not employ these intrusive methods. Instead, H-P is famous for its use of 'Management By Wandering Around' (MBWA), which represents a more informal and less intrusive form of monitoring that ostensibly enables managers to communicate trust and concern, rather than distrust and suspicion.

We noted above that an organization's culture may limit the sorts of monitoring and control strategies it wishes to deploy. Yet it is worth noting that H-P does use metal detectors to screen production workers at some facilities outside the United States (e.g., in Singapore). Such tactics, if employed in the United States, would presumably be inconsistent with the basic message of trust that H-P aims to cultivate. But in some East Asian countries, such as Korea and Singapore, where citizens confront more extensive governmental control over their lives, there is probably little contradiction between H-P's reputation as a progressive, caring, trusting employer on the one hand, and, on the other hand, using metal detector technology on the shop floor to deter theft. In other words, when we measure consistency of HR practices in terms of consistency with a standard pattern of social relationships, the society within which the enterprise is embedded can greatly affect internal consistency.

To summarize: H-P's human resource policies and value statements communicate a remarkably consistent set of messages about what the firm and employees have a right to expect of one another, to the point that employees can (and do) characterize reliably whether or not a given action or decision was undertaken in accordance with 'the H-P way'.

References

1. **Gloet, M.** and **Berrell, M.** (2003) 'The dual paradigm nature of knowledge management: Implications for achieving quality outcomes in human resource management'. *Journal of Knowledge Management*, Vol 7 No 1, pp. 78–89.
2. **Drucker, P.F., Dyson, E., Handy, C., Saffo, P.** and **Senge, P.M.** (1997) 'Looking ahead: Implications of the present'. *Harvard Business Review*, Vol 75 No 5.
3. **Cohen, D.** (1998) 'Toward a knowledge context: Report on the first annual U.C. Berkeley forum on knowledge and the firm', *California Management Review*, Vol 40 No 3, pp. 22–39.
4. **Ruggles, R.** (1998) 'The state of the notion: Knowledge management in practice'. *California Management Review*, Vol 40 No 3.
5. **Zack, M.H.** (1999) 'Developing a knowledge strategy'. *California Management Review*, Vol 41 No 3.
6. **Smith, A.F.** and **Kelly, T.** (1997) 'Human capital in the digital economy'. In Hasselbein, F. et al. (Eds.) *The Organisation of the Future*, Jossey-Bass: SF.
7. **Wright, P.M., McMahan, G.C., Snell, S.A.** and **Grehart, B.** (2001) 'Comparing line and HR executives' perceptions of HR effectiveness: Services, roles and contributions'. *Human Resource Management*, Vol 40 No 2, pp. 111–23.
8. **Ulrich, D.** (1997) *Human resource champions: The next agendas for adding value and delivering results*, Harvard Business School Press: Cambridge, MA.
9. **Watkins, K.E.** and **Marsick, V.** (1992) 'Building the learning organisation: A new role for human resource developers'. *Studies in Continuing Education*, Vol 14 No 2, pp. 115–29.
10. **Horibe, F.** (1999) *Managing knowledge workers*, Wiley: Toronto.
11. **Walker, J.W.** and **Stopper, W.G.** (2000) 'Developing human resources leaders'. *Human Resource Planning*, Vol 23 No 1, pp. 38–44.
12. **Delery, J.E.** and **Doty, D.H.** (1996) 'Modes of theorizing in strategic human resource management: Tests of universalistic, contingency, and configurational performance predictions'. *Academy of Management Journal*, Vol 39 No 4, pp. 802–35.
13. **Mueller, F.** (1996). 'Human resources as strategic assets: An evolutionary resource-based theory'. *Journal of Management Studies*, Vol 33 No 6, pp. 757–85.

14. **Truss, C.** (2001) 'Complexities and controversies in linking HRM with organisational outcomes'. *Journal of Management Studies*, Vol 38 No 8.

15. **Gratton, L., Hope-Hailey, V., Stiles, P.** and **Truss, C.** (1999) 'Linking individual performance to business strategy: The people process model'. *Human Resource Management*, Vol 38 No 1, pp. 17–32.

16. **Pfeffer, J.** (1998) 'Seven practices of successful organisations'. *California Management Review*, Vol 40 No 2, pp. 96–124.

17. **Pfeffer, J.** (2001) 'Pitfalls on the road to measurement: The dangerous liaison of human resources with the ideas of accounting and finance'. *Human Resource Management*, Vol 36 No 3, pp. 357–65.

18. **Drucker, P.** (2002) 'They're not employees, they're people'. *Harvard Business Review*, February.

19. **Brockbank, W.** (1999) 'If HR were strategically proactive: Present and future directions in HR's contribution to competitive advantage'. *Human Resource Management*, Vol 38 No 4, pp. 337–52.

20. **Conger, J.A.** (1997) 'How generational shifts will transform organisational life'. In Hasselbein, F. et al. (Eds.) *The Organisation of the Future*, Jossey-Bass: SF.

21. **Bellary, A.** Personal observations during review of manuscript.

22. **Lepak, D.P.** and **Snell, S.A.** (1999) 'The human resource architecture: Toward a theory of human capital allocation and development', *Academy of Management Review*, Vol 24 No 1, pp. 31–48.

23. **Hippel, C., Mangum, S.L., Greenberger, D.B., Heneman, R.L.** and **Skoglind, J.D.** (1997) 'Temporary employment: Can organisations and employees both win?' *The Academy of Management Executive*, Vol 11 No 1, pp. 93–104.

24. **Agrawal, N.M.** and **Thite, M.** (2003) 'Human resource issues, challenges and strategies in the Indian software services industry'. *International Journal of Human Resource Development and Management*, Vol 3 No 3, pp. 249–64.

25. **Thite, M.** (2000) 'Leadership styles in information technology projects'. *The International Journal of Project Management*, Vol 18 No 4, pp. 235–41.

26. **Sapsed J., Bessant J., Partington D., Tranfield D.** and **Young M.** (2002) 'Teamworking and knowledge management: A review of converging themes'. *International Journal of Management Review*, Vol 1 No 1, pp. 71–85.

27. **Brown, J.S.** (2002) An epistemological perspective on organisations and innovation. Keynote address to the 3rd Organisational Knowledge and Learning Conference (OKLC), 2002.

28. **Huselid, M.A.** (1995) 'The impact of HRM practices on turnover, productivity and corporate financial performance'. *Academy of Management Journal*, Vol 38 No 3, pp. 635–72.

29. **MacDuffie, J.P.** (1995) 'Human resource bundles and manufacturing performance: Organisational logic and flexible production systems in the world auto industry'. *Industrial and Labour Relations Review*, Vol 48 No 2, pp. 197–221.

30. **Osterman, P.** (1994) 'How common is workplace transformation and how can we explain who adopts it?' *Industrial and Labour Relations Review*, Vol 47 No 2, pp. 173–88.

31. **Arthur, J.B.** (1992) 'The link between business strategy and industrial relations systems in American steel minimills'. *Industrial and Labour Relations Review*, Vol 45 No 3, pp. 488–506.

32. **West, M.** and **Patterson, M.** (1999) 'People management and the productivity gap'. *New Economy*, Vol 6 No 1, pp. 22–27.

APPENDIX 1: Literature Review of High-performance Work Practices

Pfeffer (1998) [16]	Huselid (1995) [28]	MacDuffie (1995) [29]	Osterman (1994) [30]	Arthur (1992) [31]	Delery & Doty (1996) [12]	West & Patterson (1999) [32]
• Employment security	• Personnel selection	• Work teams	• Teams	• Broadly defined jobs	• Internal career opportunities	• Selection and recruitment
• Selective hiring	• Performance appraisal	• Problem-solving groups	• Job rotation	• Employee participation	• Formal training systems	• Induction
• Self-managed teams and decentralization as the basic principles of organizational design	• Incentive compensation	• Employee suggestions	• Quality circles	• Formal dispute resolution	• Appraisal measures	• Training
	• Job design	• Job rotation	• Total Quality Management	• Information sharing	• Profit sharing	• Appraisal
	• Grievance procedures	• Decentralization		• Highly skilled workers	• Employment security	• Skill flexibility
• Comparatively high compensation contingent on organizational performance	• Information sharing	• Recruitment and hiring		• Self-managed teams	• Voice mechanisms	• Job variety
	• Attitude assessment	• Contingent compensation		• Extensive skills training	• Job definition	• Job responsibility
	• Labour management participation	• Status differentiation		• Extensive benefits		• Teamworking
• Extensive training	• Selection ratio	• Training of new employees		• High wages		• Communication
• Reduce status differences	• Average training per employee per year	• Training of experienced employees		• Salaried workers		• Quality improvement teams
• Sharing information	• Promotion criteria (seniority versus merit)			• Stock ownership		• Harmonization
						• Comparative pay
						• Incentive compensation systems

Source: Williamson, S. (2002) 'The contribution of HRM to organisational performance in the Australian recreation industry'. Ph.D. Research Proposal, School of Management, Griffith University, Brisbane, Australia.

Management Philosophy: Foundation of People-centric Culture

Human relations are fragile and uncertain. There is no formula that can guarantee lasting relationships, be it in marriage, parenthood, friendship or employment. But people in successful relationships have a few things in common: They trust each other, they are fair (and more importantly, seen by each other to be fair), and make compromises to accommodate their differences. The moment any of these elements—trust, fairness and compromise—disappear, the relationship starts cracking. Once the crack appears, the originality or purity of the relationship is lost and any patchwork becomes susceptible to further damage.

Employment relationship brings in additional complexities, as it is more impersonal and multi-dimensional. When people are asked what they think about their employer, it is not the external image projected by the company that flashes across their mind. People think about whether their boss treats them well, has trust in their abilities, allocates and evaluates work fairly and also whether their colleagues are a good bunch of people to hang around with. People consider and judge employment more as a social relationship than as a contract. As they spend most of their waking hours with their colleagues, the quality of their employment relationship is heavily influenced by their perception of trust and fairness of not only their 'faceless' employer but also of the 'real' people they work with.

Therefore, no organization has full influence over the social aspect of employment relationship. Even in physical aspects, i.e., the terms and conditions of employment and organizational policies and procedures, people read between lines and see whether they are implemented in letter and spirit. Like the organization, the policies are faceless. It is the individual managers who are the real face of the company for the employee and it is in their actions and attitudes that lies the litmus test of the employment relationship.

It is obvious that success of people management depends on whether the parties involved trust each other and treat each other fairly. Of course, everybody is aware of it but unfortunately, very few pause to reflect on this fundamental reality before they formulate and implement any HR policy. Every organization makes the right noises about the importance of people. But the naked reality is quite different. No amount of sweet talk and publicity by the management can disguise the true nature of the relationship, but people managers continue to trade the real image for the borrowed.

Trust—A Casualty of Management Madness

Trust evolves over time and its true test is during a crisis. With decreasing market protection and increasing globalization of markets and competition, businesses, large and small, face demanding times. Governments can no longer afford to continue public welfare programmes on the scale they used to and businesses can no longer be paternalistic towards their employees. Tough times call for tough actions and painful decisions. But how tough should that tough be, how far is too far, and who will ensure that the pain is equitably spread? These are some of the uncomfortable questions that people ask when a Chief Executive Officer (CEO) announces tough measures.

Leaders feel lonely at the top and more so during a crisis. When they take charge, their credibility clock starts clicking. The glare of the spotlights can be quite testing for their ability and character. They quickly establish their authority by issuing vision statements, announcing new appointments, and set about to create a new order by reorganizing and reengineering policies, processes and people. Many of them sincerely believe that the more changes they make to the existing order, the better is the impact of their leadership. They are aware of their limited tenure and are in a hurry to bring about the desired change. Certain measures, like laying off people, closing loss-making units, and selling off assets are very popular with some CEOs as they bring quick results. The gloss of short-term success shines brighter under the spotlight and cracks, if any, are hidden.

Many CEOs believe that globalization calls for bigger and better enterprises and so, the search begins for mergers and acquisitions. Impatient investors, uncertain markets, growing resentment within the company bring the situation to a boiling point and puts pressure on the CEO to do something spectacular, quickly. So, a string of acquisitions are made and mergers are announced and anybody who questions is asked to put up or shut up. Armed with savvy (and expensive) publicity and clever accounting (remember, Enron), the CEO promises the future is now secure and the painful past behind. As the share price inches upward, the CEO and the senior managers pocket hefty performance bonuses.

The workers of course have to wait and further tighten the belt because the battle is not over and many more sacrifices are still needed. Any hint of industrial action by trade unions is countered by threats of further job cuts by relocating the plants elsewhere in the world. Plum positions in the merged and acquired units go to the CEO's blue-eyed boys at the cost of merit. As the initial effects wear off and the company starts looking shaky again, it is the end of the term for the CEO who has already negotiated a new lucrative posting. If the cracks appear too quickly before the CEO's term expires, and the outside world gets wind of them despite best attempts to suppress, there is always a golden parachute clause that guarantees that the CEO departs with a handsome package.

The facts are too powerful to ignore the 'ugly face' of organizational life:

- The gap between managerial and non-managerial remuneration is widening at an alarming rate. From 80 per cent in the 1980s, it rose to nearly 400 per cent in the 1990s. *Time* magazine reports that the top five executives account for a staggering 75 per cent of stock options, the top 5 per cent account for another 15 per cent and the rest of the employees account for hardly 5 per cent. The figures make people wonder whether the CEOs are busy managing the company or the share prices.
- Many CEOs and the senior managers grant themselves hefty salary increases and bonuses even when they know that the company is sinking. In one Australian firm, the Chairman even refused to sign the proxy forms opposing hefty salary increases to directors.
- Many companies announce massive increases in profits but tell their workers they cannot expect to get any salary increases nor assume that their jobs are safe.
- Many companies dip into workers' superannuation entitlements before going bust.
- Majority of mergers and acquisitions fail because of lack of cultural compatibility arising out of inadequate and improper due diligence process.
- Research on downsizing and outsourcing shows that they have not only failed to deliver the promised results but have eroded the skill base within.

Unfortunately, trust has been the biggest casualty in the recent waves of management actions, such as downsizing, delayering, outsourcing and reengineering. They have led to unintended consequences by demoralizing and demotivating employees who work harder and under increasing stress. Middle management ranks have almost disappeared and with that the experience they accumulated over the years. For example, the effects of radical privatization in New Zealand were felt recently when Auckland was plunged into darkness due to electricity failure but the local energy companies had no answer as they had let go of people who had the skills. The city had to wait for fifteen agonizing days before outside engineers were brought in.

The near abandonment of career management responsibilities by employers is another barrier to creating or rebuilding an atmosphere of trust. Their transactional attitude to employment relationship fails to deliver transformational outcomes expected by them. This 'help us but help yourself' attitude to career management prevents employers from developing the psychological attachment necessary in a learning organization.[1] Further, considering today's employment profile where more and more people work as contractors or on part-time/casual basis and are therefore, outside the boundaries of standard employment, securing their trust and commitment is quite challenging, to say the least.

Trust—The Prerequisite of Knowledge Society

In the current environment of mistrust, it is a paradox that securing the trust of employees has never been so important. Trust and fairness are at the very heart of knowledge management. Without them, there is no sharing of tacit knowledge. Since knowledge resides in individuals who have the discretion to use and share it as and when they want, organizations have to create an HR philosophy that 'restores people to the heart of organization'.[2] No HR strategy can succeed unless the organization has an overarching HR philosophy that assures its employees that they are working for a caring, nurturing, trustworthy organization.

A survey of knowledge employees in leading-edge companies revealed that psychological contract and those organizational processes relating to procedural justice, such as meritocracy and equity, directly affect two critical organizational outcomes, namely, employee commitment and intention to remain with the organization.[3]

Since voluntary co-operation is the only way to unlock tacit knowledge, it is obvious that only organizations that are known as trustworthy and fair can persuade knowledge workers to share their experience and promote innovation. These organizations become 'employers of choice' amongst the highly networked knowledge workers. To recruit and retain best talent, organizations not only need to be high performing but also seen to be of high character, credibility and integrity and value driven.[4]

The literature on knowledge management stresses the need for 'communities of practices' within and outside of the learning organization. In an organization characterized by a here-and-now attitude to employment relations, it is hard to think of creating communities or hubs of voluntary co-operation.

How do we secure trust that leads to commitment? The process begins with the management philosophy that underpins the organizational culture, i.e., its shared attitudes, values and beliefs about people. Lessem and Neubauer describe culture as a tree, with the 'leaves' depicting surface behaviour, attributes and attitudes, the 'trunk and branches' portraying institutions and ideas, and the 'roots' representing the deeper cultural influences.[5] The tree metaphor depicts a complex interaction between cultural, institutional and behavioural factors.

Like tacit knowledge, philosophy and culture are difficult to describe but easy to experience. They are embedded in the physical and social artefacts of an organization and people can narrate their experience with them through storytelling. For example, one can distinguish between the culture of Microsoft and IBM or Ford and Toyota or General Electric and WalMart. To feel the management philosophy and culture of an organization, one has to go beneath the surface of public image, CEO's personality and stated policies and look for real-life experiences of people throughout the organization.

The management of people in an organization is the direct result of management philosophy as reflected by key indicators, such as attitude towards time horizon, employment security, fair play and expectation management.

Indicators of Management Philosophy

Time Horizon

An outlook towards time is critical in one's philosophy or culture as it shapes the decision-making process. Cross-cultural management researchers have long recognized that while Western countries focus on the short term, Asian countries look to the long term. Several studies have suggested that Japanese managers, unlike Americans, generally focus on the long-term success of the company, rather than the short-term wealth of the shareholders.[6] Fears that American companies were losing their competitive edge due to their shortsightedness even prompted the United States Congress to hold a hearing in 1989 on corporate time horizons.

National and organizational attitudes towards time invariably influence the performance expectations and decisions of individual managers. A CEO who signs a three-year contract with a company will be less inclined to look beyond three years and concentrate on measures that yield maximum results in the short term. Such CEOs would tend to conveniently ignore any long-term negative consequence of their decisions. A CEO with a long-term horizon is not likely to rush while taking important decisions, such as mergers and acquisitions, retrenchments, and asset sales. It is no surprise that CEOs with longer individual time horizons have been found to frame strategic issues with longer consequence spans than CEOs with shorter individual time horizons.[7]

An outlook towards time also influences the propensity to taking risks or avoiding uncertainty. Those who value long-term outcomes take time in making decisions and are generally averse to risks. For example, in Chinese and Japanese markets, relationship is more valued than written contracts and decision-making is often painfully slow. Many rightly argue that in today's turbulent economy, decision-makers have to be quick in taking decisions lest the opportunities are lost. While risks are inherent and unavoidable in the global economy, the consequences of a rushed judgement can be catastrophic, particularly for a large organization. Those who rushed towards the dotcom boom by dumping old economy stocks are now nursing their wounds after losing more than three-quarters of their stocks' worth. Enron, Arthur Andersen, WorldCom . . . the list of casualties of corporate greed continues to shake world markets. Thus, one has to balance short-term benefits with long-term consequences.

As in investment decisions, time horizon is a critical element in people management. An organization with a short-term focus regards HR as a cost or a profit centre and demands quick returns on investment. In contrast, an organization with a long-term focus regards HR as an investment to be reaped over time.

Management Ethics

In the rush to dominate the 21st century, many organizations seem to have suspended ethical judgement of their decisions for the sake of business expediency. Such organizations seem to believe that in a dog-eats-dog world of cut-throat competition, one needs to focus on survival at any cost and there is no time to indulge in moral debates. Even government departments, public sector and non-profit organizations that have an explicit mandate for public welfare are mired in ethical dilemmas. In his classic book, *Images of Organization*, Gareth Morgan uses the metaphor of 'organizations as instruments of domination' to explain the double-edged nature of rationality that leads to the question 'rationality for whom?'[8]

Controversial decisions such as arms sales to a war-ravaged country or trading with a country notorious for human rights abuses or business partnership with a powerful but corrupt politician are often justified by governments and businesses as beneficial for businesses, jobs and the future. It is difficult to resist the temptation of a business opportunity, particularly when there are other competing countries or organizations waiting to service such customers. But such decisions certainly test the ethical boundaries of leaders and send clear signals to other decision-makers. While there are many examples of countries paying the price for dealing with a dictator or a corrupt partner, there are also examples of organizations who were nearly destroyed in disgrace for their unethical, immoral and illegal conduct.

Enron, WorldCom and Andersen Consulting are just recent examples. In all these companies, short-term gains were followed by near extinction. Analysts now point out, with the benefit of hindsight, that the same mutual funds and other shareholder bodies that are calling for retribution are responsible for the actions of these companies. They supported only those companies that were churning out double-digit returns on investment and in the process, pushed them over the line.

The crisis is evident even in those institutions which are supposed to be the symbol of ethics, trust and morality. Consider the current child abuse crisis engulfing the Catholic Church from Australia to America. Many church leaders have disgraced themselves by putting the interests of church finances and the offending priests above those of the victims, the most vulnerable sections of society. Instead of offering help and solace to victims and punishing the offending priests, church leaders simply shunted priests from parish to parish until exposed. In the process, many went further than corporate sharks and signed secrecy deals with victims.

Time and again, organizations have suffered from the false notion that they could hide unpleasant facts from the public, only to let the situation deteriorate further and then get exposed by whistle blowers or media. In the recent past, many automakers have faced public wrath after being exposed that data on customer complaints affecting safety of vehicles was suppressed. The tobacco industry has a notorious reputation in this regard. Dyson warns that in today's networked world, 'organizations will have to learn to live with increased visibility and, perhaps even more scary, a loss of control over corporate image'.[9] No amount of public relations stunts can forever hide 'every slipup, every policy, every practice'. Dyson suggests that 'when so much about you is known or knowable, candour is the best way to earn credibility'.

Ethics in People Management

While corporate ethics is hotly debated in relation to the external community, it is surprising that very little discussion is taking place about ethics in managing internal customers, i.e., employees. Once again, people managers face the challenge of introducing ethics in HRM amidst the popular clamour for bottomline strategic objectives. Dyson again warns that 'in a company's relations with customers and employees, the boundaries of what can be held private are narrowing'.[9]

As employee champions, people managers have a natural role and right to play in ensuring ethical people management philosophy and practices. It is the essential, and not an optional, requirement of a people manager to be an 'ethical steward'. The HR profession itself evolved as a welfare function and has been heavily influenced by human relations movement, motivation theories, and concepts of employee participation, job enrichment, empowerment, etc. However, several popular people management practices are under attack for being unethical.

Many companies have been exposed for employment discrimination based on race, gender, age, disability, pregnancy, sexual orientation, etc. Fears are being expressed that advances in genetics will lead to discrimination based on gene mapping of job applicants. The management of diversity is still an elusive concept with many organizations, as their focus is more on legal compliance of equal employment and affirmative action provisions than on genuine commitment to the process. Bullying in the workforce is another concern that is frequently ignored until exposed.

Similarly, managements have been accused of making people work excess and odd hours in the name of 'flexibility'. Some survey findings suggest that many employees, particularly managers, are averaging 50–60 work hours per week. While the past century was marked by a gradual decline in working hours, the present century is witnessing a reversal of the trend. Similarly, measures such as electronic surveillance and supervision of work (as in call centres), empowerment for cost-cutting but pushed in the name of delegation, enterprise bargaining, and increasing 'at risk' or performance-based portion of pay, raise concerns about 'the scope of employer's duty of care, about individual rights to autonomy, privacy, dignity and self-esteem, and the boundaries between organizational demands and employee subjectivity'.[10]

As more and more companies collapse due to corporate greed and employees feel more uncertain about their jobs and future, conspiracy theories about 'vampire-like capitalists sucking living labour' (Karl Marx) gain more credibility and words like trust and commitment sound hollow. People managers need to realize that perception is reality and hence, the importance of ethical sensitivity and reasoning.

Organizations which adopt the 'people as partners in progress' policy demonstrate a distinct HR philosophy characterized by employment security, company flexibility, sharing of financial success with the workforce, development of good communication and consultation, and representative employee voice.[11] Woodall[11] and others, therefore, conclude that 'there are ethical positions that may not always coincide with the "business case" but which still need to be heard and with which HR specialists need to engage'.[10]

Employment Security

With the changing employment profile towards short-term relationships, it is now almost taken for granted by employers that employment security is no longer an issue to be debated. After all, even Japan is shedding its much-valued lifelong employment policy. The gulf between what employers offer and what employees expect is nowhere as wide as it is on this issue. While employees today generally accept the fact that in today's environment, employability is a more realistic expectation than employment, the importance of employment security has not diminished.

Downsizing has been a frequently used management tool since the 1980s. It has been used as part of cost-cutting, restructuring and reengineering exercises to improve organizational efficiency, productivity and competitiveness. However, the results of downsizing are nowhere near the stated goals and often, downsizing firms have performed worse than those that have not downsized. Similarly, firms that have resorted to outsourcing have had mixed results. Studies also point out that the survivors of downsizing exercises suffer from increased insecurity resulting in low morale and high stress.[12] Frequently, employees pay the price for the corporate greed and lack of long-term vision of top management.

Pfeffer and Veiga believe that 'employment security is fundamental to the implementation of most other high performance management practices'.[13] To support their argument, they quote Herb Kelleher, the CEO of Southwest Airlines:

> Our most important tools for building employee partnership are job security and a stimulating work environment . . . Certainly there were times when we could have made substantially more profits in the short-term if we had furloughed people, but we didn't. We were looking at our employees' and our company's longer-term interests . . . [A]s it turns out, providing job security imposes additional discipline, because if your goal is to avoid layoffs, then you hire very sparingly. So our commitment to job security has actually helped us keep our labour force smaller and more productive than our competitors.

Pfeffer recognizes employment security as one of the practices of successful organizations and cites the examples of Lincoln Electric, General Motors and New United Motors.[14] He lists many advantages of incorporating employment security as an integral part of people management philosophy: Motivational tool for innovation and productivity improvement, decreased likelihood of layoffs that put strategic assets on the streets for the competition to employ, careful and leaner hiring, builds trust, increases co-operation and encourages people to take a longer-term perspective on their jobs. Pfeffer adds a caveat that employment security should be provided to guard people against economic downturns and strategic mistakes of management and not against poor performance.

The move towards flexible employment options away from full-time employment is equally contentious. Apart from the difficulty in 'make-and-buy' employment decisions that are based on the valuation of human capital, as discussed in the previous chapter, we need to consider the legal issues on benefits and entitlements and vicarious liability for non-traditional employees. For example, in many countries, any casual employee who works on a regular basis for more than six months is entitled to same benefits as a part-time and full-time employee. Further, the costs of recruitment and training of frequently changing temporary employees and the impact of ill-trained personnel on customer service, health and safety, etc. further dilute the advantages of flexible employment. Increased use of temporary employees also affects the morale of permanent employees.[15] Thus, both in terms of direct and indirect costs, firms that offer employment security as part of a psychological contract stand to gain in the long run.

Recognizing that new forms of organization have their dark side, Kanter believes that 'new policies must reflect new forms of security while embracing the merging realities of flexibility, mobility and change'.[2] Accordingly, Kanter urges organizations of the future to write a new social contract with their employees, incorporating new motivational tools such as providing employable skills; giving control of the career agenda (e.g., allowing to choose the next project); access to training, mentoring, and challenging projects; enhancing professional reputation by providing abundant public recognition of achievements; and sharing of value creation through company share ownership, etc.

It is difficult for the HR profession, which is under attack for lack of contribution to business results, to argue the case for employment security in lieu of the popular notions of downsizing and outsourcing.[16] Here again the success of HR advocacy depends on the time horizon adopted by the management. The HR department has to argue the case that instead of adopting a minimalist ethical position which suggests that shareholder interests outweigh those of individuals and that the ends (of business interests) justify the means, the management has to embrace a broader ethical framework that treats people as ends in themselves and puts feeling and empathy ahead of economic rationalization.[10] Unless human resource management is shown to be humane, communities of practices and hubs of voluntary co-operation cannot flourish. In this context, the assessment of effectiveness of people management needs to be on a footing other than traditional accounting and auditing principles.

Fair Play

Fairness is another key ingredient to creating a trustworthy HR philosophy. People care as much about the fairness of the process as they do about the outcome itself. Kim and Mauborgne (1999) assert that 'fair process builds trust and commitment, trust and commitment produce voluntary co-operation, and voluntary co-operation drives performance, leading people to go beyond the call of duty by sharing their knowledge and applying their creativity'.[17] They identify engagement, explanation and expectation clarity as the bedrock elements of a fair process.

An organization can demonstrate its fairness by involving people and being transparent about its goals and means, openly admitting and rectifying its mistakes, sharing rewards equitably, clearly explaining the rationale behind changes to structure, HR policies, etc. and above all, walking the talk and leading by example. Fairness rests on the basic ethical principle: Do unto others as you would be done by.

Expectation Management

Promises create expectations and the failure to fulfil promises without justification lead to breakdown in trust and co-operation. Many organizations print glossy recruitment advertisements and promise the moon to prospective employees. While there is no dearth of organizations gloating on their achievements, very rarely do they admit their weaknesses or even identify areas of improvement. Very few organizations 'underpromise and overdeliver' to both external and internal customers.

Most organizations are content in the rhetoric of politically correct posturing on HR philosophy and policies. But it is the practice that speaks for itself. An organization which claims to value people will be judged by job applicants on how objective the selection process is and how sensitively the rejected candidates are treated. Similarly, an organization that claims to value diversity will be judged by the actual number of women, disabled and migrants employed at different levels.

In one instance, when a new CEO announced in his first meeting with employees that he would shortly conduct an employee climate survey, he was taken aback to see people laughing. He later realized that the company routinely conducted employee surveys but hardly acted on it. Thus, when expectations are created, they need to be honoured; otherwise, the company will lose face and be viewed cynically by employees.

It is common practice amongst employers to take seriously any false claim made by job applicants. However, many employers routinely make grand statements and promises about business growth, employment prospects, and HR policies on performance assessment, training opportunities and remuneration. It is only after joining the organization that the employee realizes the truth. Broken promises lead to disappointment, demotivation and low morale. Dissatisfied employees become cynical and adversely influence the mood and motivation of others around them. In the current war on talent, the image of the employer in the network of knowledge workers is crucial in determining an organization's ability to attract and retain key staff. Organizations that create and promote realistic expectations succeed in their efforts to become employers of choice.

Values in Practice

One of the organizations that have successfully deployed value-driven management philosophy into their strategic

HRM practice is Herman Miller Inc. (HMI), a US-based manufacturer of office furniture that has been consistently ranked as one of the best places to work in America.[18]

> HMI has always been a values-driven company, with a historical reputation for innovation in its relationships with employees as well as in its products. It has a rich history of leaders with strong religious beliefs and a culture that evolved from their philosophy. This culture includes a significant focus on the obligation of management to become open to ideas from all employees, the importance of design and its principles in the development of products, employee participation, and employee ownership. In addition, HMI has adopted an 'open-book management' approach, wherein employees are trained in company operations; employee input is sought and acted upon; and employees share financial gains when goals are met.[18]

Why are values so important to an organization? Because they are the rallying cause for people; they keep an organization focused on its core capabilities by linking every action to cherished values; they act as a 'litmus test for solving the inevitable perplexing problems that arise', and they 'provide a cornerstone for the design of a selection process that helps attract the right types of people'.[19] After analysing the business and people practices of companies such as Southwest Airlines, Cisco Systems, and the SAS Institute, O'Reilly and Pfeffer identify the common elements hidden in their success:

> First, each of these companies has a clear, well-articulated set of values that are widely shared and act as the foundation for the management practices that build the core capabilities that in turn provide a basis for the company's competitive success. Second, each of these organisations has a remarkable degree of alignment and consistency in the people-centred practices that express its core values. Finally, the senior managers in these firms, not just the founders or the CEO, are

leaders whose primary role is to ensure that the values are maintained and constantly made real to all of the people who work in the organization'.[19]

Leo Tolstoy said that all happy families have something in common but each unhappy family is unhappy in its own way. The same can be said about organizations and employees. Each organization has its own history of employee relations with unique strengths and weaknesses. People managers need to reinforce those strengths and rectify the weaknesses.

Agenda for Managerial Action

Points to Ponder . . .	. . . Steps to Consider
Employees are increasingly angry, frustrated and cynical about management motives and actions.	Honesty is always the best policy for all stakeholders. Executive remuneration has got to be equitable, transparent and tied to long-term performance.
With many CEOs initiating change for the sake of change, employees are change fatigued.	Commitment, communication and transparency are at the heart of a successful change process. Employees need to clearly understand the what, why and how of the intended change and be convinced that it is in the best interests of the organization with no hidden agenda and will affect everybody in a fair and equitable manner.
HR philosophy is more a rhetoric than reality.	No amount of impression management and image building will help if there is no genuine commitment to people. HR without ethics is like a body without a soul.
Today's managers focus on success in the short term.	The challenge is to respond quickly to emerging opportunities without

	losing sight of the big picture and long-term implications.
In a hyper-competitive global environment, ethics is regarded as relative and negotiable.	An organization that compromises on basic and universal values gambles on its very future.
People managers are expected to be ethical stewards.	Encourage managers to be the ethical role models. Do not tolerate unethical managers no matter how important they are to the company. Treat all complaints about unacceptable work practices, be it bullying, sexual harassment or racism seriously and swiftly.
More and more employers are abandoning employment security.	Commitment to reasonable employment security and employability is one of the key reasons behind organizations that succeed in recruiting and retaining best talent.
Employers are offering less (such as, security, wages, and training) but demanding more (such as, productivity, commitment and competence).	Kanter[2] recommends new social contract with motivational tools, such as employability, training, challenging work, frequent feedback and recognition (see case scenario in Ch. 6).
Manage employee expectations by underpromising and overdelivering.	Employees prefer honest answers over shallow promises. Ensure that any promise by a manager is realistic, equitable and implemented in time.

Case Scenario: SAS Institute—Philosophy and Values

The fundamental way that SAS Institute operates has been the same since its inception and is premised on a small, consistent set of values and beliefs. One is the desire to 'create a corporation where it was as much for the workers as for top management'. Two principles are inherent in that statement. The first is the principle that *all* people at SAS Institute are treated fairly and equally. In its practices and day-to-day operations, the company is a very egalitarian place. Neither Jim Goodnight (the company's CEO) nor anybody else has a reserved parking space. His health plan is no different from that of the day care workers. There is no executive dining room—everyone regardless of his or her position can eat at one of the on-site company cafeterias, where high-quality, subsidized food is accompanied by a pianist playing during the lunch hour. Everyone at SAS Institute has a private office not a cubicle. Dress is casual and decided by what the person feels comfortable wearing.

The second important principle is that the workplace should be fun and people should be treated with dignity and respect.

Essentially, SAS Institute believes in the power of reciprocity—that people feel obliged to return favours that are done for them. Or, more prosaically stated, if you treat your people well, they will treat the company well by being loyal and dedicated in return.

A third, interconnected part of the philosophy that guides SAS Institute is a belief and reliance on intrinsic, internal motivation. A part of trusting people is treating them like responsible adults and relying on them to do a good job. Barrett Joyner, the Vice-President of North American sales and marketing, noted that 'the emphasis is on coaching and mentoring rather than monitoring and controlling. Trust and respect—it's amazing how far you can go with that.'

The final part of SAS Institute philosophy comes from an important insight about the business and economic benefits that come from creating an environment in which both the physical aspects of the workplace and the services offered to employees relieve the stress and the day-to-day concerns of people. 'The point of the strategy is to make it impossible for people not to do their work' by removing as many distractions and concerns as possible.

The ideas that people are important, that if you take care of them they will take care of the company, and that taking care of them involves treating them as you yourself might want to be treated are not particularly novel or complicated. What makes SAS Institute fairly unusual is that it actually lives by these simple precepts. Implementing this philosophy requires taking a long-term approach. Goodnight commented, 'We only take a long-term view of all issues. Since any project will take at least one to three years to come to fruition, a long-term perspective is required.' This long-term perspective extends to the management of people at SAS Institute.

References

1. **Thite, M.** (2001) 'Help us but help yourself: The paradox of contemporary career management'. *The Career Development International*, Vol 6 No 6, pp. 312–17.
2. **Kanter, R.M.** (1997) 'Restoring people to the heart of the organisation of the future'. In Hasselbein, F. et al. (Eds.) *The Organisation of the Future*, Jossey-Bass: SF.
3. **Flood, P.C., Turner, T., Ramamoorthy, N.** and **Pearson, J.** (2001) 'Causes and consequences of psychological contracts among knowledge workers in the high technology and financial services industries'. *The International Journal of Human Resource Management*, Vol 12 No 7, pp. 1152–65.
4. **Smith, A.F.** and **Kelly, T.** (1997) 'Human capital in the digital economy'. In Hasselbein, F. et al. (Eds.) *The Organisation of the Future*, Jossey-Bass: SF.
5. **Lessem, R.** and **Neubauer, F.** (1994) *European management systems: Towards out of cultural diversity*, McGraw-Hill: London.
6. **Beldona, S., Inkpen, A.C.** and **Phatak, A.** (1998) 'Are Japanese managers more long-term oriented than United States managers?' *Management International Review*, Vol 38 No 3, pp. 239–56.
7. **El Sawy, O.A.** (1988) 'Temporal biases in strategic attention'. Working paper DS-88-1, University of Southern California.

8. **Morgan, G.** (1997) *Images of organisation*, Sage: Thousand Oaks, CA.
9. **Drucker, P.F., Dyson, E., Handy, C., Saffo, P.** and **Senge, P.M.** (1997) 'Looking ahead: Implications of the present'. *Harvard Business Review*, Vol 75 No 5.
10. **Woodall, J.** and **Winstanley, D.** (2001) 'The place of ethics in HRM'. In Storey, J. (Ed.) *HRM: A Critical Text*, Thomson Learning: UK.
11. **Involvement and Participation Association (IPA)** (1997) 'Towards industrial partnership: Putting it into practice'. London, *IPA* (No. 3—Welsh Water).
12. **Doherty, N., Bank, J.** and **Vinnicombe, S.** (1996) 'Managing survivors: The experience of survivors in BT and the British financial sector'. *Journal of Managerial Psychology*, Cranfield University: Bedford.
13. **Pfeffer, J.** and **Veiga, F.** (1999) 'Putting people first for organisational success'. *Academy of Management Executive*, Vol 13 No 2, pp. 37–48.
14. **Pfeffer, J.** (1998) 'Seven practices of successful organisations'. *California Management Review*, Vol 40 No 2, pp. 96–124.
15. **Davis-Blake, A., George, E.** and **Broshak, J.** (1994) 'When temporary solutions create permanent problems: How use of contingent workers affects full-time, permanent employees'. Paper presented at the 1994 Annual Meeting of the Academy of Management, Dallas.
16. **Sahdev, K., Vinnicombe, S.** and **Tyson, S.** (1999) 'Downsizing and the changing role of HR'. *International Journal of Human Resource Management*, Vol 10 No 5, pp. 906–23.
17. **Kim, W.C.** and **Mauborgne, R.** (1999) 'Fair process: Managing in the knowledge economy'. In Magretta, J. (Ed.), *Managing in the New Economy*, Harvard Business School Press: Boston, MA.
18. **McCowan, R.A., Bowen, U., Huselid, M.A.** and **Becker, B.E.** (1999) 'Strategic human resource management at Herman Miller'. *Human Resource Management*, Vol 38 No 4, pp. 303–08.
19. **O'Reilly, C.A.** and **Pfeffer, J.** (2000) *Hidden value—How great companies achieve extraordinary results with ordinary people*, Harvard Business School Press: Boston, MA.

4

Institutionalizing Learning to Learn—Key to Leverage Intellectual Capital

I think; therefore, I am

—René Descartes

Organizations have always faced the challenge to improve efficiency and effectiveness. The industrial economy has sought to achieve this largely through industrial engineering and used technology and process knowledge to boost productivity and profitability. Peter Drucker estimates that in the 20th century, there was a fifty-fold increase in the productivity of the manual worker in manufacturing. However, today the latest technology and process methodology are available off the shelf and at a fraction of the original cost and hence, they are no longer sustainable competitive advantages. It is the intellectual capital that fills the gap in the knowledge economy. Thus, the evolution of work organizations can be traced from 'agriculture through the industrial revolution to *manufacture*; through the knowledge revolution to *mentofacture* (made by the mind); and through the quality and learning revolutions to *spiroculture* (the creation of meaning and identity)'.[1]

Today, the necessity for people to question the very fundamental assumptions or mental models about their work and enterprise is quite evident. Most industries today testify to the fact that their environment is changing more rapidly than ever before. They are affected by a variety of factors, such as technology breakthroughs, decreasing government funding, globalizing markets and competition, changing profile and preferences of shareholders and customers and so on. In many countries, large companies operated as monopolies or dominant market leaders in banking, telecommunication, aviation, pharmaceuticals, etc. but today, they are as vulnerable to environmental uncertainty as anyone else. Size and/or technical, market, and financial dominance no longer assure future success.

Thus, circumstances are forcing organizations and people to alter their way of thinking and working. And those who can think and work better, smarter and faster survive and prosper. This requires them to become learning organizations.

Learning: The New Imperative

The initiative to enhance productivity has shifted from management executives to knowledge workers. Instead of directing and controlling work and workers, the management has to facilitate teams of workers to work on their own and figure out the best way of doing things. Further, the management needs to persuade workers to share their knowledge with others and empower the entire organization to benefit from the generation and application of new knowledge. As more and more manual work is automated, workers have to use their brain more than their hands, to think ways and means of responding to fast-changing demands with speed and agility. It requires learning to learn better ways of doing things and servicing the customer in the best way possible every time, all the time.

As Gareth Morgan demonstrates in his classic book, *The Images of Organisation*, comparing organizations to living brains opens up fascinating avenues for organizational discovery.[2]

There is nothing like the brain as an ultimate symbol of creativity and complexity. The interaction between parts and whole of the brain is equally intriguing as many scientists believe that memory is distributed throughout the brain and thus can be reconstituted from any of the parts. Using organizations as brains, we can analyse how information is processed and decisions made, whether they need to be centralized or decentralized, and how different parts can learn like the brain.

The concept of learning to learn is qualitatively different from the traditional notion of 'training', which merely focused on skills imparted by a trainer to meet immediate work requirements. As Zuboff explains, 'Learning is not something that requires time out from being engaged in productive activity; learning is the heart of productive activity. To put it simply, learning is the new form of labour'.[3]

Today, the focus is on competencies that enable people to self-manage, work in teams, think globally, boldly and unconventionally, and deploy the power of intuition and emotional intelligence. Competencies also include character, as without the latter, people will not share their knowledge.

The growing literature on learning organizations, organizational learning and management of innovation and creativity highlight how the concept of learning has changed in the knowledge economy. The literature focuses on the shifting emphasis to competencies, lifelong and double-loop learning, shedding organizational defensive routines and cultures as a prerequisite to a learning mindset, managing failure in a high-risk environment, and creating and sharing knowledge in cross-functional and cross-cultural teams.

Brains Wide Open

In today's globalized and networked marketplace, any idea from anybody that contributes to continuous improvement is welcome. It can come from a far-off corner of the world or the juniormost employee. The challenge for the organization is to encourage people to unleash their power of thinking and apply it in their daily work. In the process, ideas help organizations to break new grounds and acquire global excellence. For example, in the printing industry, well-established boundaries and mental models are being broken by a prototype that envisions a printer in which the ink never dries and the nozzle is never subject to wear and tear.[4]

When organizations apply the power of learning, they are empowered to successfully face the global competitive pressures. However, it is a daunting task to become a learning organization. Doing so requires fundamental changes in the thinking process and the ability and adaptability to be open-minded to the extent that well-established mental models may have to be sacrificed and painful readjustments made. This has to happen at the individual, group and organizational levels.

Albert Einstein once faced this litmus test by a junior scientist and admitted that his long-held and cherished belief was flawed. Filkin narrates the story under the title 'Einstein's red herring'.[5] Einstein was a firm believer in the Newtonian idea of an infinite unchanging universe and accordingly, advocated the concept of a 'cosmological constant'. However, Georges Lemaitre, a Belgian Jesuit priest and the leading theoretical cosmologist working at the Vatican observatory, wanted to find some new evidence to suggest that the universe was finite. When Lemaitre came to know about new scientific evidence by another scientist, Hubble, to suggest that the universe was expanding, he managed to corner Einstein and Hubble together to attend his presentation. When he had finished he could not believe his ears. Einstein stood up and announced that what he had just heard was 'the most beautiful and satisfying interpretation I have listened to' and went on to confess that creating the 'cosmological constant' was 'the biggest blunder of his life'.

Lemaitre continued to face opposition from eminent scientists and the debate continues, as it should in a typical learning organization. What is important, however, is that people like Einstein are needed to advance the cause of learning by admitting that they can make mistakes and be open to other's ideas, no matter how small they are and where they come from. Thus learning to unlearn is as important as learning to learn.

Approaches to the Learning Organization

There are different definitions of and approaches to a learning organization. Peter Senge, in his acclaimed book, *The Fifth Discipline*, describes a learning organization as a place 'where people continually expand their capacity to create the results they truly desire, where new and expansive patterns of thinking are nurtured, where collective aspiration is set free, and where people are continually learning how to learn together'.[6]

Senge offers five ways to becoming a learning organization:

- 'Systems thinking' that involves studying all the patterns of a system instead of snapshots, to get a holistic and deeper view of the big picture.
- Developing 'personal mastery' to continually clarify and deepen our personal vision, of focusing our energies, of developing patience and of seeing reality objectively.
- Constantly questioning and testing deeply ingrained 'mental models' about the company, the markets, competitors, etc.
- Developing a 'shared vision' by unearthing shared 'pictures of the future' that foster genuine commitment rather than compliance.
- 'Team learning' through dialogue.

Senge advocates that the heart of a learning organization lies in learning that results in a 'shift of mind', something that transforms who we are and what we do.

Chris Argyris is another major contributor to the concept of organizational learning.[7] He argues that when an environment is so uncertain that cause and effect cannot be reasonably established, single-loop (corrective) learning that involves correcting errors against set norms, becomes ineffective. Such an environment calls for double-loop (generative) learning that allows and encourages people to constantly question and test existing norms, beliefs, values and even goals to ensure alignment with fast-changing scenarios. In Senge's words, this involves changing mental models. Thus, learning to learn involves the self-questioning ability. However, in a bureaucratized environment, people are rarely encouraged to question the standard operating norms and procedures, and organizations face an uphill battle to change the mindset of people.

How is organizational learning different from individual learning? According to Argyris and Schon, 'There is no organizational learning without individual learning, and that individual learning is a necessary but insufficient condition for organizational learning. We can think of organizational learning as a process mediated by the collaborative enquiry of individual members'.[8]

Thus, organizational learning is more than the sum of individual learning. However, the challenge here is to convert individual learning into organizational learning as otherwise 'the processes and insights evaporate (when a long-time employee leaves an organization) because they were not shared or made a part of collective memory'.[9]

Morgan borrows from the principles of cybernetics and holography to describe a learning organization.[2] He argues that 'the core insight from cybernetics is that a system engages in self-regulating behaviour based on "negative feedback". Systems of negative feedback engage in error detection and automatic correction in such a way that movements beyond specified limits in one direction initiate movements in the opposite direction to maintain a desired course of action.' Similarly, he uses the metaphor of the hologram to think of systems 'where qualities of the whole are enfolded in all the parts so that the system has an ability to self organize and regenerate itself on a continuous basis'.

Morgan designs a learning organization based on the following principles of holographic design:

- Build the 'whole' into the 'parts'(using visions, values and culture as corporate DNA, networked intelligence, structures that reproduce themselves and holistic teams).
- The importance of redundancy (i.e., variety of functions in information processing, skills and the design of work).
- Requisite variety (i.e., internal complexity must match that of the environment).
- Minimum specs (i.e., define no more than is absolutely necessary).
- Learn to learn (i.e., scan and anticipate environmental change, double-loop learning, and emergent design).[2]

Garvin (1993) defines a learning organization as 'an organization skilled at creating, acquiring, and transferring knowledge, and at modifying its behaviour to reflect new knowledge and insights'.[10] He traces three overlapping stages in the process of learning: cognitive stage where people are exposed to new ideas and begin to think differently; behavioural stage where people internalize new insights and start altering their behaviour; and finally, performance improvement stage when altered behaviour results in marked improvement. The shorter the learning cycles, superior is the performance. Garvin proposes that successful organizational learning occurs through

- systematic problem-solving,
- experimentation with new approaches,
- learning from own experience and past history,

- learning from the experiences and best practices of others, and
- transferring knowledge quickly and efficiently throughout the organization.[10]

Pedler et al. (1997) prefer to use the term 'learning company' (to emphasize collective endeavour) and define it as 'an organization that facilitates the learning of all its members and consciously transforms itself and its context'.[11] They develop a 'identikit' of a learning company with the following characteristics:

- A learning approach to strategy: Where policy and strategy formulation are consciously structured for learning.
- Participative policy-making.
- Informating: Where information technology makes information available to frontline staff in order to empower them to act on their own initiative.
- Formative accounting and control: Where systems of budgeting, reporting and accounting are structured to assist learning for all members about how money works in the business.
- Internal exchange: Where all internal units see themselves as customers and suppliers to the end-user or client.
- Reward flexibility: Where flexible and creative rewards, both monetary and non-monetary, cater for individual needs and performance.
- Enabling structures: Where structures can easily be changed to meet the job, user, or innovation requirements.
- Boundary workers as environmental scanners: Where all employees engage in scanning the environment and bring back the information into the company.
- Inter-company learning: Through joint ventures and other learning alliances for mutual exchange.

- A learning climate: Where all managers see their primary task as facilitating employees' experimentation and learning from experience, through questioning, feedback and support.
- Self-development opportunities for all: Where people take responsibility for their own learning and development and the organization provides resources and facilities for self-development to all members.

As we can see from the different perspectives discussed above, there cannot be one best way of becoming a learning organization, as each organization differs in terms of its issues and challenges, environment, abilities and motivation of people. Any managerial action in this regard can only be seen as an 'experiment rather than as the "right answer" because there are no quick fixes to solve complex organizational problems and it is only by "learning, action and further learning" that an organization can find its own right way.'[11] The process begins with finding out the 'learning disabilities' of the organization. Some companies establish experimentation groups or pilot projects and after learning from them, they are later rolled out to the entire organization. People who show initiative, drive and enthusiasm in the initial learning process become mentors for others to follow.

Learning to learn orientation demands a new set of competencies as against a fixed set of skills required in a single-loop orientation. These individual-related competencies are discussed in the next chapter. In an organizational context, an ideal learning organization 'includes notions of organizational adaptability, flexibility, avoidance of stability traps, propensity to experiment, readiness to rethink means and ends, inquiry orientation, realization of human potential for learning in the service of organizational purposes, and creation of organizational settings as contexts for human development'.[7]

Managing Innovation and Creativity

Infosys, a world-class software company based in India, believes in the following principles in managing creativity:

- Cynicism has no place in the organization. Any idea is great, deserves cheers and should be encouraged.
- For long-term success, you need to surround yourself with people who are smarter than you.
- Obsolete innovations—before the competition does it for you.
- Have a healthy sense of paranoia and respect for competition.
- Markets come and go but as long as three attributes—speed, imagination and excellence—are alive, you have a future.
- Everybody needs incentives—but not just money. People want challenges, opportunity, dignity, respect, intense competition, and quality time.
- The most powerful style of leadership is by example.
- Be transaction based to avoid groupism. The organization should have one goal, one vision.

Merely generating ideas without providing a channel to implement them can be both unproductive to the organization and demoralizing to employees. As O'Dell and Grayson recommend, 'Make sure that every plane you allow to take off has a runway available for landing' (with sufficient resources, etc.).[12]

According to Amabile, creativity is a function of three components: expertise, creative thinking skills and motivation.[13] She suggests the following managerial practices to promote creativity in organizations:

- Match assignments to people's expertise, skills and motivation.
- Provide freedom to work around the process and to meet goals that are reasonably consistent.

- Provide sufficient time and resources.
- Create mutually supportive groups with a diversity of perspectives and backgrounds.
- Encourage with enough and timely praise to make people feel that their work is important.
- Design appropriate organizational systems and procedures to make clear that creative efforts are top priority. This could be done with financial and non-financial incentives, mandating information sharing and collaboration, and ensuring that political problems do not fester.

It is true that all managers have to compete for scarce resources and cannot throw money to let people do things that they are passionate about. But by communicating the strategic direction of the company and by working with people to understand the practical implications of their ideas and the feasibility of turning them into marketable products and services within a reasonable time-frame, managers can productively channellize the creative flow. It is the difference between playing God and coach.

Managers need to understand that different people have different thinking styles: 'Analytical or intuitive, conceptual or experiential, social or independent, logical or values driven.' They need to allow for 'creative abrasion' and 'deliberately design a full spectrum of approaches and perspectives into their organizations and understand that cognitively diverse people must respect other thinking styles'.[14] Thus, 'to innovate successfully, managers need to hire, work with and promote people who are unlike them'.

The research divisions that reinvent their company to be innovative believe that

- research on new work practices is as important as research on new products,
- innovation is everywhere; the problem is learning from it,

◻ research cannot just produce innovation; it must 'co-produce' it with partners, and the research department's ultimate innovation partner is the customer.[15]

The difference between the processes and practices creates tension that can be very difficult for managers to handle. 'Lean too much toward practice and new ideas may bubble up and evaporate for lack of a structure to harness them. Lean too much toward process and you may get no new ideas at all. The goal, then, is to tap into the creativity at work in every layer of an organization with a combination of process and practice'.[16]

Barriers to Learning

Not many companies succeed in their attempt to become a learning organization due to powerful barriers to learning. The most visible force that inhibits learning is what Chris Argyris calls 'organizational defensive routines'.[17] When questioned, people take defensive positions and use their power and knowledge to uphold their decision or viewpoint, even when they are aware that their stand does not serve organizational interests. Argyris argues that 'organizational defensive routines encourage individuals to bypass the causes of the embarrassment or threat and to cover up the bypass. They also encourage making this action undiscussable and the undiscussability undiscussable.' He cites politicking, game playing, layering, and creating unnecessary structures as a few such examples.[17]

People learn from their leaders and imitate them. In one instance, the Managing Director wanted to close down a factory and the finance department made a case favouring his viewpoint. After several months, when a new MD arrived, he wanted to retain the factory and the same finance officials did a U-turn and reversed their case!

In their obsession with defensive routines, organizations tend to ignore the power of the unknown. A single customer or a journalist or an employee can rock the boat and bring out the dirt in the open. When that happens, the first reaction is to defend the action, no matter how ridiculous it looks. Everybody in the company runs for cover and point the finger elsewhere.

Senge rightly points out that due to severe learning disabilities, most organizations die before the age of forty. He gives the example of a 'boiled frog', i.e., how a frog gets used to a very slowly rising temperature to the extent that it sits quiet even when the temperature reaches boiling point, to illustrate how people and organizations get accustomed to slow decay and miss out on the early warning signals.

By learning to unlearn well-entrenched organizational defensive routines, people can question past routines and create new knowledge. Organizational learning mainly depends on its employees' willingness to 'cast off or unlearn past practices' that are no longer relevant.[18] 'Core competencies can become core rigidities' and therefore how to learn is more important than what to learn. HR professionals may sometimes unwittingly reinforce organizational defensive routines through inappropriate HR policies and procedures rather than helping organizations overcome unproductive assumptions.[19] Thus, unlearning is an integral part of the learning process and is even more so in a knowledge economy as knowledge becomes obsolete very fast and its context and application change all the time.

The present models of leadership that are power and control driven are another stumbling block to strategic learning. First of all, leadership needs to be diffused at all levels. Second, leaders need to provide enough space for people to experiment and challenge existing mental models. Third, leaders need to lead by example. They have to show the way to become open-minded and self-reflective. They also need to ensure that the learning to learn orientation does not remain at the strategy table and flows on to operational levels through frontline managers who can act as change agents. Frontline managers play a key role and their leadership effectiveness should be assessed on how soon they make themselves redundant by empowering, mentoring and coaching others. Motorola defines leaders as those who 'envision, energize and enable'.

Being open to ideas also requires tolerance towards criticisms. When a junior employee or a customer criticizes the present practices, the managers should be able to take it on the chin and objectively evaluate competing ideas.

Managing learning, however, is not without its share of politics. Davenport cautions that 'if knowledge is associated with power, money, and success, then it is also associated with lobbying, intrigue, and backroom deals' and advises that effective knowledge management involves political alliances and deals between those who have knowledge and those who use it.[20] This involves a firm commitment on the part of those who work on latest skills, technologies, processes and emerging markets to pass on their knowledge to other members of the organization by doubling up as in-house trainers. Sharing actually enriches and enhances one's knowledge. HR should publicly recognize and reward people who share knowledge and create interactive forums to facilitate the process.

The learning culture evolves over time. In many organizations executives are so busy working on day-to-day operations that they hardly have time to introspect and look at the big picture. Their typical reaction is, 'Oh! I love to read, think and discuss, but where is the time'? It is estimated that fully 90 per cent of managers squander their time in "active nonaction", being procrastinators, disengaged and distracted, and only 10 per cent managers are purposeful, i.e., they spend their time in a committed, purposeful, and reflective manner.[21] Taking time to read, reflect and review is both a matter of individual initiative and organizational support.

One of the paradoxes of the new economy is that while speed and agility define success, learning to succeed is a gradual and time-consuming process. According to Nordstrom, the proponent of funky business, 'Even though the new economy comes without speed limits, creativity cannot be forced upon people. To be creative we need slack. We need resources and time. We need time to sit down and reflect. We need time alone. We need time to play around. We need time to experiment. We need time to have casual conversations with others'.[22]

Lack of systems thinking is another barrier to deep learning. Organizations often resort to short-term problem fixing and patching, without realizing that such hasty repairs cause problems elsewhere and deepen the problem in the long run. For instance, by resorting to widespread retrenchment in a downturn, organizations end up losing critical knowledge sources that have been developed painstakingly over the years and as a result, lessen their ability to face future challenges. Thus, as Senge says, 'today's problems come from yesterday's "solutions"'.

Managing Failure . . . and Success

Philosopher Santayana said, 'those who cannot remember the past are condemned to repeat it'. Behind every successful person or venture, there are tales of previous failures that were used as building blocks for improvement.

Learning involves tolerance towards failure. Research shows that the majority of innovative ideas fail to become commercial reality. Storey and Quintas argue that 'innovation is about diversity, untypicality and uncertainty, and it therefore, carries a considerable degree of risk'.[23] HR has to ensure that people are encouraged to boldly experiment and share their views without any fear or apprehension. At Motorola, the corporate culture allows constructive conflict that enabled an engineer to take his ideas on the

Iridium project to top management after being rejected at lower levels.

Nadler argues that the management of failure involves 'a mindset that enables companies to recognize the value of productive failure as contrasted with unproductive success. A productive failure is one that leads to insight, understanding, and thus, an addition to the commonly held wisdom of the organization. An unproductive success occurs when something goes well, but nobody knows how or why.'[24] David Kelley, the CEO of IDEO Product Development, puts it in another way: 'Enlightened trial and error outperforms the planning of flawless intellects.' Similarly, Watkins and Marsick argue that 'a zero defect culture where mistakes are high risk is highly unlikely to encourage learning'.[25]

However, organizations are too reluctant to admit failure. Even companies known for excellence in management, talk eloquently about their success stories but fall silent when asked to identify areas of weaknesses that need improvement. So organizations should ask themselves: How do we deal with failure? Mere encouragement to generate new ideas is not enough. When people make genuine attempts to implement their ideas and fail, they need to be encouraged, not discouraged, to try further. Otherwise, they will never bother to think and try again; they will merely follow their managers. Infosys describes this process as 'celebrating failure'.

Fear of failure can cause untold damage. Managers with a command and control style use fear as their main weapon to make employees compliant and suppress freedom of thought and expression. Therefore, to drive away the fear of failure, managers who foster it should be driven away first. In this process, leaders at the top play a crucial role as it is the test of their commitment to the learning process.

Similarly, success also needs to be managed effectively. One may think that success feeds success and therefore, does not need to be managed. But there are many traps hidden in managing success. It may lull people into thinking that they know everything there is to know and stop learning. Success may be attributed to wrong persons or teams as some people are shy to blow their own trumpet while some others are experts at it. It could be due to cultural background as in Asian societies, modesty is preferred over self-promotion. Further, lessons from success may be applied to inappropriate situations, locations or times.

Benchmarking Against Best Practices: Adapt, Adopt or Reject?

Once an idea is turned into a successful innovation, it becomes common knowledge and others will start noticing it. Learning organizations are keen to learn both from within as well as from outside. Sometimes, ideas are borrowed from totally unrelated organizations or situations. Today, many organizations build enduring relationships with contractors, suppliers and customers to learn from each other. Often, customers provide critical insights and a comparative picture of competing products and therefore, keeping the eyes and ears open for customer feedback is a prerequisite to benchmarking practices.

Internal and external benchmarking can serve a number of purposes: leveraging knowledge, breaking established paradigms, creating a readiness for action, and providing models of excellence.[10] However, researchers point out that transferring best practices is easier said than done. Szulanski reasons that the slow process could be due to the ignorance of the source and the recipient about the existence and utility of knowledge (a case of the left hand not knowing what the right hand is doing), lack of resources to implement new practices, lack of personal relationship and rapport between the parties and the lag of over two years for the new practice to spread and bear fruit.[26]

Similarly, O'Dell and Grayson observe that the natural desire of people to learn and share is thwarted by a variety of organization-related reasons, such as structures that promote 'silo' behaviour, culture that promotes personal knowledge over sharing of knowledge, poor social networks between people, overreliance on transmitting what is already known rather than what is unknown, and lack of rewards for people to learn and share knowledge.[12] They point out that in consulting organizations, despite having best-in-class online databases, consultants hesitate to share knowledge because of the culture that rewards individual success over team success and competitive pressures that leave no time to share.

Mentoring

Employees tend to model their behaviour based on the star performers in the organization. Despite what the organization says about what is valued and desirable in the organization, people seek out on their own what it takes to succeed in the organization. In some cases, it occurs naturally with either the individual taking the initiative and approaching a manager or a manager taking the initiative and teaching his/her members formally and informally. Mentoring is often seen to be distinct from coaching on the basis that coaching aims to teach specific work-related skills to improve work performance whereas mentoring is seen to be more long-term oriented as it includes personal and career support.

A large part of learning in the workplace is informal. However, 'informal learning is harder both to identify and mould. By its very nature, it doesn't occur in neat time slots or locations where you can grab it and leverage it. However, while you can't formalize *what* learning takes place, you can set up conditions which can encourage it'.[27]

Considering that in a knowledge economy, learning is no more an option but an imperative and that learning by doing is the best way to learn, mentoring assumes critical importance as it is direct, face to face and context specific. Therefore, organizations need to take proactive steps to institutionalize the process. If left to be completely informal, the opportunity becomes selective and managers would assume that mentoring is an option and not an integral part of their work. By making it a formal management practice, organizations can harness the potential of mentoring. At the same time, making the system too formal runs the risk of depriving the managers and their mentees of making the process customized and innovative. By defining only the 'minimum spec' and leaving the rest open, mentoring can be an enriching experience.

One cannot assume that a formal system of mentoring will be automatically accepted and followed by managers. They need to have the genuine desire to share their knowledge and help build organizational competencies. Organizations should actively seek people with such traits at the time of recruitment and recognize and reward them frequently. The senior management team again needs to set the example by becoming mentors to demonstrate their commitment to the process. Narayana Murthy, co-founder of Infosys, recently gave up his executive responsibilities and designated himself as 'Chief Mentor'.

With regard to matching mentors with mentees, research suggests that it is helpful if they are from different work groups. As long as mentors have the right understanding of the organizational environment and have demonstrated the desirable competencies, they can mentor any employee. However, not all mentors are skilled in transferring their knowledge and need appropriate training in aspects such as emotional intelligence, questioning, reflection and providing feedback. Ibarra emphasizes that 'chemistry is the key ingredient in true mentoring relationships . . . and cannot be mandated by the HR department or a leadership team'.[28]

Institutionalizing the mentoring process involves unflinching management commitment, an elaborate administrative and HRM process and continuous improvement based on past experience and benchmarking against best practices. Any half-hearted attempt is likely to backfire with dissatisfied mentees, unconvinced and uncommitted mentors, and wastage of resources. However, if well done, mentoring can be an invaluable tool in enhancing individual and organizational learning.

We have Knowledge. What Next?

Corporations routinely invest time, effort and money to seek knowledge. Organizational consultants keep giving the same advice based on time-tested principles that are already known to their clients. Thus, it is not difficult to access knowledge. What is difficult is implementing and utilizing it. Within the same organization, one can observe wide variation in quality and performance. Pfeffer and Sutton call this the 'knowing–doing gap' and caution that knowing what to do is not enough.[29] They argue that 'the gap between knowing and doing is more important than the gap between ignorance and knowing', primarily because knowledge about best practices cannot remain a secret for long and therefore, what defines success is the ability to implement and the understanding that it is not the practice per se but the philosophy behind it that is important.

To remedy the performance paradox of why so many organizations know what to do but very few actually do it, Pfeffer and Sutton suggest that organizations should understand that

- 'why' comes before the 'how'
- knowing comes from doing and teaching others how
- action counts more than elegant plans and concepts
- there is no doing without mistakes
- fear (of failure) fosters knowing–doing gaps, and
- co-operation and collaboration foster innovation rather than competition with each other in the organization.[29]

Thus, more than knowledge itself, what matters is the ability to turn knowledge into action by identifying and transferring internal and external best practices throughout the organization through people-to-people interactions, creating new knowledge all the time and developing capabilities that set the stage for a successful culture of sharing, transfer and change.[30]

Sharing Knowledge

Garvin suggests many measures to facilitate knowledge sharing: written, oral and visual reports, site visits and tours, personnel rotation programmes, education and training programmes and standardization programmes.[10] Experiential learning is the best way to learn and therefore, Garvin recommends personnel rotation programmes as one of the most powerful methods of transferring knowledge. Ideally, star performers need to be rotated across different divisions and locations to pass on the benefit of their personal expertise. He also cautions that mere encouragement for new ideas is not good enough. Ideas need to be applied or implemented, recognized and rewarded, for the cycle of creativity and innovation to be repeated and institutionalized.

Communities of practices in learning organizations facilitate transfer of knowledge through extensive use of knowledge repositories, such as intranets and data warehouses. They offer expertise mapping to indicate the contact details of sources of specific knowledge, both within and outside the organization, and discussion forums amongst people with similar interests, tasks and challenges. For example, when a mainframe programmer is stuck with a problem in writing complex COBOL programs, he/she could send an email to concerned experts within the company or post a message on the Special Interest Group (SIG) bulletins run by the company or manufacturer (in this case, IBM) or the professional IT association. It is amazing how people from all over the world respond to such professional queries and go out of their way to help others. Such mechanisms simply tap the natural desire of people to share knowledge and help.

While technology can provide a useful avenue for communication, it is only the first step. Not all knowledge can be put in writing. Some knowledge may require close social interaction between people to facilitate meeting of minds. A survey indicated that up to 70 per cent of workplace learning is informal. Many companies encourage such interactions through mentoring, job rotation, periodic conferences, award and recognition programmes, and share fairs where people showcase their best practices and offer help.

Instead of hiring somebody to write the case and put it up on the intranet, it is important that those who are most familiar with the knowledge act as 'part-librarian, part-consultant, and part-coach'. This requires that such people and teams are given specific time to disseminate information rather than expecting them to do it naturally. To institutionalize the process, documentation should be made part of their work and assessed and rewarded accordingly. 'Learning history' is another approach suggested by scholars to capture institutional experience, disseminate its lessons, and translate them into effective action.[29] It is a 'written narrative of a company's recent critical event' narrated by participants of the event and codified by 'learning historians—trained outsiders and knowledgeable insiders—who identify recurring themes, pose questions and raise "undiscussable" issues'.

Corporate University

Establishing corporate universities is another approach followed by large multinational corporations. For example, Motorola University with its fourteen locations around the world and an annual budget of more than $120 million, aims to create a culture at Motorola that values quality, technological innovation and learning.[31] It has spearheaded the company's passion for Total Customer Satisfaction (TCS) through its Six Sigma campaign that aims to reduce defects in the company's products to no more than 3.4 units per million. It has grown with partnerships established around the world with colleges and universities. Within the company, it welcomes good ideas no matter where they come from and spreads the best practice around the world. It also customizes training to suit specific national and cultural learning styles.

Every Motorolan is required to undertake at least forty hours of education each year in functional, interpersonal and business skills. The university follows action-learning strategies that involve matching the training technique and tools to the topic and encouraging interaction between different units and people throughout the world. To address technological obsolescence, the company's technicians are sent around the world to get hands-on training on latest technologies.

The advantage of a corporate university is that it customizes training and learning to the specific tasks and responsibilities of the company's employees, suppliers and customers. Many companies that spend a lot of money on training fail to understand why their return on investment is low and employees have to be pushed to undergo training. One possible reason could be that employees see no direct relevance of such training to their job and career. Many external training consultants talk in the air and do not care to find out and address the real issues and challenges faced by people at work. The issues vary widely depending on the industry, organization occupation and location. Therefore, companies have to cultivate internal trainers who are in touch with specific organizational issues and lead training sessions in collaboration with external trainers. Collaboration with universities and community colleges is an effective and efficient way of forging learning alliances and customizing learning initiatives.

Role of Human Resources in Facilitating Learning

In an organizational context, learning takes place at the individual, group and organizational levels and HR can facilitate learning at all these levels. At the individual level, HR is entrusted with the responsibility of recruiting and retaining knowledge workers who can develop the right competencies both in technical and behavioural areas. They need to be motivated through a range of performance management and reward measures to convert their expert mental models into explicit knowledge. At the group level, HR needs to enable people to work in autonomous teams both within and outside the organizational boundaries sharing mental models. At the organizational level, strategy, system, style and staff need to work in tandem to create an atmosphere that is conducive to learning. By making expert mental models explicit through training and development, HR can transform novice performance into expert performance. Watkins and Marsick believe that 'human resource developers who are systematically and developmentally increasing the learning capacity of the organization are creating learning organizations'.[25]

As we move away from the concept of training to the concept of learning, HR professionals need to facilitate rather than control the process and motivate employees to 'accept a move from dependence to independence, from passive and reactive learning to active and proactive learning and from viewing learning as a single event managed by others to continual lifelong, self-managed learning'.[32] While it is easy for HR managers to shift the responsibility for learning to individuals, they need to recognize that people will be overwhelmed by the responsibility without adequate support and encouragement in the form of training in self-management, helping identify future trends, giving time off to learn and encouraging collaborative effort.

'The old mental model that construes training as an independent administrative function is fatally flawed in that it tries to separate what a systems view of performance tells us cannot be separated'.[33] It is clear that there is a qualitative difference in the changing role of HR professionals from 'organizers of training' to 'facilitators of learning'. The latter role recognizes that learning is a shared responsibility and that not all learning can be and need be controlled, as much of what people learn, particularly tacit knowledge, takes place in informal social networks, also called communities of practices, with little or no environmental support. 'The paradox of such communities is that although they are self-organizing and thus, resistant to supervision and interference, they do require specific managerial efforts to develop them and integrate them into an organization. Only then can they be fully leveraged'.[34] Therefore, more than directing learning, HR professionals have to help create a nurturing culture and structure that facilitate self, team and organizational learning on a continuous basis. As learning is today a critical competitive advantage, the responsibility for learning should be shared by all managers and not just left to HR practitioners. Therefore, organization-wide learning policies need to be integrated with business strategy.[35]

One of the challenges for HR in the new learning environment is to justify the business case for training and development efforts and investment. It is clear that traditional accounting measures simply fail to tap the hidden value of learning initiatives, such as mentoring, on-the-job learning and communities of practices. Measures such as number of hours of training per employee do not mean much, as it is the quality not the quantity of learning that really counts. Any learning that is tied to business objectives and strategies naturally contributes to improvement in business performance. Balanced scorecard methods can address the challenge of measurement of learning to some extent with their holistic approach. However, learning is too complex a process to be managed by measurement.

In a learning organization, learning becomes as natural and easy as breathing. That is why premier learning organizations, such as Royal Dutch Shell (RDS) are described as a 'living company'.[36] It was at Shell that 'scenario forecasting' became a useful tool to anticipate and prepare for unexpected environmental changes. Shell believes and practices 'servant leadership' whereby leaders humbly admit that they donot have all the answers and seek the co-operation of all employees to help them find the right answers. By boldly allowing free flow of information, knowledge and people within and outside of organizational boundaries, learning organizations pave the structural way to harness human capital.[27]

Learning is an ongoing process. In an environment characterized by discontinuity and hyper-competition, learning to be creative and innovative is always a work in progress. As Peter Senge says, 'You can never say, "we are a learning organization" any more than you can say, "I am an enlightened person". Pursuit of excellence is like chasing a moving target.'

Agenda for Managerial Action

Points to Ponder . . .	*. . . Steps to Consider*
Today, learning to learn is a key strategic weapon and deserves utmost and ongoing attention. It is the heart of knowledge management and the yardstick of the knowledge economy.	Learning needs to be embedded in all aspects of organizational life. Unlike training, learning has to have more breadth and depth by being hands on, mentor and self driven, ongoing, double-loop oriented, flow in all directions and involve wider community, such as customers, suppliers, universities and even competitors.
Brains wide open.	Conduct an organizational climate survey to examine how conducive is the learning atmosphere in your organization.
	• Are the leaders humble enough to admit that they don't have all the answers and open-minded enough

	to honestly accept others' suggestions?
	• Does everybody in the organization feel that their opinion matters and is taken seriously?
	• Is there enough breathing space in decision-making, communication channels, structures and processes?
Lack of systems thinking due to 'boiled frog' mentality erodes the ability to sense and act on early warning signals.	Are your people too busy to pause and introspect? Consider devoting one day a month for deliberate organization-wide learning when people stop their routine work and engage in a 'dialogue' with people from different units and external experts or just sit and read in the well-stocked company library.
A learning organization could be built on the principles of holographic design.	• How well networked are different parts of your organization, technologically and socially, to complement each others' strengths?
	• Are they equipped to perform multiple tasks instead of pursuing narrow and rigid specialization?
	• Does their internal complexity match that of the environment?
	• Has the organization given them enough autonomy by defining no more than what is absolutely necessary?
Barriers to learning.	Identify the learning disabilities in your organization.
	• Is there too much bureaucracy, politicking or groupism that forces people to engage in organizational defensive routines?
	• Is the top management setting right examples for being open-minded, tolerate constructive criticism, and genuine enthusiasm for ideas without cynicism? Do you reward those managers who exhibit such

	qualities and reprimand those who do not?
	• How does the organization treat whistle blowers—punishing them or admitting and correcting mistakes?
	• Do you encourage ongoing innovation to suit changing times by letting people question past practices so that core competencies do not become core rigidities?
Managing creativity.	• Do you give employees a real say in assigning tasks so that they get to do what they are really passionate about?
	• Is there a fair and equitable process in work allocation so that everybody gets an opportunity to update and acquire employable skills?
	• Do employees have a real say in setting deadlines, allocating resources, choosing team members and work as they see fit?
	• Do people with new ideas get a second hearing after initial rejection?
	• Do they get enough praise and in time?
	• Do they get their fair share of the productivity gains?
Learning involves tolerance towards failure.	• When people in your organization fail in their experiments to innovate, are they encouraged to introspect and carry on or made to pay for their failure?
	• Do they understand the difference between unproductive success and productive failure?
Benchmarking against best practices.	• Does your organization have a close and continuing relationship with key customers, contractors and suppliers to learn from each other? This could be achieved through means such as periodic

meetings, access to each others' database, and feedback from frontline staff.

- Are people in the organization aware of each other's area of work and expertise? The process of knowledge sharing could be facilitated through technology mediated forums, periodic conferences, and other informal social networks.
- Do you regard sharing knowledge as a key performance indicator and assess and reward it as such? For example, do you encourage and reward people for successful mentoring, presenting papers in internal and external conferences, or engaging with educational institutions?

Mentoring.

The mentoring process needs to be formal enough to be considered an important managerial activity and at the same time, be informal enough to let the mentor and mentee find their own level of comfort and involvement. The process requires commitment of enough time, efforts and resources.

'The gap between knowing and doing is more important than the gap between ignorance and knowing.'[29]

Ensure that

- No action is initiated without the input and involvement of people concerned.
- More attention is paid to implementation than rhetoric.
- People can experiment without the fear of failure.
- Those who share knowledge are rewarded over those who hoard knowledge.
- Star performers are periodically rotated across functions and locations to acquire and share knowledge.
- Frequent meetings of minds take

	place to satisfy natural desire to share and gain peer recognition. • Training has direct relevance to people's tasks and trainers have intimate knowledge of the task and environment. • Learning alliances are forged with community colleges and universities through customized programmes, internships for students, staff exchange and involvement in curriculum development.
HR needs to play the role of a facilitator and change agent in institutionalizing learning to learn.	In their changing role from 'organizers of training' to 'facilitators of learning', people managers need to focus on nurturing rather than directing the learning culture with the active involvement of the entire management team.

Case Scenario: Nokia Leads Change through Continuous Learning

The Nokia Corporation is a leading supplier of mobile, fixed and IP networks, including related services. It has net sales of $30 billion and employs over 50,000 people. In its distinctive management approach, Nokia relies on a strong corporate culture and the company values: customer satisfaction, respect for the individual achievement, and continuous learning. The following account highlights how the Nokia value of continuous learning is put into action today.

Continuous learning is a true value at Nokia, and this is the result of the top management's genuine commitment to it. It has helped acculturate the attitude that continuous learning is non-negotiable. This is reflected in Nokia's performance management, in which an integral part is called 'investing in people' or the IIP process. IIP is the responsibility of each and every manager. It consists of four parts: objective setting, coaching and achievement review, competence analysis and personal development plan, and finally, performance evaluation.

The IIP discussion starts with a review of the previous six months. After setting objectives for the next six months, the manager and subordinate perform a coaching and achievement review. In their role as coaches, managers facilitate professional learning and development of their subordinates and monitor their effectiveness. The IIP process ends with an evaluation of individual competencies and by drafting of the relevant personal development plan. Employees can pick up their profile from the intranet, evaluate themselves, create a personal development plan and tap into a variety of learning solutions offered at Nokia's learning centres around the world.

Learning centres form one joint learning platform for the entire corporation. By mixing participants from across different business groups, Nokia enhances corporate knowledge creation by letting them widely share their traditions and experiences. Learning centres are a networked, internal service provider and offer programmes for more junior-level managers in professional competence development, which is a continuous challenge for Nokia, as it operates in multi-cultural settings. They use both internal and external assistance in design and delivery of managerial and leadership programmes. The programmes on offer are quite blended solutions; they include e-learning elements, face-to-face learning facilitation, self-managed learning and small action-learning projects. However, much learning at Nokia takes place on the job level, where managers coach their people in professional development. There is also a lot of job rotation at Nokia. Learning on a day-to-day basis is very much a part of the mindset of Nokia's culture.

Nokia derives outside input by working with a variety of leading business schools, universities of technology and professional consultants. The programmes for senior managers have a much stronger in-house flavour. Reflecting top management's commitment to continuous learning, the business group presidents are the leading 'owners' of all global management and leadership programmes. They bring their personal input to these programmes and also appoint 'godfathers' from their management teams. These godfathers are the content owners of the various topics selected as the focal themes of the programmes. In most cases, the programmes feature a strong action-learning element, which is implemented through strategic projects carried out in conjunction with the programme. The top management team is personally involved in the generation of project themes to make sure that they are aligned with the strategic direction of the company.

Nokia does not see the evaluation of learning as a science. It uses different methods to monitor results, such as a 360-degree feedback, to ensure continuous improvement. Nokia's top managers emphasize networking as an important aspect of measurement of learning as it increases social capital and organizational cohesion and facilitates continuous reinforcement of corporate culture and values. Continuous learning is a central issue at Nokia and the corporate culture and practices strongly support it.

Source: Excerpts reprinted with permission from interview with Sonja Weckstrom-Nousiainen, VP—HRD, Nokia Mobile Phones by Leena Masalin. Published in *Learning and Education*, Vol 2 No 1, pp. 68–72. Copyright © 2003 by the Academy of Management. All rights reserved.

References

1. **Burgoyne, J.** (1995) Quoted in Peddler, M., Burgoyne, J. and Boydell, T. (1997) *The learning company*, McGraw-Hill: London.
2. **Morgan, G.** (1997) *Images of organisation*, Sage: Thousand Oaks, CA.
3. **Zuboff, S.** (1988) *In the age of the smart machine*, Basic Books: New York.
4. **Brown, J.S.** (2002) An epistemological perspective on organisations and innovation. Keynote address to the 3rd Organisational Knowledge and Learning Conference (OKLC).

5. **Filkin, D.** (1997) *Stephen Hawking's universe: The cosmos explained*, BBC Books: London.
6. **Senge, P.M.** (1990) *The Fifth Discipline: The art and practice of the learning organisation*, Random House: London.
7. **Argyris, C.** (1999) *On organisational learning*, Blackwell: Oxford, UK.
8. **Argyris, C.** and **Schon, D.A.** (1978) *Organisational learning: A theory of action perspective*, Addison-Wesley, Chapter 1, pp. 8–29.
9. **Nevis, E.C., DiBella, A.J.** and **Gould, J.M.** (1995) 'Understanding organisations as learning systems'. *Sloan Management Review*, Vol 36 No 2, pp. 73–85.
10. **Garvin, D.A.** (1993) 'Building a learning organisation'. *Harvard Business Review*, Vol 71 No 4.
11. **Pedler, M., Burgoyne, J.** and **Boydel, T.** (1997) *The learning company*, McGraw-Hill: London.
12. **O'Dell, C.** and **Grayson, C.J.** (1998) 'If only we knew what we know: Identification and transfer of internal best practices'. *California Management Review*, Vol 40 No 3.
13. **Amabile, T.** (1998) 'How to kill creativity'. *Harvard Business Review*, September 1998, pp. 77–87.
14. **Leonard, D.** and **Straus, S.** (1997) 'Putting your company's whole brain to work'. *Harvard Business Review*, July–August 1997.
15. **Brown, J.S** (1991) 'Research that reinvents the corporation'. *Harvard Business Review*, January–February 1991.
16. **Brown J.S.** and **Duguid, P.** (2000) 'Balancing act: How to capture knowledge without killing it'. *Harvard Business Review*, May–June 2000.
17. **Argyris, C.** (1997) 'The next challenge'. In Hesselbein, F. et al. (Eds.) *Organisation of the future*, Jossey-Bass: SF.
18. **Inkpin, A.C.** and **Crossan, M.M.** (1997) 'Believing is seeing: Joint ventures and organisational learning'. In Rus-Eft, D., Preskill, H. and Sleezer, C. (Eds.) *HRD review: Research and implications*, Sage: Thousand Oaks, CA.
19. **Argyris, C.** (1986) 'Reinforcing organisational defensive routines: An unintended human resources activity'. *Human Resource Management*, Vol 25 No 4, pp. 541–55.
20. **Davenport, T.H.** (1997) 'Ten principles of knowledge management and four case studies'. *Knowledge and Process Management*, Vol 4 No 3, pp. 187–208.
21. **Bruch, H.** and **Ghoshal, S.** (2002) 'Beware the busy manager'. *Harvard Business Review*, February.

22. **Nordstrom, K.** quoted in Pickett, L. (2003) 'Funky business'. *HR Monthly*, March 2003. Australian Human Resources Institute: Melbourne.

23. **Storey, J.** and **Quintas, P.** (2001), 'Knowledge management and HRM'. In Storey, J. (Ed.) *HRM — A Critical Text*, Thomson Learning: UK.

24. **Nadler, D.** (1989) 'Even failures can be productive'. *The New York Times*, 23 April 1989.

25. **Watkins, K.E.** and **Marsick, V.** (1992) 'Building the learning organisation: A new role for human resource developers'. *Studies in Continuing Education*, Vol 14 No 2, pp. 115–29.

26. **Szulanski, G.** (1994) *Intra-firm transfer of best practices project*, American Productivity and Quality Centre: Houston, TX.

27. **Horibe, F.** (1999) *Managing knowledge workers*, Wiley: Toronto.

28. **Ibarra, H** (2000) 'Making partner: A mentor's guide to the psychological journey'. *Harvard Business Review*, March–April 2000.

29. **Pfeffer, J.** and **Sutton, R.** (1999) 'Knowing "what" to do is not enough: Turning knowledge into action'. *California Management Review*, Vol 42 No 1.

30. **Kleiner, A.** and **Roth, G.** (1997) 'How to make experience your company's best teacher'. *Harvard Business Review*, October 1997.

31. **Botelho, F.** and **Ryan, M.P.** (1996) Motorola University and the learning organization. Case 714, Institute for the Study of Diplomacy, Georgetown University, Washington, DC.

32. **Grieves, J.** and **Redman, T.** (1999) 'Living in the shadow of OD: HRD and the search for identity'. *Human Resource Development International*, Vol 2 No 2, pp. 81–102.

33. **Brinkerhoff, R.** quoted in Cameron, F. (2002) 'Fuzzy logic: Measuring the intangible value of learning'. *HR Monthly*, September 2002, Australian Human Resources Institute: Melbourne.

34. **Wenger, E.C.** and **Snyder, W.M.** (2000) 'Communities of practice. The organizational frontier'. *Harvard Business Review*, January–February 2000

35. **Gardiner, P., Leat, M.** and **Sadler-Smith, E.** (2001) 'Learning in organisations: HR implications and considerations'. *Human Resource Development International*, Vol 4 No 3, pp. 392–405.

36. **Brenneman, W.B., Keys, J.B.** and **Fulmer, R.M.** (1998) 'Learning across a living company: The Shell companies' experiences'. *Organisational Dynamics*, Vol 27 No 2, pp. 61–69.

5

Attracting Talent

A learning organization requires a fundamental shift in the mindset. There is no better way to begin the change process than by revisiting our attitude and policies towards recruitment. The recruitment process is vital to organizations for many reasons. There is a saying that a person is known by the friends he/she keeps. Similarly, an organization is known by the people it employs. By itself, an organization is faceless. It is the people in the organization who create the identity, character and personality of an organization. As times, leaders and strategies change, organizations require different mix of people. Recruitment provides the opportunity to cater to changing needs for people by either repositioning current employees or injecting fresh blood into the organizational veins.

Recruitment is more of an art than science. By ensuring that the recruitment and selection process results in attracting, identifying and inducting the 'right kind' of people, organizations make a solid start. Having recognized that the intellectual calibre of employees is a core competitive advantage in the knowledge economy, organizations need to engage in deep thinking and strategizing about:

□ What kind of employees do we need: What are our expectations of them in terms of the skills, competencies and characters required in a knowledge economy

□ How do we get them: What are 'their' expectations of us as an employer and how we can position ourselves to persuade them to join hands with us

□ How do we retain them: Once we get them, how we can work together for mutual benefit and persuade them to share their future with us.

Companies typically apply precise and rigorous guidelines for capital allocation but do not show the same commitment when it comes to recruiting people, despite the fact that hiring decisions involve enormous costs when one takes into account the recruitment costs, training costs, salary and benefits over the tenure of employee and replacement costs.[1] Hiring a wrong or mediocre person can be very damaging to an organization, financially and socially. Therefore, recruitment and retainment of high performers are so vital to the future of an organization today that they can no longer be treated as support or staff functions managed by the HR department. They need to be an integral part of the strategic business plan and the entire management team should be held responsible for planning and execution of suitable strategies.

The process begins with mapping an 'ideal employee' profile . . .

From Left Brain to the Right

In the industrial economy, which operated in a relatively more stable environment, an 'ideal employee profile' read something like this:

□ Aim to grow with the company and develop a long-term and stable career

- Comfortable with hierarchy, well-established company policies and procedures and work within defined limits of the job, position, roles and responsibilities
- Compliant with organizational culture and decision-making process
- Well-developed, rational and logical decision-making capability to gather all the relevant data and information, scan alternatives and recommend the best possible solution to the next authority
- Specialized skills
- Ability to abide by and implement the management decisions without stepping the boundaries of authority
- Ability to mentor and groom subordinates and mould them to fit with the organizational culture, and
- Leadership ability to maintain discipline, order and control with strict adherence to standard operating procedures.

With the above mandate in mind, recruiters would carefully look for candidates who have or likely to have a stable career, well-developed specialized skills and references that testify to the candidate's loyalty. A candidate who has changed jobs many times is likely to be frowned upon. So is the candidate who has held different types of jobs with no speciality in any particular skill set. The tendency in such companies is to define a job as closely as possible with emphasis on specific skills needed, and the hierarchy is focused on a set of 'cherished capabilities, such as clear accountability, legitimate authority, established routines, division of labour and specialization'.[2] Similarly, the selection procedure in such companies is well laid out with extensive tests of cognitive ability and academic intelligence. Any sign of out-of-the box thinking or tendency to question established authority would hurt the candidate's chances of success.

The scenario described above is very much alive, if not thriving. One can notice that it is quite out of sync with what we understand of the knowledge economy. Many recruitment managers might jump to defensive routines in justifying the process, described above, on the grounds of legal requirements, fairness and the need for bureaucracy, particularly in government organizations. However, today, we are operating in a global, multi-cultural, hyper-competitive, fast-changing and knowledge-intensive environment as against a local, stable, homogeneous environment that characterized the industrial economy. In a world of unpredictable change and educated employees and consumers, the capabilities and expectations, described above, will not work and those who continue to cultivate such outdated capabilities will fall into the trap of 'doing the wrong work, but doing it very well'.[2]

Change in the environment calls for change in the employee profile. One of the principles of a learning organization, as discussed in Chapter 4, is that 'the internal complexity must match that of the environment'. Today, organizations need people who are comfortable to work with blurred boundaries of employment, tasks, authority, market and organization. As a consequence of this need, we are today witnessing discernible shifts from employment to employability, training to learning to learn, ethnocentric attitude to geocentric attitude, independent work to teamwork, narrow specialization to multi-tasking, organized organization to self-organization, and adherence to rules to flexibility that arises from constant questioning of assumptions and mental models. Therefore employees need to master the art of managing chaos and uncertainty in their immediate and outside environment. The new economy demands the emergence of a new set of capabilities, i.e., the collections of organizational competencies that describe what organizations are able to do and how they are able to do it.[2]

Call for Competencies

The terms skills and competencies are sometimes used interchangeably. Generally, skills are referred to more in operational settings and competencies in knowledge-intensive settings. It is argued that skills offer operational flexibility (breadth) whereas competencies offer strategic flexibility (depth).[3] However, all jobs from the boardroom to the shop floor, require both breadth and depth of knowledge and therefore, overemphasizing the distinction between skills and competencies is likely to result in preserving entrenched hierarchy and class system between blue- and white-collar jobs—the very system we want to move away from.[4] Therefore, it is desirable to take a broader approach to the definition of competencies by including 'skills, knowledge and behaviours' necessary for the successful performance of a task.[5]

Today, it is generally recognized that it is not the technical / functional expertise but behavioural / managerial expertise that plays a dominant role in the successful execution of most tasks. It is because an overwhelming number of jobs are in the service industry where customer service is the key to business performance. Further, an increasing number of people are working in strategic business units and self-managed teams where competencies, such as business orientation, team building, interpersonal relations, and cross-functional understanding play an important role.

For example, in interactive service work, such as call centres, technical skills are seen as less important than aesthetic and social competencies in customer service representatives.[6] In these settings, 'workers need to develop an understanding of themselves that allows them to consciously use their emotional and corporeality to influence the quality of the service'. Even in a highly technical field, such as IT, research suggests that lack of soft skills is one of the key reasons for the high rate of failure in information systems projects.[7] So is the case with expatriate failure.

Despite the growing evidence, employers still tend to recruit and reward people mainly on their technical skills and accomplishments to the detriment of soft skills. To correct the imbalance, recruiters need to attract and select people with the competencies and capabilities that really drive the business performance of the organization. While the required competencies differ from organization to organization, depending on their environment, goals and strategies, the following are generally regarded as those essential in the new economy.

Emotional Intelligence

From early childhood, typically parents, teachers and superiors encourage us to suppress emotions and take cool-headed rational decisions based on facts. Yet we know that emotions have a powerful impact on our decision-making process. Employees often react emotionally and not rationally in a range of situations, such as receiving negative feedback, denial of promotion and making a choice between a salary cut and redundancy. Such situations call for understanding, analysing and managing emotions by all the parties rather than a clinical emphasis on rationality.

In today's environment of uncertainty, chaos and paradox, managers have a greater need to explore multiple solutions and understand their own and others' emotional reactions to problem-solving. Emotional labour is becoming an important part of interactive service jobs in industries such as entertainment, fast food, airlines, and call centres. In an attempt to portray positive emotions, people in these jobs may experience depersonalization, emotional drain and exhaustion. Therefore, they require the ability to control their own emotions and positively influence the emotions of customers while at the same time efficiently handling the volume of work. That is why emotional intelligence is gaining prominence as a necessary competency.

According to Mayer and Salovey, emotional intelligence involves the ability to understand, analyse, express and regulate emotions of self and others.[18] They argue that by employing emotional knowledge, one can promote emotional and intellectual growth. People high in emotional intelligence are able to

- accurately identify and express emotions and feelings of self and others
- use their emotional knowledge to prioritize thinking by directing attention to important information and as an aid to judgement. They realize that emotional mood swings from happiness to sadness lead to multiple points of view and encourage specific-problem approach, such as when happiness facilitates inductive reasoning and creativity
- interpret the meanings that emotions convey (such as understanding that sadness often accompanies a loss), understand complex feelings (such as simultaneous feelings of love and hate), and recognize likely transitions among emotions (such as from anger to satisfaction)
- stay open to feelings, reflectively engage with emotion, depending upon its judged informativeness and manage emotion in oneself and others by moderating negative emotions and enhancing pleasant ones.

Emotional intelligence represents the core aptitude or ability to reason with emotions. Some view it as a lifelong educational process rather than a psychological aptitude. Psychologists agree that general intelligence or IQ accounts for between 10 and 20 per cent of life success. It is argued that emotional intelligence or EQ may explain a small portion of the remaining.[8]

Some have extended the scope of emotional intelligence to cover self-awareness, self-regulation, motivation, empathy and social skill.[10] EQ 'can be thought of as one member of an emerging group of potential hot intelligences that include social intelligence, practical intelligence, personal intelligence, non-verbal perception skills, and emotional creativity'.[11] Research shows that it definitely increases with age. As to whether it can be learned or acquired by birth, the answer is the same as with any personality-related skill, such as leadership. A poem on leadership reads: '. . . No combination of talents can guarantee it. No process or training can create it where the spark does not exist.'

Not many people are aware of the importance emotions play in a workplace. It is thought to be a personal matter that does not have concern with work. It is important to create that awareness first and then help people to interpret and regulate emotion and use it as a tool in decision-making through coaching, mentoring, experiential exercises, role play, introspection and honest dialogues in a trusting environment. To measure emotional intelligence, many organizations rely on a person's self-description of how emotionally intelligent he/she is. However, it can be deceptive as people generally exaggerate their capability in understanding and dealing with emotions.[8] A Multifactor Emotional Intelligence Scale (MEIS), empirically developed by Mayer et al. assesses three primary facets of EQ, namely, perception, understanding and managing of emotion.[11]

As with other management concepts, there is a lot of hype about EQ in terms of what it is and what it can do. There is no consensus on how to measure it and nurture it. The concept is still at the beginning of the learning curve.[8] However, it has succeeded in exposing the over-emphasis on IQ or rational decision-making and underemphasis on emotions.

Self-leadership

Today, organizations are consciously attempting to move away from the command and control managerial style to empowering employees through a range of employee involvement and participation processes, such as autonomy, debureaucratized and decentralized structures, and bottom-up communication. This transition can only succeed when employees learn how to manage themselves and utilize their creative energy in problem-solving rather than solely relying on their managers. A team environment can play a supporting role in the process but ultimately, it is self-management, self-organizing and self-leadership, or what Senge calls personal mastery, that has a major impact on the success of contemporary management initiatives towards employee empowerment.

Those with an aptitude for and demonstrated experience in self-leadership can effectively play the role of a change agent in transforming employees' mentality from (managerially) organized organization to self-organization. Therefore, this competency is highly valuable and deserves attention at the time of recruitment and selection.

Systems Thinking

An uncertain and fast-changing environment calls for a big picture mentality and a sense of how a seemingly good move from one part of the organization may land the entire organization in a checkmate situation. Senge's example of a boiled frog, discussed earlier, illustrates how a lack of systems thinking leads people to miss the crucial early warning signals and go down the path of no return. Similarly, Morgan highlights the importance of building the whole into the parts.

Learning to Learn

In the previous chapter we discussed some of the key traits of employees in a learning organization, namely, lifelong learning attitude, keeping an open mind to divergent ideas, shedding defensive routines, adapting double-loop orientation, propensity for risk taking, learning from experience of self and others, benchmarking against best practices, and natural desire to share knowledge through mentoring. The knowledge economy requires 'career-resilient' workers 'who not only are dedicated to the idea of continuous learning but also stand ready to reinvent themselves to keep pace with change; who take responsibility for their own career management; and last but not the least, who are committed to the company's success'.[13] By looking for and selecting people with such competencies, employers can inject fresh blood into the organization and reinvigorate the enthusiasm of current employees.

Intuitive Decision-making

Even though intuition can be regarded as part of learning to learn competency, it deserves special mention. In times of unprecedented change, there are very few proven solutions and very little time to scan alternatives and decide the best course of action. In such circumstances, those who are able to balance between reason and intuition in their decision-making process are the ones who are most likely to succeed.

At a strategic decision-making level, the need for intuition becomes even more important as strategies commonly have no precedent nor can be easily analysed. Decisions, such as mergers and acquisitions, alliances with competitors, entering a foreign market, introducing a brand new product or service, investing in R&D of an idea never thought of before, involve heavy reliance on intuition.

Intuitive individuals rely on gut feelings, hunches, inspiration and insight to solve problems. It is a distilled experience and is called upon, often unconsciously, in times of decision-making in an uncertain environment. It is not an irrational process as it is acquired over years of experience in problem-solving. Thus, intuition is not only compatible with rationality, but employs it, possibly at a faster rate than the speed of thought.[14,15]

Cross-cultural Sensitivity

It is obvious that in an increasingly global environment, organizations need to develop a global orientation and cross-cultural sensitivity. Gone are the days when firms could choose an international market based on their cultural preferences. For example, Australia is a Western country caught up in an Asian surrounding. For its economic and political survival, Australia has to constantly engage with its Asian partners. It has been a painstaking journey for Australian political and business leaders who are constantly criticized by their Asian counterparts for doing too little and too late in reconciling cultural differences.

Today, organizations need employees with cross-cultural awareness and empathy, developed through multiple linguistic skills, frequent overseas travel and community interactions with other cultures. Such people are aware of cultural prejudices and stereotypes and make a conscious effort to block them from influencing their decision-making process. 'The recognition that other cultures do not necessarily share the same values and beliefs as one's own is a critical asset'.[16]

Capacity for Change

According to Ulrich, 'capacity for change focuses on agility, flexibility, and speed'.[2] He argues that 'both losers and winners will face uncertain futures. While losers are forming teams and task forces to study change, winners will already have adapted.' Today's environment calls for enormous capacity for change to grapple with uncertainty, complexity and hyper-competition. Therefore, Microsoft's Bill Gates calls for people who can conduct business at the speed of thought.

Other equally important competencies, required in the new economy, are:

- Knowledge management: Ability and aptitude to generate, share and utilize knowledge (as discussed in Chapter 1)
- Team management: Involves interpersonal skills, conflict resolution skills, etc.
- Customer focus
- Innovation and creativity (as referred to in Chapter 4).

The list of competencies varies depending on the business environment of the organization, its culture, strategies, current and desired core capabilities, occupation category and the position. Each organization has to, therefore, identify its own set of competencies through introspection rather than blindly adapting the ones in vogue.

How to Identify Competencies?

Many companies tend to bundle a group of popular competencies into a position, irrespective of their relevance and level of significance. For example, in one organization, the HR department added a list of soft competencies, namely, customer relationship and service delivery, business planning and organizing, results orientation, developing knowledge, entrepreneurial spirit, continuous professional development and teamwork as key performance indicators (KPIs) into the position of IT analyst/programmer. While the position did require these soft competencies, the major task was still technical work. The IT personnel found it very difficult to highlight their contribution by addressing the KPIs. As a result, they were justifiably upset about the criteria applied to judge their performance.

Therefore, it is important to engage in extensive consultation, particularly with those who are doing the job, before finalizing the competencies required to perform a job. Spencer believes that the best way to identify the knowledge, skills, or other abilities needed to perform competently in a job is

1. to identify the most effective performers in that job
2. study what these people actually do that distinguishes them from average performers, and
3. identify the specific skills, abilities or characteristics which are responsible for this difference.[17]

Spencer argues that traditional job analysis methods can identify *what* people do, but not the nuances of professional skill that enable some persons to perform a task more effectively than others. Further, they tend to be too detailed to be practical and are not selective. He quotes the Pareto rule, which indicates that only a critical 20 per cent of the functions a person performs on the job account for 80 per cent of performance and therefore, it is essential to differentiate superior performance from average performance.

Further, he describes a job competence assessment procedure that was successfully used to identify soft skill competencies in the United States Foreign Service officers and later expanded to fifty other professions. For example, the study pointed out that in the US Foreign Service Office, superior performers exhibited such soft skills as

- non-verbal empathy (ability to 'hear' what a person from a foreign culture was really saying or meaning in a negotiation),
- speed in learning about and developing political network (find out who 'actually' calls the shots in a foreign capital and how to get to that person), and
- positive expectations (a strong belief in the underlying dignity and worth of others different from oneself, and the ability to maintain this positive outlook under stress).[17]

A possible danger of identifying competencies by separating superior performance from average performance is that it yields a set of criteria that ensured success in the past.

Considering that past performance does not necessarily guarantee future success, the identified set of criteria may become obsolete by the time they are operationalized, implemented and institutionalized through HR mechanisms, such as performance management and remuneration. Hence, generic competencies, such as learning to learn, have more enduring value than situation-specific competencies.

How to Measure Competencies?

People managers are increasingly realizing the limitations of relying heavily on traditional psychometric and personality tests measuring cognitive ability. According to Sternberg et al., 'Even the most charitable estimates of the relation between intelligence test scores and real-world criteria such as job performance indicate that approximately three-fourths of the variance in real-world performance is not accounted for by intelligence test performance.'[18] As they point out, there is a big difference between academic intelligence (book smarts) and practical intelligence or common sense (street smarts).

Unlike the intelligence tests which are well defined and follow a single method to find a single correct answer, real-life challenges are unpredictable, ill-defined and offer multiple methods and solutions. Therefore, the attention is now shifting to problem-solving ability in a real-world situation to help organizations identify, operationalize and test those qualities that really matter.

Most of the competencies, discussed above, seem to improve with age, experience and maturity of individuals. Emotional intelligence or practical intelligence, intuition-based decision-making, cross-cultural sensitivity, self-leadership are the kind of competencies which require individuals to experience over a period of time, introspect and learn from experience. These are hardly the kind of competencies that one can claim to have attained by attending a training programme or a university qualification.

According to Sternberg et al.:

> There is reason to believe that whereas the ability to solve strictly academic problems declines from early to late adulthood, the ability to solve problems of a practical nature is maintained or even increased through late adulthood. The available evidence suggests that older individuals compensate for declining fluid abilities by restricting their domains of activity to those they know well and by applying specialized procedural and declarative knowledge.[18]

Such competencies cannot be tested by traditional cognitive measures. They are better tested by problem-solving tasks involving real-life situations such as, 'If you are a customer service representative in a "000" emergency call centre and you receive a distress call saying an armed intruder has entered the home, what would you do?'

Thus, recruiters need to be aware that jobs that require the competencies discussed above may need to be staffed with people with real-life experiences and not necessarily high qualifications. These competencies can be viewed as part of tacit knowledge, which is procedural and acquired with little help from others. Procedural knowledge is difficult to articulate. Further, to quote Polanyi, individuals know more than they can tell. To that extent, it is difficult for recruiters to effectively tap and test tacit knowledge at the time of selection.

While research on how to test practical intelligence or tacit knowledge is still in its infancy, Sternberg et al. believe that it can be effectively measured.[18] According to them, such measurement instruments typically consist of

> □ a set of work-related situations, each with between five and 20 response items. Each situation poses a problem for the participant to solve, and the participant indicates how he or she would solve the problem by rating the various response items;

- statements describing actions taken in the workplace, which participants rate for how characteristic the actions are of their behaviour; and
- descriptions of complex open-ended problem situations where participants are asked to write plans of actions that show how they would handle the situations.[19]

Sternberg et al. further suggest that for the foreseeable future, the most viable approach to testing common sense or tacit knowledge is to supplement existing intelligence and aptitude tests with selection of situational tests and interviews, such as above.

Recruitment Practices

In the so-called war on talent, organizations will have to compete fiercely for the best talent. For some, the best talent means nothing but the top rank holders from prestigious universities whereas for some others, it refers to those with the right attitude and competencies, no matter where they come from. Recruitment refers to attracting suitable talent whereas selection refers to choosing the best of the short-listed talent. Therefore, it is necessary to attract a sufficiently large applicant pool to choose from. Filling vacancies by promoting from within provides opportunities for advancement and is an effective way of motivating and retaining current employees. However, by recruiting talent from outside, organizations can inject fresh blood, minimize inbreeding and address current critical shortages in skills and competencies. The emphasis on external and internal recruitment flows from the type of talent required and the cultural change necessary to drive the business strategy and the employment profile (core/contract/casual) that the organization wants to pursue. New technologies, in the form of intranet and internet, also called e-cruitment, offer cost-effective and speedy options, on a global scale, to search for best talent within and outside the organization.

An organization needs to consider the following aspects while designing its recruitment strategy.

Harnessing Diversity

In a globalized and knowledge-intensive economy, employers have no option but to abandon ethnocentric approach to recruitment and select people solely on merit, irrespective of their national or cultural background. Companies need to adopt equal employment opportunity (EEO) policies, not just to comply with law but with the genuine interest in and appreciation of the benefits that diversity can bring to the organization.

By not encouraging a diverse workforce, organizations only stand to lose. Research suggests that companies that actively promote diversity, in terms of gender, ethnicity, age, disability, marital status, etc. get an enormous boost to their community image and succeed in harnessing the hidden potential within socially disadvantaged groups, such as women, minorities, older and disabled people. With the ageing population, recruiters have to cast their net far and wide without being constrained by stereotypes and prejudices.

Recruitment practices that promote diversity include training all managers on the benefits and practice of diversity, removing selection criteria that directly or indirectly promote discrimination, advertising positions in areas and newspapers that are accessed by target groups (e.g., advertising in childcare centres to attract the attention of women), encouraging current employees to inform the target groups about the company's employment policy and vacancies, and choosing women and managers from minority groups as members of the selection panel to boost the confidence of candidates from underrepresented groups and also to ensure non-discriminatory behaviour by other members of the panel.

Cultivating the Image as an Employer

Each company has a particular image in the eyes of the public. For example, Microsoft is seen as a technology- and innovation-driven company, IBM as service oriented, WalMart as a conservative but solid company and Virgin as a fun-loving company. Building a positive image that conforms to the business strategy and culture of the organization is very important to attract the right talent.

When Virgin Blue started its aviation operations in Australia in 2000, it received thousands of applications even before the formal advertisement of vacancies. The company's recruitment strategy was bold and unconventional. It is said that when the company wanted to recruit pilots, it approached an ex-union official of another airline who had spearheaded a strike a few years ago that ultimately failed and resulted in the sacking of pilots. Those pilots had later spread all over the world to get employment but were keen to return home. When Virgin approached them through the ex-union official, they jumped at the opportunity. Some other employers would have perhaps shunned the same pilots for their past record.

Some recruiters suffer from a false sense of belief that a flashy advertisement is all that is needed to attract attention. This is particularly so when they try to convey that they possess the corporate values that the applicants typically look for. Most job advertisements claim that employees are their best assets and that they invest heavily in their development. In many instances, it is the advertising agency which writes the copy and the recruiters simply hope that people will believe what they see in the advertisement.

Rather than a glossy advertisement and a passionate speech during recruitment drives, today's knowledge workers are more interested in knowing the company's stand, in unambiguous words, on policies such as training, opportunity to work on challenging assignments, flexible working, criteria for judging performance and the basis for a range of monetary and non-monetary rewards. Using their extensive professional network, knowledge workers typically check the reality before making up their mind. In other words, it is not the rhetoric but the actual performance of the company as an employer that shapes its image in the employment market and determines its success in recruiting and retaining the best talent.

Employers should clearly and imaginatively convey their corporate vision, business strategy, management philosophy and psychological contract with employees. For example, those looking for employment with Amazon.com will learn that it was 'born in a Chevy travelling West on Interstate 90', referring to how Jeff Bezos thought of the idea of setting up the Earth's Biggest Bookstore in 1994 while on his way to Seattle. The company explains on its website why people should choose to work with them: 'At Amazon.com, you get to

- work with and learn from an unusually high proportion of smart, focused people who are passionate about their work;
- work on challenging, interesting projects that have a huge impact on our success;
- work in a casual but accountable environment in which hard work, initiative, and smart decisions are rewarded;
- play an important part in continuing our leadership in e-commerce by bringing new ideas to the table and launching new businesses;
- be rewarded with great career opportunities and the chance to participate financially in the company's long-term success; and
- have fun'!

Such positioning attracts the kind of people that Amazon is looking for—smart, hard-working, unconventional, risk taking and above all, fun-loving.

People also appreciate companies providing a realistic picture of the position being advertised. When Sir Ernest Shackleton wanted to recruit men for his daring Trans-Antarctic expedition in 1914, he advertised: 'Men wanted for an expedition. Low wages, harsh working conditions and low chances of survival.' More than 500 men applied for 28 positions. While never accomplishing its goal of the first crossing of the Antarctic continent as the ship was caught in packed ice and crushed, this expedition became a 'larger than life testament to heroism and human endurance, with all the 28 men surviving nearly two years in the barren, frigid Antarctic'.

Recruitment strategies should aim at exciting the creative imagination and passion within people to embrace the company's mission and goals and share the rewards, rather than spinning a fairy tale of imaginary corporate values and work environment.

Cultivating the Image as a Responsible Corporate Citizen

Few companies realize that a recruitment campaign is closely tied to their overall image as a responsible corporate citizen. A company known for dubious work practices, such as discrimination in employment, authoritative work culture, bullying, extreme pressure to perform at any cost, promotions based on favouritism, tax avoidance, environmental vandalism and poor customer relations will naturally have a poor image as an employer. No marketing guru can change that image.

An ethically responsible organization would run its recruitment campaign in an ethical way—advertisements that tell the truth rather than promising the moon, honest comparison with competitors in employment conditions rather than juggling the figures to give a distorted picture, following ethical principles in poaching employees from competitors, enabling the successful job applicant to provide sufficient employment termination notice to present employer so as not to disturb current work commitments, etc.

Employees as Ambassadors

Knowledge workers not only work in a networked environment, they are also highly networked. If a company wants to attract a person who is highly valued by his/her current employer, it is not the advertisement nor the head-hunter but the word-of-mouth reference by existing employees that is most likely to do the trick. Employees have a better idea of the kind of people that the company needs and are likely to influence such a person that they know of. They are also best suited to explain the real-life scenario of an employment position to prospective applicants in a recruitment drive. Word-of-mouth referrals 'seem to attract employees who show longer tenure and lower turnover'.[20] Therefore, a company with happy employees, who are willing to act as its ambassadors, is the one that attracts the right talent with the least recruitment expenditure.

To obtain such a reference though, companies have to do more than offering a referral bonus. They have to show genuine care and concern for employees in meeting their career expectations. This is how a sound management philosophy turns into a sound investment in people.

Catch Them Young as Interns

It is difficult to choose knowledge workers with the right competencies in a campus interview. Qualities that employers look for, such as learning to learn and capacity for managing change and complexity, are difficult to identify in just a day-long selection process with tests and interviews. It is equally difficult for the organization to demonstrate to a valuable candidate as to how it is different from and preferable to the competitors. A possible solution is to provide internships to bright campus students and make them work on live projects. The intern gets a first-hand experience of company culture and appreciates the opportunity for work experience. In return, the company gets to closely watch the intern's aptitude and capabilities in action as a prospective employee rather than relying on hunches in employment interviews. Even if the intern does not join the company on completion of studies, any positive impression about the company, generated during the internship, will remain strongly with the person, spread as word-of-mouth publicity and may prompt the person to consider the company as a future employer.

At General Electric Company (GE), one of the most admired corporations in America, the company scouts for best candidates to participate in its Human Resource Summer Internship Programme while still in graduate school. 'The three-month internships give students the opportunity to complete a value-added human resource project as well as participate in day-to-day human resource activities. Upon completion of the internship, both the students and GE are able to evaluate more clearly the potential future fit of the individual into GE'.[26]

The policy to consider internships as an employment strategy may have little immediate benefit. However, it will appeal to those organizations that have a long-term view of their HR philosophy and consider HRM function as an investment centre.

Managing Quantity and Quality

The challenge of the recruitment exercise is to attract the right number and type of people. Depending on the occupation, position level, company's image as an employer and labour market conditions, recruiters have to sometimes manage too many or too few employment applications.

From the cost and efficiency point of view, the internet provides an excellent opportunity to manage the flow of recruitment. Employers can now provide enough and instant information about the company and the position to a potentially worldwide applicant pool without being constrained by prohibitive advertisement costs. The intranet can do the same to internal employees looking for growth opportunities within the company. The position description (what the job involves) and the position specification (what the job demands in terms of competencies) can be made available to all the applicants helping them to self-judge the fit between position requirements and their ability and expectations.

The World Wide Web is also increasingly facilitating global network of professionals looking for employment opportunities. The professional associations now provide an opportunity to both employers and candidates to link up with each other. For example, for academic positions, one of the best available web links is free online access to *The Chronicle of Higher Education* published from the USA. Universities worldwide list their positions through this paper. The web site enables readers to customize their requirements and get a weekly email posting of positions of their choice. Thus, electronic networking provides organizations instant access to global talent at an incredibly low cost. As a result, e-cruitment has expanded rapidly in recent years.

Treat Applicants Like Customers

While today customer service is an integral part of business strategy for most companies, it is surprising that the same attitude and commitment are rarely seen while dealing with potential employees. Despite the availability of technologies that help manage even a large pool of applicants, very few companies show interest in acknowledging applications, providing relevant information about the position and the company, informing candidates of the progress and result of their application. In many instances, candidates are dismayed at the arrogance of and lack of interest by recruiters and interviewers in keeping appointments and answering queries. In the selection interviews, inappropriate and offensive questions are often asked with open display of stereotypes and prejudices.[22] Obviously, such negative experiences tarnish the image of an employer and put off candidates from applying again.

Tread Carefully in Outsourcing Recruitment

Companies that consider recruitment as a key strategic weapon would like to drive the process themselves rather than handing it over to another firm. Outsourcing recruitment makes sense only when it involves a global search of key managers with extensive international exposure or seeking skills that are highly specialized but in short supply, such as new IT technologies or filling positions that are new and unfamiliar to the company.

The advantages of specialist hire firms is that they know their business well, have long-established contacts with key people who do not reply to newspaper advertisements, have a well-developed and updated candidate database built over a long time and a better knowledge of labour market conditions, such as compensation trends. However, many recruitment firms place profit before service and are more eager to clinch a deal in a hurry than in taking time to understand and marry the needs of the employer and employee. The hire firms are not entirely to blame. In many instances, HR managers treat hire firms with scant respect and spend little time in explaining the nature and requirements of the position. Companies that have a successful relationship with hire firms almost always spend considerable time in choosing them based on sound criteria and then establishing a long-term relationship so that they understand each other well enough to service the recruitment needs.

Finally, attracting best talent depends on meeting their expectations. These expectations are discussed in the next chapter on retaining talent.

Selection Practices

To facilitate quick and objective scanning of applications, companies can post an online application form that is simple to fill up and asks applicants to provide the information relating to essential selection criteria. For example, if a sales position requires the job incumbent to be at least a university graduate, have sales experience in recreation industry, and possess a valid driver's licence, the online application form can shortlist the applicants who meet these basic criteria.

To make a preliminary assessment of soft competencies, the application form should ask open-ended questions allowing the candidate to describe a situation when the desired competency was demonstrated. For example, to measure teamwork capability, applicants may be asked: 'Please tell us about a time you worked in a team in about 100 words. Try to cover: a short description of the team and its goals, your role in the team, how you realized that other team members needed motivating, what exactly you did and what the result was'.[23] The challenge here is to develop a good sense of judging open-ended answers.

Apart from asking applicants to fill up a standard application form, it is also desirable to ask them to submit a curriculum vitae (CV), written in their individual style, so that interviewers can better appreciate the candidate profile rather than just referring to a standard form.

Interviews have been and will continue to be the most important method of employee selection. In many instances, particularly when candidates and recruiters are geographically dispersed, telephone and video-conferencing can substitute or complement face-to-face interviews. However, even in a technology-intensive environment, the human touch will still play a critical role in selection. The more structured the interview process, the more is its validity and reliability. In unstructured interviews, selection managers often have their favourite set of questions, such as, 'what are your strengths and weaknesses' or 'where do you want to be five years from now' and have a favourite answer to them.[24] Such interviews are obviously unproductive.

Who should be on the interview panel? Traditionally, senior managers have dominated the interview panel solely on their position of authority. However, it is logical that the selection panel also consist of people who most closely interact with the position. For example, team members should have a say in the selection of a new team member. However, in such a situation, the possibility of choosing a like-minded person and killing diversity needs to be minimized. The interview panel members need to have cross-cultural sensitivity and genuine commitment to promoting diversity both in the thinking and composition of the organization. They should be able to effectively block out their stereotypes and prejudices about people who are different than them. This includes avoiding the trap of selecting people who think the same as the selection manager(s).

As regards the focus on a candidate's personality, 'a consensus has been achieved with regard to the importance of the "Big 5" personality dimensions, with recent questionnaires being developed around the dimensions of conscientiousness, emotional stability, neuroticism, agreeableness, and openness to experience'.[20] The ability to judge intangible competencies, such as emotional intelligence and intuitive decision-making, is a big challenge to interviewers today. As yet, there are no proven techniques to judge them accurately and interviewers have to develop the skill through experiential learning. The acquisition of soft competencies is a matter of exposure. Therefore, interviewers have to examine whether the applicant is exposed to and has learnt from situations that demanded the competencies in question. Structured interviews using both the situational questions (e.g., 'Assume that you were faced with the following situation . . . what would you do?') and past experience questions (e.g., 'Can you think of a time when . . . what did you do?'), demonstrate high levels of criterion-related validity, particularly when used with descriptively anchored answer rating scales.[25]

Extensive research suggests that a battery of selection techniques, such as general mental ability, integrity test, work sample tests and structured interview, rather than any single method alone, is the most successful way to select the best candidate for both entry-level as well as senior positions.[26] Assessment centres that provide a range of such selection methods are becoming increasingly popular.

Interviewers should have a realistic expectation of candidates with regard to their technical skills and behavioural competencies. Each person has his/her strengths and weaknesses and personality orientation. The interviewers should focus on the strengths and see whether the person is flexible to learn the competencies that he/she seems to lack. Many times, the interviewers fall into the trap of preferring those who fulfil the immediate technical needs of the job to those who have well-rounded experience and behavioural competencies that are not of immediate relevance to the job. For example, if an organization needs a marketing manager for a consumer product and needs to make a choice between two candidates—one, with relevant experience but uncertain credentials as a team leader and a strategic thinker and another, with less relevant experience but impeccable credentials in team leadership and strategic thinking, the general tendency is to choose the former. By subjecting the interviewee to narrowly defined criteria, the interviewers will miss the big picture and fail to appreciate the broader skills and competencies of the person.

In one instance, a personnel manager interviewed a candidate who did not have the qualifications or finesse of other applicants but having ventured into his own business at a very young age and failed, he appeared to have developed a mature and well-rounded personality. The manager prevailed on the other selection committee members to give a chance to this candidate who later proved to be an extremely valuable employee with his entrepreneurial instincts and customer focus.

With regard to the references furnished by candidates, they generally tend to be positive and do not really contribute to the selection process. To address this problem, employers should ask the candidates to provide the list of only those referees who had a close working relationship with them in the recent past. The HR manager should speak to such referees and elicit detailed information about when and how they interacted with the candidate. If the interaction is not long or deep enough, such references should not be given serious consideration. Referees should be encouraged to explain the work situation in detail in terms of the main demands of the work, delegation of tasks, difficulties encountered and the candidate's contribution in overcoming problems, etc. By going into minute details of the previous job with the referee, reliable and useful information can be obtained to help make the right selection.

Extensive international research suggests that most of the popular selection techniques, such as intelligence tests, interview (particularly unstructured), prior experience, reference checks, education, and personality tests 'may have a probability of success that is little more than chance'.[27] Such findings raise serious questions about the validity of selection methods and organizations need to find their own way by maintaining selection records and carefully reviewing their experience with different methods.

Designing Recruitment Strategies Around Core, Contract and Casual Employees

Organizations need to be mindful of the changing employment profile and design their recruitment strategies accordingly. The core, contract and casual employees cater to different needs of the organization with different set of competencies and also have a different set of expectations of their employer.

Core Employees

These are employees for the long term and are committed to the goals and vision of the organization. They possess firm-specific core competencies and act as corporate DNA passing on their knowledge through successive generations of employees. They are the custodians, champions, trustees and torchbearers of organizational culture and competencies. They are expected to play the role of mentors, corporate ambassadors and role models and move across different locations and divisions of the company to help spread best practices across the organization. They offer 'greater stability and predictability of a firm's stock of skills and capabilities, better coordination and control, enhanced socialization, and lower transaction costs'.[28] Obviously, 'outsourcing these kind of skills might jeopardise the competitive advantage of the firm by eroding its stock of core skills',[29] and therefore, core employees need to be developed internally.

To attract core employees, organizations need to develop a long-term-oriented recruitment and retention strategy that goes beyond cost considerations. Typically, large organizations recruit bright graduates from university campuses and provide them in-depth induction. After a few years, they identify high-potential candidates from amongst them, who are then rotated across functions and locations to be groomed as future senior managers. Multinational enterprises (MNEs) develop a global pool of such managers, drawn from parent-country, host-country and third-country nationals (as discussed in Chapter 9). To recruit and retain core employees, organizations need to offer reasonable employment security, employability through continuous training, mentoring and career management, development-oriented performance management, competitive and long-term-oriented remuneration that includes stock ownership and performance incentives, and generous rewards to cater to personal needs and circumstances. Overall, the retention strategy should focus on how best to align organizational requirements and individual goals and needs.

Contract Employees

These employees typically have a short- to medium-term employment relationship that remains for the duration of the contract. They possess readymade, latest and specialized skills that are in demand in the market. They move from one firm to another, consolidating, broadening and deepening their experience as they move along their entirely self-directed and self-managed career path. They take greater risks and invest heavily in time, money and efforts to keep themselves up to date and accordingly, command a premium in the market.

To recruit top-quality contractors, firms have to not only offer a competitive price but also meet their expectations of the position in terms of challenge, interest, relevance, convenience and often, duration. Recruitment firms can be of great help in sourcing the right type of contractors as they typically specialize in particular occupations and have a comprehensive, up-to-date database with a personalized approach to recruitment. However, to get better value out of recruitment firms, employers should conduct a proper and thorough due diligence process, shortlist a few preferred suppliers and establish a long-term relationship with them with relatively steady business and periodic quality audit.

Many contractors prefer to become permanent employees at some point in their career. It provides a good opportunity to employers to consider recruiting contractors, with proven skills and right attitude, as core employees. Over a period of time, the skills of the former contractors can become firm specific and provide sustainable competitive advantage to their employers. This option is particularly attractive to those firms that cannot afford to hire fresh graduates and groom them over a long period. However, employment of contractors may lead to dissatisfaction amongst permanent employees who may feel that they are underpaid and deprived of opportunities to work on latest skills affecting their employability.[30]

Part-time/Casual Employees

These employees typically possess generic and relatively lower-level skills in administrative, support, operational and maintenance types of operations. They typically work under close supervision with little operational discretion. They can cater to temporary needs of the organization arising out of cyclical business needs.

The surge in employment of casual/part-time employees testifies to their significance in the new economy. The majority of such employees are recruited through outsourcing firms as is evidenced by the surge in the growth of such firms. It is mainly because of the prohibitively high administrative costs and statutory benefits payable to them, which can push their wage bill by as much as 25 per cent if they were to be directly employed. 'In these cases, using outside workers enables organizations to reduce overhead costs and retain a significant degree of flexibility concerning the number of workers employed, as well as when they are employed.'[28]

Part-time and casual employees are attracted by competitive remuneration, flexibility in working conditions and opportunity for permanent positions. As in the case of contractors, firms need to establish long-term and quality-oriented relationship with outsourcing firms that provide such employees. They also provide a rich source for permanent recruitment with a proven and easily verifiable track record.

While employment of casual/part-time workers seems to make economic sense, motivating them with short-term transactional employment relationship is very difficult and challenging. The deprivation of employment benefits and career opportunities available to regular employees creates a sense of inequity, injustice and unfairness in the minds of casual/part-time employees leading to demotivation and low morale. The quality of their work, in their varied roles, such as call centre staff, tellers, check-out operators and security guards, is as crucial as that of permanent employees in providing customer service. Majority of the firms experience high turnover of such employees and the cost of replacement, training and poor customer service will significantly reduce the benefits of employing them on a non-permanent basis. Many firms try to address the problem by offering permanent part-time work and provide regular benefits and training after a certain period. Some others provide multiple casual positions to increase the hours of employment. For example, a theme park in Australia allows its employees to work in different roles, such as clown, cleaner, canteen operator and stunt assistant, throughout the day, to align the needs of the business and the individual.

Thus, employers have to weigh the pros and cons and design suitable recruitment and retainment strategies around core, contract and casual employees.

Agenda for Managerial Action

Points to Ponder . . .	. . . Steps to Consider
Recruitment is a holistic process.	Recruitment should flow directly from business strategy with active commitment and participation from all levels of management. It should focus as much on employee needs and expectations as those of the organization. It also needs to be closely tied to retention policies and strategies.

Change in the environment calls for change in the employee profile.

Today, organizations need people who can manage ambiguity, change and complexity. These qualities require a different set of skills and characteristics that were frequently frowned upon in the industrial economy. Organizations need to overhaul their HR planning, job analysis, recruitment and selection procedures to be able to identify, recruit and retain people with the right competencies.

There is no set of competencies that is universally applicable to all organizations and positions.

The best way to identify competencies required in a position is to involve and brainstorm with all stakeholders to seek those qualities that contribute to overall and ongoing superior performance.

Effective recruitment practices are grounded in reality rather than fantasy, harness diversity, enthuse employees to act as ambassadors and treat applicants with professionalism and respect.

Does your organization
- have a diversity management policy and action plan that harnesses the potential of women, minorities, immigrants and older workers?
- consciously cultivate its image as an employer of choice and a compelling place to work, based on its true and unwavering commitment to developing people and their communities in the way it treats them in good and bad times and by letting them have a say in organizing their work and working environment?
- let employees and employment practices speak for themselves in what it is to work for this organization?
- use internships as an important means of recruitment and selection?
- effectively leverages technology to manage the recruitment flow?
- have a professional and dignified approach to recruitment?

There are very few selection techniques that have convincingly demonstrated their validity and

In the absence of proven methods of selection, organizations have to rely on their own experience and

reliability. The challenge is even greater when it comes to measuring soft competencies.	historical data in choosing a set of selection techniques that work best for them. Recruiters need to be well trained and well experienced to be able to judge the quality of tacit knowledge and soft skills based on a multitude of tests that encourage applicants to practically demonstrate their credentials.
Core, contract and casual employees have a different set of abilities and expectations and require customized approach to recruiting and retaining them.	Organizations should carefully weigh the pros and cons of outsourcing and then manage each type of employee to suit their profile with the underlying belief in and respect for the dignity and contribution of all.

Case Scenario: Recruiting at Southwest Airlines

To ensure that the company hires the right people, Southwest is extraordinarily selective in recruiting. Because of the company's outstanding reputation as a great place to work, it does not need to rely on headhunters or employment agencies. The company receives a lot of resumes over the transom, and its employees also encourage their friends and families to apply. In 1998, Southwest had almost 200,000 job applicants. Of these, roughly 35,000 were interviewed and over 4,000 hired. The company recruits primarily for attitude, believing that skills can be learned.

To ensure fit, there is an emphasis on peer recruiting. For example, pilots hire other pilots, baggage handlers hire baggage handlers, and so on—even if this means coming in to work on their day off to do background checks. Teamwork is critical. If applicants say 'I' too much in the interview, they don't get hired.

The hiring process consists of an application, a phone screening interview, three additional interviews (two with line employees), and a consensus assessment and a vote. During the interview process, the applicant will come into contact with other Southwest employees. These people are also invited to give their assessment of whether the person would fit in at the company. To further screen for the Southwest spirit, Southwest will let its best customers become involved in the interviewing process for new flight attendants. The entire process focuses on a positive attitude and teamwork.

As befits a company where selection is important, Southwest has spent a lot of time identifying the key components comprising effective performance and behaviour. It uses a hiring approach developed by Development Dimensions International, Inc. (DDI):

- Use past behaviour to predict future behaviour
- Identify the critical job requirements (target dimensions) for the position
- Organize selection elements into a comprehensive system
- Apply effective interviewing skills and techniques
- Involve several interviewers in organized data-exchange discussions
- Augment interview with observations from behavioural simulations

The company does not use personality tests, but instead emphasizes previous actual behaviours. Southwest believes that most skills can be learned and doesn't screen heavily for these except for certain specialist jobs, such as pilots and mechanics. Attitudes are what count.

An important awareness on the part of the People Department is that the company rejects literally tens of thousands of applicants each year. These are all potential customers. Therefore, the recruiting process is designed to not make any applicants feel inferior or rejected. Some applicants who were turned down have claimed that they had a better experience being rejected by Southwest than they did being hired by other companies.

The company hires very few people with MBAs, and even those that do get hired are selected for their fit, not for their credentials. In fact, Southwest prefers people without extensive industry experience. For example, 40 per cent of their pilots come directly from the military, 20 per cent to 30 per cent from small commuter airlines, and the rest from major airlines.

Southwest also actively encourages nepotism and has 820 couples who work for the company. One woman described how she had gotten her son a job with the airline, but then described how he had been fired. 'He didn't deserve to work here,' she said. Thus, when these people describe the company as 'family', a common reference throughout the airline, they really mean it.

Source: Excerpts reprinted by permission of Harvard Business School Press. From *Hidden Value: How great companies achieve extraordinary results with ordinary people* by Charles A. O'Reilly III and Jeffrey Pfeffer. Copyright © 2000 by the Harvard Business School Publishing Corporation; all rights reserved.

References

1. **Bartlett, C.A.** and **Ghoshal, S.** (2002) 'Building competitive advantage through people'. *MIT Sloan Management Review*, Vol 43 No 2, pp. 34–41.
2. **Ulrich, D.** (1997) 'Organising around capabilities'. In Hasselbein, F. et al. (Eds.) *The Organisation of the Future*, Jossey-Bass: SF.
3. **Kochanski, J.T.** and **Risher, H.** (1999) 'Paying for competencies'. In Risher, H. (Ed.) *Aligning pay and results*, AMACOM: NY.
4. **Crandall, N.F.** and **Wallace, M.J.** (1999) 'Paying employees to develop new skills'. In Risher, H. (Ed.) *Aligning pay and results*, AMACOM: NY.
5. **Zingheim, P.K.** and **Schuster, J.R.** (2000) *Pay people right!* Jossey-Bass: SF.
6. **Thompson, P., Warhurst, C.** and **Callaghan, G.** (2001) 'Ignorant theory and knowledgeable workers: Interrogating the connections between knowledge, skills and services'. *Journal of Management Studies*, Vol 38 No 7.

7. **Agrawal, N.M.** and **Thite, M.** (2003) Nature and importance of soft skills in software project leaders. Working Paper 214, Indian Institute of Management, Bangalore, India, September, 2003.

8. **Mayer, J.** and **Salovey, P.** (1997) 'What is emotional intelligence?' In P. Salovey and D. Sluyter (Eds.) *Emotional development and emotional intelligence: Implications for educators,* Basic Books: New York.

9. **Mayer, J., Caruso, D.R.** and **Salovey, P.** (2000) 'Emotional intelligence meets traditional standards for an intelligence'. *Intelligence,* Vol 27 No 4, pp. 267–98.

10. **Goleman, D.** (1998) 'What makes a leader?' *Harvard Business Review,* November–December.

11. Anonymous. Published in an IBM publication around 1974.

12. **Waterman, R.H., Waterman, J.A.** and **Collard, B.A.** (1994) 'Toward a career-resilient workforce'. *Harvard Business Review,* July–August.

13. **Anderson, J.A.** (2000) 'Intuition in managers: Are intuitive managers more effective?' *Journal of Managerial Psychology,* Vol 15 No 1.

14. **Khatri, N.** and **Ng. H.A.** (2000) 'The role of intuition in strategic decision making'. *Human Relations,* Vol 53 No 1, pp. 57–86.

15. **Prahalad, C.K.** (1997) 'The work of new age managers in the emerging competitive landscape'. In Hasselbein, F. et al. (Eds.) *The Organisation of the Future,* Jossey-Bass: SF.

16. **Spencer, L.M.** (1983) *Soft skill competencies,* Scottish Council for Research in Education, Edinburgh.

17. **Sternberg, R.J., Wagner, R.K., Williams, W.M.** and **Horvath, J.A.** (1995) 'Testing common sense'. *American Psychologist,* Vol 50 No 11, pp. 912–27.

18. **Williams, W.M.** and **Sternberg, R.J.** (1996) *Success acts for managers,* Harcourt Brace: Orlando, FL.

19. **Iles, P.** (2001) 'Employee resourcing'. In Storey, J. (Ed.) *Human resource management: A critical text,* Thomson Learning: London.

20. **Stockman, J.E.** (1999) 'Building a quality HR organisation at GE'. *Human Resource Management,* Vol 38 No 2, pp. 143–46.

21. **Rynes, S.L., Bretz, R.D.** and **Gerhart, B.** (1991) 'The importance of recruitment in job choice: A different way of looking'. *Personnel Psychology,* Vol 44, pp. 487–522.

22. **Wood, R.** and **Payne, T.** (1998) *Competency based recruitment and selection*, Wiley: West Sussex, England.
23. **Fernandez-Araoz, C.** (1999) 'Hiring without firing'. *Harvard Business Review*, July–August.
24. **Taylor, P.J.** and **Small, B.** (2002) 'Asking applicants what they would do versus what they did do: A meta-analytic comparison of situational and past behaviour employment interview questions'. *Journal of Occupational and Organisational Psychology*, Vol 75, pp. 277–94.
25. **Schmidt, F.L.** and **Hunter, J.E.** (1998) 'The validity and utility of selection methods in personnel psychology: Practical and theoretical implications of 85 years of research findings'. *Psychological Bulletin*, Vol 124 No 2, pp. 262–74.
26. **Nankervis, A., Compton, R.** and **Baird, M.** (1999) *Strategic human resource management*. Nelson Thomson Learning: Australia.
27. **Lepak, D.P.** and **Snell, S.A.** (1999) 'The human resource architecture: Toward a theory of human capital allocation and development'. *Academy of Management Review*, Vol 24 No 1, pp. 31–48.
28. **Bettis et al.** (1992) Quoted in Lepak, D.P. and Snell, S.A. (1999) 'The human resource architecture: Toward a theory of human capital allocation and development'. *Academy of Management Review*, Vol 24 No 1, pp. 31–48.
29. **Pearce, J.L.** (1993) 'Toward an organisational behaviour of contract labourers: Their psychological involvement and effects on employee co-workers'. *Academy of Management Journal*, Vol 36, pp. 1082–96.

Retaining Talent

It is obvious that the retention of high-performing employees is better than a long and expensive search for new employees with uncertain outcomes. Unfortunately, companies think of retention only when the labour market is tight and ignore it during a downturn. Pfeffer describes the futility of such an approach:

> By laying off employees too quickly and too readily at the first sign of financial difficulty, (firms are) buying high and selling low (and, in the process, incur unnecessary cost having done a) good job selecting, training and developing their workforce . . . They lay off people in cyclical downturn and then, when the entire industry is booming and staff is scarce, they engage in often fruitless bidding contests to rehire the skills that they not that long ago sent packing. (Thus, in many cases), layoffs put important strategic assets on the street for the competition to employ.[1]

Steel et al. recommend that the retention policy should be based on well-informed data, such as quit rates at the organizational, departmental and job category levels as compared to industry rates which throw light on where exactly excessive bleeding is occurring.[2] This should be complemented with data from exit interviews, surveys of former and present employees, compensation surveys, and best practices in retention in order to formulate appropriate retention strategies.

Exit interviews are the most widely used method to gather information on why people quit. However, this may not always be reliable.[3] For instance, if a person is quitting because the boss is autocratic and bullying, it is unlikely to be mentioned in the exit interview because of its repercussions on the release, payment of dues or future employment prospects. Therefore, the employee is most likely to give a harmless reason, such as better pay or personal circumstances. It is dangerous to rely and act on such superfluous data. The information from exit interviews needs to be followed up, some time later, by an independent source to validate earlier data.[2]

Interestingly, research suggests that both high and low performers have higher quit rates than average performers (ibid.). High performers typically quit for reasons such as lack of training and promotion opportunities, inadequate compensation commensurate with performance and outside opportunities. Often, organizations delude themselves into believing that people quit for higher pay. It is a typical sign of lack of systems thinking. Those who have changed jobs know that it is a painful decision with repercussions on a family's stability, spouse's career, children's education, social network in the present location and employment, and uncertainty about the prospects in the next job.[4] Unless a person feels quite strongly about issues such as equity, morale, relation with the immediate superior, and opportunities outside, he/she is unlikely to change jobs. 'Research consistently finds that employees show a strong preference for the status quo' and only when the relative attractiveness of a new job far outweighs that of the existing job, they overcome the built-in resistance to change.[2]

While retention strategies depend on the particular circumstances of the focus group, some generic solutions at the macro level can be designed, as suggested below, to specifically manage employee expectations and morale as they are considered to be the biggest influencing factors affecting the employees' decisions to stay on.

Aligning Organizational Goals with Employee Needs

As previously discussed, each generation has its own way of defining life and careers. Generation Xers are less loyal to organizations and more committed to their profession. For them, an employer is just another passage in their career path that is primarily defined by them. They also clearly mark the boundaries of their personal and professional life and use the latter as a means to enrich the former. However, the twenty-something generation has only a 'hazy sense' of their identity.

Individuals are now increasingly aware that lifelong, full-time employment is fast disappearing and being replaced by contract, casual or part-time employment in a variety of functions and with a variety of employers. Against this reality, what do they expect from their employers?

Reasonable Security of Employment

Evidence suggests that the security of employment is still a major issue for employees and has a considerable impact on their morale, motivation and intention to stay. Their attitude to any organizational restructuring exercise is mainly influenced by their consideration of 'what is in it for me?' 'Employment security encourages people to take a longer-term perspective on their jobs and organizational performance' and motivate them to be 'more productive because they know they are helping to ensure a result that benefits them—having long-term job and career'.[1] Thus, recruiters have to be aware that any spin on employment flexibility needs to be grounded in the realization that employment security cannot be brushed aside as an outdated expectation.

Employability

Individuals are concerned not only about employment for today but also about employment in the medium to long term, as employment stability affects the choice and the quality of their lifestyle. They realize that to secure their future, they need a robust portfolio of skills and competencies that they can transfer from one job to another. Accordingly, they prefer employers who give them the opportunity to work on skills that are in demand today and in the foreseeable future. Those employers who are committed to providing ongoing training and reskilling and those who practise internal job rotation and promotion are the ones who are likely to be treated as the employer of choice.[5] Whether employees are motivated by fear or acceptance of job insecurity, performance commitment is likely to be influenced by the availability of opportunities for developing their 'employability'.

Competitive and Contingent Remuneration and Rewards

Compensation needs to be internally consistent and externally competitive. High-performing employees are scarce, in great demand and do not come cheap. Firms that recruit and retain such employees almost always offer contingent compensation that include gain sharing, profit sharing, stock ownership, pay for skill and various other forms of individual, team and organizational incentives. 'When employees are owners, they act and think like owners'.[1] However, as we will discuss in Chapter 8, the success of reward strategies rides on the overall HRM climate and goes beyond monetary considerations. Recognition rewards that celebrate success and the competencies that contribute to the success, abundantly, frequently, equitably and in time, go a long way in reinforcing employee commitment and intention to stay. Recognizing and rewarding people who acquire new skills is another way to make the workforce more productive as well as to keep them.

Transparency

With the recent exposure of corporate greed and excesses, people are sceptical and cynical about the sincerity of employers in treating their employees. The level of trust in corporations, in the eyes of employees and investors alike, is generally so low that people tend to rely more on rumours and conspiracy theorists than published management policy and statements. The more the corporations hide the truth about how they manage their company and employees, the more ugly it gets. And with networked communication, people are empowered to unearth the truth faster and better than in the past.

Thus, employers have no choice but to be candid in providing information about the company and 'fully disclose such things as executive compensation, hours involved in an average work week, the probability and speed of advancement, and the *real* mission and values of the organization'.[6] The company's intention to exit or outsource any particular line or part of business is another vital information that employees need, to plan and manage their career. Without this information, it is difficult for employees to see how they fit in the company's scheme of things. Many companies fear that if they tell employees that they are exiting from a particular business, they will panic and jump ship. It is similar to a doctor's fear of telling a patient of his/her illness. Employees expect employers to treat them like adults.

Mukesh Ambani, Chairman of the India-based multinational enterprise Reliance Industries summarizes contemporary employee expectations:

In the past, public standing of a company was the magnet, promotions and increment the source of motivation and the fear of financial uncertainty the glue that bound an efficient hand to the job. In the knowledge age, excitement of the challenge in a job attracts the talented. It is a powerful magnet. Creative and democratic environment are the source of motivation and the opportunity of continuous growth the glue that binds the talent to a company. As for reward, it is the talent that dictates the terms.[7]

Managing Careers

The career management process is caught in the whirlpool of environmental, organizational, and HRM changes. The paradox of contemporary career management is evident in the here-and-now employment policies and 'help us but help yourself' attitude of many employers. It is an irony that the career-conscious employee is being asked to offer more and more, while the employer is in no position to offer the scale and the kinds of rewards that were available in the past.[8]

Today, people looking for employment 'need to be more flexible and versatile in their skills and knowledge, and must be willing to go anywhere, at any time, and at a moment's notice, to do anything'. The world of work is changing so fast that most individuals seem to have no clue on how to react, let alone being proactive.[9] 'It is hard for someone being swept downstream in a fast-moving river to make sense of where they are, let alone where they are going.'[10] Whymark and Ellis caution that 'too cavalier an attitude by employers may have detrimental long-term effect on the health of the organization and its ability to attract and retain talented managers'.[8] Some organizational theorists, therefore, recommend a pluralistic approach by incorporating older, more static career concepts along with newer, more dynamic career concepts on the ground that 'the repeated cycle of out-with-the-old-and-in-with-the-new is likely to increase rather than reduce pandemonium'.[9]

Further, if employees' performance falls short of expectations because of organizational shortfalls, such as failing to adapt to new organizational forms due to incompatibility in organizational systems, they cannot be held responsible. 'Many managers see the rhetoric of the new organization as running well ahead of its practice and are fatigued by change, insecure, defensive in their career strategies, and highly political in their behaviours. Some organizations falsely believe that they can be reengineered overnight'.[11]

Stratford recommends 'new contracts' with employees, changing management activities to retain employee commitment, organizing career profiling services for internal redeployments and outplacement services for the redundant.[12] Only then can they secure long-term employee commitment and retention. 'The role of career development is less clear now than it was in the traditional organization. This should not be a sticking point of nostalgia however, but rather the incentive for developing new models of career development'.[13]

The provision of 'employable skills' is a key success factor in contemporary career management. Organizations can provide necessary assistance to employees to fulfil this key criterion by way of helping them identify these skills and supporting continuous learning through mentoring schemes, virtual career development centres, computer-based training (CBT), flexi-hours and so on. When vacancies for 'hot skills' arise, organizations can reinforce their commitment to employees by recruiting internally to the extent possible. This also helps organizations to provide the bridge between the present and the future. We also need to question organizational expectations of super heroic qualities in all employees. Instead of expecting everything from everybody, organizations need to identify the key strengths in each individual and assign tasks and responsibilities accordingly.

It is clear that even in the new economy, organizations have a clear role and responsibility in career management. The nature and level of this responsibility may vary depending on organizational size, organizational life cycle, industry, type and level of employees, occupation, top management philosophy, national and organizational culture, etc. Removal of hierarchical, functional and organizational boundaries, through delayering, multi-skilling and outsourcing activities have resulted in boundary-less careers and increased labour turnover, thus, limiting long-term career management. However, organizations can still play a proactive role in career management by removing internal boundaries for career movements, individualizing career planning, mentoring employees in self-management and overhauling the HR philosophy.[14] Any way one looks at the new economy, there is scope and a window of opportunity for organizations to play a constructive role in career management.

Selective Retention

In today's uncertain and competitive world, it is neither possible nor desirable to aim at retaining all the employees. The competitive environment calls for employees who perform beyond expectations or well above the ordinary contractual obligations. It is these employees that organizations should identify and try to retain.

This policy is similar to the controlled burning exercise carried out by the Fire Services to minimize the potential damage from an all-out bush fire. Bartlett and Ghoshal explain:

> As any good gardener knows, to promote healthy growth, in addition to fertilizing and watering you also must prune and weed. That is a metaphor Jack Welch used often in describing the performance ranking process he introduced to cull chronic underperformers at GE.[15]

Indeed, whether the decision of an employee to stay is a positive event or to quit is a negative event depends on the performance of that employee because companies want good performers to stay and poor performers to leave.[2] The policy of selective discrimination in retention also recognizes the fact that both employers and employees can make mistakes in selecting each other or that their needs may change over time requiring readjustment in the relationship.

Today, organizations are pushed to the wall to perform at their best to survive and prosper. The standards of performance have gone beyond the local or national level. Today, one needs to be globally competitive and remain so all the time. Under the circumstances, employers simply cannot afford to adopt paternalistic employment policies and need to differentiate between superior and mediocre performance. They need to realistically assess how long they want their employees to stay with them and design their retention strategies accordingly.[16]

For example, many multinational IT companies have a practice of identifying the top and bottom 20 per cent of performers in their organization during the annual performance review. The top 20 per cent are star performers and the companies go out of their way to retain them through rapid promotions, top performance bonuses, continuous training, mentoring and career management. Their employment-related grievances are immediately dealt with by their manager, with the active involvement of the top management. To fulfil a star performer's need for acquiring a portfolio of skills in demand, employers often sacrifice their immediate interests to retain them.

For instance, a key employee might be a critical resource in a function or location but if the person wants to relocate to another function or location to suit his/her interests and circumstances, the manager has to release the employee sooner or later. If this is not done, the organization will lose the person altogether. In such cases, a compromise is reached to accommodate the needs of both parties instead of rejecting the request of the employee altogether. The organization needs to make every effort to design the job to suit the employee's career interests, personal strengths and circumstances. Ideally, this should happen for every employee, but considering today's harsh realities, at least the top performers should be singled out for creating tailor-made employment conditions. The bottom 20 per cent are given friendly warning to improve performance along with additional help, such as more frequent feedback, training and mentoring to facilitate performance improvement. However, if their performance is deemed to be unsatisfactory even after an extended period, they will be asked to look out for employment elsewhere while being relegated to routine tasks.

While it is relatively easy to identify the superior and poor performers and design appropriate positive and negative reinforcement measures, it is the large percentage of 'average' employees who may remain as 'unsung heroes'.[17] They put in solid, day-to-day performance but typically, get insignificant performance incentives and insufficient rewards. Considering the 'resounding failure' of the present performance appraisal system and the limited resources available for reward schemes (as discussed in Chapters 7 and 8), the average employees are, in many cases, justified in feeling unjustly, inequitably and unfairly appraised and compensated for their contribution. They need the support of their managers in mentoring, career counselling and skill/competency improvement to cross the thin line between average and superior performance. The performance and reward management systems also need to be sensitive to their potential limitation in recognizing the contribution of average performers and adopt holistic and inclusive approaches in addressing their genuine grievances.

The Power of the Immediate Manager

In many companies, the CEO, the senior managers and the HR department show genuine commitment to people and formulate elaborate policies to reinforce their commitment.

However, it is the immediate manager who provides the direct and constant management interface with all the employees and is most influential for their morale and motivation. Some of these managers say what the management wants to hear but practice what they actually believe. Managers who are autocratic, power hungry, deeply suspicious and highly political, effectively hide their true personality from the eyes of the top management. They also prevent employee grievances and suggestions from reaching higher management levels.

The senior management needs to understand that the reality on the ground might be quite different from what they are led to believe by frontline managers. They need to directly gather feedback on how their policies are working on the ground by talking directly to the employees, as often as possible, and checking whether frontline managers are following the policies in letter and spirit. 'Hewlett-Packard is famous for its use of "management by wandering around" which represents a more informal and less intrusive form of monitoring that ostensibly enables managers to communicate trust and concern'.[18]

In one instance, the CEO of a company emailed his employees telling them how seriously he considered the issue of work-life balance, particularly on female employees and how he is determined to help them by offering flexible employment options. Believing his rhetoric, one female employee in the IT section, who was regarded a star performer, approached her manager with a request to let her work from home using the laptop computer, as she did whenever she was on call after hours. The request was promptly turned down without reason. When she persisted, the manager promised to do something after she completed an important project but kept postponing the decision. The employee was obviously disappointed and demoralized and started looking for employment elsewhere.

If the CEO of the company had come to know of this incident, he would have wondered why the employee did not approach the higher management, including himself. This is another classic management delusion that employees readily approach the higher management when they are dissatisfied with the decision of their immediate supervisor. The reality is that employees are generally apprehensive about upsetting their day-to-day relationship with their manager whose decision is most likely to be upheld anyway for the sake of managerial unity. Unfortunately, those who question the manager are often labelled as whingers and even though the company policy might be to seek frank employee feedback, the practice might shut them up from speaking out openly. When whingers turn whistle blowers and expose the management practice in public, it might be too late for the management to prevent the potential damage to its image.

Therefore, instead of unrealistically expecting employees to take their grievances further up, the senior management should independently ensure that it has the full support of the frontline managers and reprimand those who act against the stated policies. Since a positive relationship with the immediate supervisor is a very important element of job satisfaction and therefore, retention, it should be regarded as an important yardstick in measuring managerial effectiveness. Studies on employee turnover emphasize the 'importance of employee expectations and morale (i.e., feelings of well-being, job satisfaction) in contributing to employee decisions to stay'.[2] The morale–turnover relationship is seen to be particularly strong among high performers. That is why organizations such as Microsoft hold their senior managers accountable for their subordinates' morale.[19]

In one of the units of Lucent Technologies, managerial bonuses are based on financial (20 per cent), customer (20 per cent), and people (20 per cent) dimensions.[20] Similarly, at Sears, Roebuck & Company, a retailing giant, the variable pay for managers is based, in equal proportion, on financial performance, measures linked to creating a compelling place to work and a compelling place to shop.[21] It is not easy to define and measure people dimensions, such as subordinates' satisfaction with managerial style, but that should not deter managements from emphasizing the importance of people management in any manager's job. Similarly, managerial selection should also favour those who have an inherent aptitude for taking responsibility for employee morale.

Fit the Job to the Person, Not the Other Way Round

While assigning employees to different tasks, rarely do managers keep the employee's interests and needs in mind. They tend to allocate human resources on the assumption that the person should fit the job and not the other way round.

Literature on career anchoring[22] and job sculpting[23] suggests that people have deep-rooted personality orientations. Some people excel in strategic thinking and dealing with ambiguity whereas others in the meticulous execution of clearly defined strategies. People have a clear preference for or against particular types of work, such as working with technology or people.

Obviously, employee preferences have to match changing organizational needs and most employees are deeply aware of this reality. While they adjust to organizational reality, they expect their managers to be aware of their strengths and personal preferences and match them to an appropriate job in the medium to long term. Providing reduced working hours, based on self-assessment of personal needs, is another way to boost employee creativity, work quality, satisfaction and retention. 'Viable reduced-hours career options require concomitant changes in the areas of compensation, assignments, and promotions'.[22]

Unfortunately, employees often become victims of their own success. Employees who excel in a particular product, location, strategy or technology get stuck with their success and their managers often refuse to release them from what they are doing to pursue what they want. The manager has a vested interest in binding the employee to the task for fear of not getting another person of such excellence. The result? An excellent performer becomes demotivated and demoralized and subsequently, the organization loses a valuable asset to competition.

Nurture Social Communities

People spend a large part of their waking hours at work. Social relations with colleagues are therefore an important consideration for people and often result in 'job embeddedness' that is characterized by links (i.e., connections with other people and groups), fit (i.e., compatibility with job, organization and community) and sacrifice (i.e., cost of what people have to give up if they leave a job).[4] Even though such relations are primarily driven by individual initiatives, the employer can play an important role by way of decentralized organizational structure, open communication channels, innovatively designed office blocks, flexibility in working conditions, etc. Many organizations actively promote humour at work, encourage employees to set up lunchtime walking groups and other hobby groups, and arrange open days and outings with family members.

'Job embeddedness can be established and maintained through careful attention to the connections employees make to people, institutions, and activities both inside and outside the organization.' For example, 'a company can sponsor (and provide time for) employees to participate in various activities, such as community clean up or beautification'.[4]

Thus, social networks are crucial for communities of practices. They act as a glue to bond and retain people. 'Since the boundaries between personal and work life are increasingly blurred, the work context provides an anchor of stability and "friendship" opportunities, nurtures a spirit of belonging, and can facilitate teamwork and cooperation'.[25]

In collectivist cultures, bonding occurs naturally and is highly regarded (as discussed in Chapter 9). Employees in these cultures avoid competition with peers and prefer group decisions and uniform compensation. In individualistic cultures, competition amongst employees is encouraged with a preference for independent decision and rewards based on individual contribution. With increasing emphasis on teamwork, organizations need to consciously influence their culture that promotes community orientation to work.

The quality of work environment is a major influence on the stability of social architecture at the workplace. The Quantum Corporation, a leading global supplier of computer hard disks, is therefore, committed to creating an 'extraordinary environment' for its employees that 'includes:

- Achieving long-term business success,
- Ensuring that Quantum's employees feel valued,
- Ensuring a sense of pride of association with the company,
- Instilling a sense of camaraderie and that "all of us are in this together",
- Ensuring that each employee has the opportunity to reach his/her highest potential personally and professionally, and
- Generating a sense of excitement and fun'.[26]

Teamwork is one of the core strategies adopted by Quantum in creating an extraordinary environment. 'Significant care in selecting team members, placing them all in close proximity (co-location), and team-based performance appraisals (and rewards) are seen as key to making the process work'.[26] Teams succeed when members share the same passion and goals, develop a sense of belongingness and feel proud of their membership of the team. Thus, developing affinity to social communities in the workplace is a powerful way of retaining people.

Facilitating a Dignified Exit

Today, both employers and employees realize that their relationship is not likely to be permanent and that both have the right and the need to decide when to sever the ties. However, it is surprising that many companies react negatively, some even with hostility, when key employees submit their resignation. In many instances, they are asked to leave immediately without serving the notice period, for fear that they may take away the company's secrets. While this apprehension may be justified in certain circumstances, it is difficult to comprehend how a valued employee can be treated with suspicion for simply exercising his/her choice of employer. Star performers, who are idolized by their employer, are shocked when they are treated with contempt after their resignation. Some employers go to the extent of making their departure as difficult as possible by refusing to issue the service letter, delaying outstanding payments, and refusing to let the employee encash leave. The attitude that the employer has the right to fire an employee to suit business needs but not vice versa, as reflected in employee exits under bitter circumstances, can only have a negative impact on employee relations.

In one instance, an employee who had just resigned, expected the company to pay him his bonus that was announced before he resigned. The only condition for payment was that the employee should be on the rolls of the company as of a particular date, and that he was. However, the company refused payment on the basis that the resignation letter was submitted before the particular date and therefore, notionally, he had already cut off his ties with the company.

In many cases, exit interviews are conducted with no real intention to use the data to improve HR policies. Some

HR managers even twist and interpret the data to suppress employee dissatisfaction. But how does facilitating a dignified exit help companies retain employees? A dignified exit shows that the company really cares even when one leaves and the positive message may induce that person to consider the company for future employment. It is received equally well by the existing employees and helps them differentiate between those employers who claim they care and those who really do. At Sun Microsystems, the career centre helps employees identify suitable career opportunities both inside and outside the organization. When there is a mismatch between the employee's strengths and organizational requirement, the employee is provided outplacement services to find a suitable job elsewhere. When requirements change, necessitating the need for the skills of former employees, they are welcomed back. Such relations are only possible when there is a genuine appreciation and respect for each other and dignified exits go a long way in establishing that relationship.

The '3 C' model adopted by Sears is grounded in the reality that making the organization a 'compelling place to work', through appropriate retention strategies, is a prerequisite to making the organization a 'compelling place to shop' as well as a 'compelling place to invest'. 'Sears has been able to show that an increase in employee satisfaction in one quarter will increase customer retention in the next quarter, which will subsequently be reflected in shareholder returns the quarter after that'.[21] Thus, effective retention strategies directly augment and multiply organizational performance.

Integrated Retention Policy

Steel et al. recommend that a fully integrated retention policy that takes into account external and internal environmental factors is more likely to succeed.[2] The retention goals need to be formulated based on data on who is quitting, the industry quit-rate statistics and projected workforce needs.

Organizations should also find out why people stay as 'the reasons people stay are not always the same as the reasons people leave'.[2] Such information mechanisms help determine whether excessive bleeding of talent is occurring and if so, how much, where and why. Steel et al. suggest two kinds of retention strategies: 'Blanket strategies' at the macro level (such as improving recruitment practices) and 'focused strategies' tailored to specific target audiences.

Blanket strategies are those that are well proven in the organization in the past and may include tried and tested methods, such as selection techniques (e.g., personality tests), realistic job previews and job enrichment. Targeted strategies require accurate information. For example, research suggests that while there is no difference between the quit rates of men and women, the latter are far more likely to quit because of family considerations. However, the quit-reasons of highly educated women are nearly the same as those of men, i.e., to improve job opportunities. Thus, effectiveness of focused strategies depends on accuracy of information.

Finally, Pfeffer cautions that fighting the war for talent could become hazardous to the organization's health if it leads to overemphasis on the individual to the detriment of team spirit, glorification of outside candidates that undermines the proven capability of current employees and labelling of star performers at the cost of the morale and mentoring of the rest of the employees.[27] In the obsession for individual talent, the wisdom of recognizing the importance of systems and culture on performance may get lost. Therefore, retention is not a set of isolated best practices but an ongoing, systemic effort in improving the overall quality of HRM climate.

Agenda for Managerial Action

Points to Ponder . . .	_. . . Steps to Consider_
Retention becomes a priority only when the labour market is tight. However, it is a direct result of overall employee satisfaction during both good and bad times.	The retention policy needs to be enduring, long-term oriented and integrated with other HRM policies.
Exit interview data is not always reliable.	Accurate and comprehensive data is very important to understand the complex psychological reasons behind employees' intention to stay or quit.
In their attempt to focus on business strategies, HRM policies often pay less attention to the need to align business goals with employee expectations.	Retention policy-makers need to focus on what is in it for knowledge workers to join and stay with the company. They should be able to make a strong and convincing case that the company has a positive brand image as a compelling place to work and an employer of choice by offering employability, competitive remuneration, recognition of contribution, a people-friendly and open culture and a demonstrable, ongoing commitment to developing careers.
Help us but help yourself attitude to career management is not helpful to retain people.	While organizations can no longer 'manage' careers, they can 'enable and empower' them through a new psychological contract that offers portfolio of critical skills, career advice and mentoring, flexible and stimulating work environment and sharing of wealth.
Selective retention is a targeted strategy to reward and retain star performers who act as role models for the rest of the employees in developing desired skills, knowledge and behaviours.	The danger in selective retention is that it may alienate the so-called average performers. This policy requires development of sophisticated systems of performance and reward management

	mechanisms for positive reinforcement.
The immediate manager wields the most powerful influence on employee satisfaction and retention.	Managers need to be held directly responsible for employee morale and assessed and rewarded accordingly. Employee communication and feedback mechanisms should encourage employees to air their grievances without the fear of retaliation by their superiors.
Social cohesiveness in employment relationship is an important determinant of employee decision to stay.	Organizational structure and culture should be such that they promote employee togetherness and satisfy their need for social recognition in the workplace.
In today's context of career management, the need to frequently change employers in one's career is understood and even stressed; however, when employees resign, they are often faced with negative reaction by employers.	Today's complex world of work requires frequent readjustments in employment relationship both by employers and employees. Progressive employers recognize that they may not always fully meet the expectations of employees and are ready to part ways in a friendly and professional way and in the process, keep the doors open for a future relationship.

Case Scenario: Writing the New Social Contract

It is time for a new social contract based on the new realities. This 'contract' should show people what the company is willing to do to help them build their own futures. It should be an explicit statement of how much people are valued. And it should be a commitment to specific actions and specific investments in people.

Imagine an agreement, which every manager would sign and give to every person in the company, that would read something like this:

'Our company faces competitive world markets and rapidly changing technology. We need the flexibility to add or delete products, open or close facilities, and redeploy the workforce. Although we cannot guarantee tenure in any particular job or even future employment, we will work to ensure that all our people are fully employable—sought out for new jobs here and elsewhere.

We promise to increase opportunity and power for our diverse workforce. We will:

- Recruit for the potential to increase in competence, not simply for narrow skills to fill today's slots
- Offer ample learning opportunities, from formal training to lunchtime seminars, the equivalent of three weeks a year
- Provide challenging jobs and rotating assignments that allow growth in skills even without promotion to higher jobs
- Measure performance beyond accounting numbers and share the data to allow learning by doing and continuous improvement, turning everyone into a self-guided professional
- Retrain employees as soon as jobs become obsolete
- Emphasize team building, to help our diverse workforce appreciate and utilize fully each other's skills
- Recognize and reward individual and team achievements, thereby building external reputations and offering tangible indicators of value
- Provide educational sabbaticals, external internships, or personal time-outs at regular intervals
- Find growth opportunities in our network of suppliers, customers, and venture partners
- Ensure that pensions and benefits are portable, so that people have safety nets for the future even if they seek employment elsewhere
- Help people to be productive while carrying family responsibilities, through flex-time, provision for sick children, and renewal breaks between major assignments
- Measure the building of human capital and the capabilities of our people as thoroughly and frequently as we measure the building and use of financial capital
- Encourage entrepreneurship—new ventures within our company or outside it that help our people start businesses and create alternative sources of employment

- Offer opportunities for meaningful community service through the company, including community service in our leadership training and team development
- Tap our people's ideas to develop innovations that lower costs, serve customers, and create new markets, as the best foundation for business growth and continuing employment and as a source of funds to reinvest in continuous learning.

Policies like these can renew loyalty, commitment, and productivity for all men and women, in organizations both large and small, as they struggle to create jobs, wealth, and well-being in the global economy.

Source: Excerpts reprinted with permission from Kanter, R.M. (1997, 2003) Rosabeth Moss Kanter on the Frontiers of Management, Boston: Harvard Business School Press. Copyright © Rosabeth Moss Kanter, Ernest L. Arbuckle, Professor of Business Administration, Harvard Business School, All rights reserved.

References

1. **Pfeffer, J.** (1998) 'Seven practices of successful organizations'. *California Management Review*, Vol 40 No 2, pp. 96–124.
2. **Steel, R.P., Griffeth, R.W.** and **Hom, P.W.** (2002) 'Practical retention policy for the practical manager'. *Academy of Management Executive*, Vol 16 No 2, pp. 149–62.
3. **Griffeth, R.W.** and **Hom, P.W.** (2001) *Retaining valued employees*, Sage: Thousand Oaks, CA.
4. **Mitchell, T.R., Holtom, B.C.** and **Lee, T.W.** (2001) 'How to keep your best employees: Developing an effective retention policy'. *Academy of Management Executive*, Vol 15 No 4, pp. 96–109.
5. **Meyer, J.P.** and **Allen, N.J.** (1997) *Commitment in the workplace: Theory research and application*, Sage, Thousand Oaks, CA.
6. **Smith, A.F.** and **Kelly, T.** (1997) 'Human capital in the digital economy'. In Hasselbein, F. et al. (Eds.) *The Organisation of the Future*, Jossey-Bass: SF.

7. **Ambani, M.** (2002) Building value through talent management. Valedictory address at the National Conference on Human Resources. 5 October, Mumbai, India.

8. **Whymark, K.** and **Ellis, S.** (1999) 'Whose career is it anyway? Options for career management in flatter organization structures'. *Career Development International*, Vol 4 No 2.

9. **Brousseau, K.R., Driver, M.J., Eneroth, K.** and **Larsson, R.** (1996) 'Career pandemonium: Realigning organizations and individuals'. *Academy of Management Executive*, Vol 10 No 4, pp. 52–66.

10. **Gunz, H.P., Jalland, R.M.** and **Evans, M.G.** (1998) 'New strategy, wrong managers? What you need to know about career streams'. *Academy of Management Executive*, Vol 12 No 2, pp. 21–37.

11. **Nicholson, N.** (1996) 'Career systems in crisis: Change and opportunity in the information age'. *Academy of Management Executive*, Vol 10 No 4, pp. 40–51.

12. **Stratford, D.** (1996) 'Outplacement is but one part of corporate change strategy'. *HR Monthly*, April.

13. **Templer, A.J.** and **Cawsey, T.F.** (1999) 'Rethinking career development in an era of portfolio careers'. *Career Development International*, Vol 4 No 2.

14. **Parker, P.** and **Inkson, K.** (1999) 'New forms of career: The challenge to Human Resource Management'. *Asia Pacific Journal of Human Resources*, Vol 37 No 1, pp. 76–85.

15. **Bartlett, C.A.** and **Ghoshal, S.** (2002) 'Building competitive advantage through people'. *MIT Sloan Management Review*, Vol 43 No 2, pp. 34–41.

16. **Cappelli, P.** (2000) 'A market driven approach to retaining talent'. *Harvard Business Review*, January–February.

17. **Henderson, R.** (1997) *Compensation management in a knowledge-based world*, Prentice Hall: NJ.

18. **Baron, J.N.** and **Kreps, D.M.** (1999) 'Consistent human resource practices'. *California Management Review*, Vol 41 No 3, pp. 29–53.

19. **Barlett, C.** (2001) *Microsoft: Competing on talent (A)*, Harvard Business School Publishing: Boston, MA.

20. **Becker, B.E.** and **Huselid, M.A.** (1999) 'Overview: Strategic human resource management in five leading firms'. *Human Resource Management*, Vol 38 No 4, pp. 287–301.

21. **Kirn, S.P., Rucci, A.J., Huselid, M.A.** and **Becker, B.E.** (1999) 'Strategic human resource management at Sears'. *Human Resource Management*, Vol 38 No 4, pp. 329–35.

22. **Schein, E.H.** (1996) 'Career anchors revised: Implications for career development in the 21st century'. *Academy of Management Executive*, Vol 10 No 4, pp. 80–88.

23. **Butler, T.** and **Waldrop, J.** (1999) 'Job sculpting: The art of retaining your best people'. *Harvard Business Review*, September–October.

24. **Bernett, R.C.** and **Hall, D.T.** (2001) 'How to use reduced hours to win the war for talent'. *Organisational Dynamics*, Vol 29 No 3, pp. 192–210.

25. **Bahrami, H.** and **Evans, S.** (1997) 'Human resource leadership in knowledge-based entities: Shaping the context of work'. *Human Resource Management*, Vol 36 No 1, pp. 23–28.

26. **Barber, D., Huselid, M.A.** and **Becker, B.E.** (1999) 'Strategic human resource management at Quantum'. *Human Resource Management*, Vol 38 No 4, pp. 321–28.

27. **Pfeffer, J.** (2001) 'Fighting the war for talent is hazardous to your organisation's health'. *Organisational Dynamics*, Vol 29 No 4, pp. 248–59.

Creating Performance Development Systems

Performance Appraisal—An Inevitable Evil?

A robust performance management (PM) system is one of the key difficult-to-imitate competitive strategies within the domain of HRM. By clearly defining, measuring and thereafter rewarding desired behaviours and competencies, organizations can set themselves apart from the competition.

Despite the obvious importance of performance management, the process has largely been a 'resounding failure', in the eyes of both employers and employees as demonstrated in numerous surveys.[1] In line with the change in its name from performance appraisal to performance management or development, the stated objectives of the process are linking performance to organizational objectives and strategies, employee feedback, identifying development needs and determining rewards. However, very few companies can successfully demonstrate the achievement of any of these goals.

With regard to feedback, the biggest concern of appraisees is that the impact of situational factors is not fully taken into account by the appraisers. As a result, they cannot agree on what needs to be improved and how, leading to demotivation.

Bernardin et al. believe that the lack of precision in measurement, customer focus, and consideration of situational constraints is the prime reason for the failure of the process.[2] In addition, the enormous administration and time burden imposed by bureaucratic systems further erodes the confidence and the buy-in required to make it meaningful and successful.

Thus, performance appraisal processes are 'typically seen by raters as extra work and by ratees as at best irrelevant, at worst demotivating'.[3] Edward Deming, father of the quality movement, denounced performance appraisal as one of the seven deadly diseases afflicting Western management.[4] According to him, the appraisal process nourishes short-term performance, builds fear, destroys teamwork and encourages politics. It has also been argued that feedback does not always help improve performance; in fact, 'a poorly implemented feedback programme could actually hurt, rather than help performance'.[5]

Some researchers trace the failure to critical design flaws in the Management By Objectives (MBO) concept, which has had a major influence on the performance appraisal system.[6] They believe that MBO was flawed because it relied too heavily on short-term, quantitative results without taking into account situational factors and discouraged risk taking. It also ignores the imbalance in the power relationship between the supervisor and subordinate. After all, MBO is just another tool and its success heavily depends on the culture and HRM climate in an organization. In a command and control culture, it fails to instil a participative approach to management and forces subordinates to withhold their views and stick to easily verifiable soft targets at the cost of innovation, creativity and risk taking. In a hard-hitting article, 'Management for whose objectives?', Levinson made a convincing argument that managers keep organizational requirements ahead of employee needs and make no effort to converge both, thus leaving the employee with little incentive to participate in the process.[7]

The role played by appraisal politics and impression management further weakens the credibility of the performance appraisal system. Research suggests that where administrative decisions (such as promotions, salary raises) are involved, raters resort to intentional distortions to maintain interpersonal relations with and trust of all the ratees.[8] It also suggests that employees can influence the process through the management of impressions.[9] Thus, the traditional appraisal process is too formal, static and disempowering—qualities inconsistent with a knowledge economy.[9]

Another reason for the dissatisfaction with the appraisal system is the common rater errors. When not trained properly, raters are prone to be influenced by

□ Recency effect (generalizing most recent performance for the entire appraisal period)
□ Central tendency (rating everybody the same)
□ Halo effect (generalizing performance on one factor for all other factors)
□ Leniency–strictness bias (rating too generously or too harshly)
□ Stereotypes and prejudices on gender, ethnicity, age, disability, marital and parental status, sexual orientation, etc.

Considering the above, it is not surprising that performance appraisals are a major source of legal battles. Legal experts advise that appraisals be based on objective criteria, raters be properly trained in anti-discrimination policies, ratees informed in writing about poor performance and given an opportunity to respond to the rating and improve performance. Any employment termination based on performance should be legally defensible.[10] The legal ramifications are becoming more pronounced with ageing population, immigrant labour, flexible work practices, teamwork, increasing job uncertainty and stress.

Performance Development—Key to Competitive Strategy

Despite the dismal performance of the performance appraisal process so far, it is obvious that the process is too important for organizations to let it fail. Companies that have introduced some form of performance management systems have achieved overall better financial performance than those that have not.[11] The reasons are many.

The PM process provides the best opportunity for organizations to convey and reinforce the desired competencies necessary to implement organizational strategies. For example, if the organization aims to be a global leader in its field through innovative and cost-effective products, it needs to have employees with a global orientation, high on creativity and innovation with a pulse on changing market trends and preferences and the ability to outsource globally for cost advantages. The rhetoric has to be firmly embedded in the PM system where the desired competencies and outcomes are clearly defined, measured and then rewarded.

Unless employees see a clear link between what is desired, measured and rewarded, they are least likely to follow them. For example, it is the experience in many universities that despite the rhetoric about equal importance given to teaching, research and service in academic positions, performance is measured mainly on research outcomes (publications, grants and supervision) with the result that academics tend to concentrate on research and underplay the importance of teaching and service. Thus, 'it is not what you want but what you measure and reward is what you get'.

People need feedback to confirm what they are doing is what is expected of them and how they can further improve their performance. They want positive reinforcement of good performance. In helping them, organizations need to be clear about whether 'the job drives the person or the person drives the job'. In hierarchical, rules-driven, mechanistic forms of organizations, jobs are clearly defined and the person is simply supposed to follow the rules. In such organizations, people can only be judged on how loyal and compliant they are. On the other hand, in organic companies, people drive the job and are given enough strategic and/or operational freedom to use creativity and innovation in performing their tasks. Such organizations also recognize that when people are given the freedom, they have to take risks and therefore, allowances are made for wrong decisions. Thus, while judging performance and rewarding people, one should remember that it is the management that sets the ground rules.

In today's competitive environment, organizations have to differentiate between different levels of performance to achieve optimum efficiency and productivity. They can no longer count on retaining the top talent with a uniform compensation and benefits structure and afford to tolerate the poor performers. They now urgently need to identify exceptional performers in order to reward them, retain them and use them as ambassadors of excellence and role models. They need to identify good performers in order to guide them in the right path and achieve better results. Further, they need to identify consistent poor performers for potential termination.

Considering the importance of the PM process, how should one proceed? In their quest for the most suitable system, organizations have to answer the important questions shown in Figure 7.1:

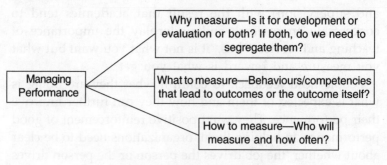

Fig. 7.1: Managing Performance

What to Measure—Means or the End?

Performance measurement involves the definition of performance as well as standards or levels of performance. While measuring performance, should the focus be on outcome or on the behaviours or competencies that are supposed to lead to the outcome?

Those who focus on outcome argue that in a customer-centric economy, outcomes based on customer satisfaction should define performance.[2] An outcome-focused measurement of performance theoretically makes sense but involves the tension between quantity and quality as well as situational influence. For example, a company that ties performance to sales may realize that the sales representatives focus too much on sales to the detriment of after sales service leading to customer dissatisfaction and long-term decline in sales.

Therefore, some argue that since outcome is situation specific and problematic to define, 'the domain of performance is best defined as a domain of behaviours rather than a set of outcomes'.[12] One way to resolve the controversy is to follow a 'mixed model' that takes into account both the outcomes as well as the behaviours or competencies that lead to the outcome.[13] Of course, the success of this balancing act depends on the nature and objective of the position under consideration.

The Balanced Scorecard is an increasingly popular approach in recent times for identifying performance measures from a holistic, long-term perspective.[14] It 'complements traditional financial indicators with measures of performance for customers, internal processes, and innovation and improvement activities'.[15] This approach directly links the strategic goals of the organization to the unit-level and individual-level goals and thus provides strategic focus to the performance measurement process. Suggested measures for different indicators include

- □ return on capital, cash flow, profitability, etc. for a financial perspective
- □ customer satisfaction index and market share, etc. for a customer perspective
- □ tender success rate, rework and project performance index, etc., for an internal business perspective
- □ percentage revenue from new services, rate of improvement index, staff attitude survey, etc. for an innovation and learning perspective.

Fairness in Appraisal

According to Gilliand and Langdon, the PM process, 'fairness perceptions arise from the evaluations of the ratings received and rewards tied to those ratings, the appropriateness and consistency of the appraisal process, and the explanations and feedback that accompany the communication of performance ratings'.[16] They believe that each stage of the performance management, i.e., system development, appraisal process and feedback, should ensure procedural fairness, interpersonal fairness and outcome fairness. They recommend the following practices to ensure fairness:

- □ Actively involve employees in identifying what, how and when to measure and in periodically reviewing the process
- □ Communicate clearly the objectives, the methodology and the criteria. Alleviate concerns before implementing the system
- □ Standardize the instrument and process to maintain consistency
- □ Reduce supervisory biases by training; asking raters to maintain records of employee performance and regularly communicating with the employee; and subjecting ratings to multiple reviews
- □ Allow self-appraisal

- Use multiraters (360-degree feedback) but ensure that they all have a reasonable knowledge of the employee's work performance
- Ensure the appraisal process is focused on the job not the person
- Do not surprise employees with bad news by ensuring that they are given continuous feedback (both positive and negative)
- Train raters and ratees in giving and receiving feedback
- While giving feedback, allow employees to express themselves
- Have a formal and effective appeal process
- Explain clearly how the appraisal process is linked to administrative decisions, such as pay rise, promotions, and incentives.

Managing Negative Emotions

One of the reasons why performance appraisal process is so unpopular and is regarded as an 'annual agony' by both raters and ratees is that, in its traditional form, it creates strong negative emotions in the workplace resulting in poisoning of relations and, in some cases, resignation from employment. It is a common experience amongst personnel managers that the frequency of employment resignation increases markedly after each performance appraisal cycle and what is worrying is that it is the good performers who quit. The biggest challenge to a manager is how to convey negative feedback and no matter how it is done, it is bound to generate arguments and disagreements.

Research suggests that the acceptance of feedback would be better if the manager clearly conveys organizational objectives, jointly sets the goals, gives periodic feedback, maintains a record of critical incidents to back up annual ratings and professionally conducts the feedback interview. One of the critical managerial competencies in this process is the ability to counter negative emotions arising out of administrative decisions following the appraisal, such as promotions, incentives, and placement of personnel in sought-after positions.

A manager high on emotional intelligence is able to minimize negative emotions, assuming that the right type of performance management process is in place. The success of the manager in this regard also depends on the ability to manage envy and jealousy in the workplace.[17] Rational decision-making models ignore the powerful influence of envy and jealousy that result from a loss of self-esteem when desired outcomes go to another person. With downsizing and constant reengineering, organizations are indirectly fostering excessive competitiveness, hostility and stress in the workplace. In the absence of objective performance criteria, employees resort to politics and impression management tactics.

A manager can minimize negative emotions in the workplace by being fair and transparent in allocating work, measuring performance and deciding on rewards; open to suggestions and divergent viewpoints; and providing personal and organizational help through mentoring and coaching to improve performance. People accept negative feedback if it is constructive, well founded, offered by a trustworthy person and accompanied by genuine opportunities to improve.

Coaching—Prerequisite for Effective Performance Development

No matter how well designed a performance management system is, its ultimate test lies in the competence of the manager administering it to his/her unit or team. While using feedback to improve performance, 'a coach can be the difference between a healthy coping reaction and learned helplessness'.[5] Right from the design phase to the implementation phase, the manager plays a critical role in enlisting suggestions, seeking support for the system, establishing goals, providing periodic feedback including constructive criticism, and offering help to improve performance.

This requires competencies, such as coaching/mentoring,[18] communication, counselling, empathy, emotional intelligence, facilitation, conflict resolution, and negotiation in conducting goal setting, performance review and feedback interviews. What is more important, however, is that the manager has to establish his/her credibility as a trustworthy person with fair, equitable, transparent, non-political behaviour and leading by example.

Managers also require periodic training in performance appraisal and management, particularly in avoiding typical rater errors. In recent years, sports psychology has been used quite successfully in business to illustrate the nature and importance of coaching for effective performance.[19]

Team Appraisal

Today, more and more organizations are using teams to counter competition through coordinated effort, address increasing task complexity, increase customer focus and to flatten structures for sharper focus and increased accountability. By definition, a team works interdependently towards a common goal. For organizations which are long used to individual performance appraisal, teams pose a new challenge.

The basic problem in a team appraisal is that the team members have different types and levels of competencies and accordingly, their contribution to team performance varies. Moreover, in most cases, employees do not have a say in selecting their team members. Social loafing is another common problem in a team setting, particularly when team members perceive that individual effort is not assessed and rewarded. Once present, social loafing can 'spread among team members like flu, poisoning the work climate'.[20] However, measuring individual performance in a team becomes difficult with the increase in interdependence of work and the need for teamwork and ownership.

Team performance measurement systems could be assessed on four criteria: attainment of objectives, reliability and validity, perceived fairness, and legal compliance.[21] They should be designed to promote the development of competencies, motivate individuals to contribute to effective team performance, and motivate the team to perform effectively as a unit.[21] As such, it is a combination of individual performance and team performance.

Competencies should be relevant to organizational and teams objectives, properly communicated and subject to accurate and fair measurement. They can be classified under broad areas covering all aspects of work and defined at different levels of performance (such as low, intermediate and high). They can be assessed by supervisors or peers or certified by competent internal or external experts.

Team performance assessment may have two components— individual assessment of technical and interpersonal competencies and team assessment of its performance. Peers and/ or supervisors may assess each team member on his/her technical competencies and team-related behavioural competencies, such as conflict resolution, collaborative problem-solving, communication, decision-making, and co-operation.[22,23]

The type of team assessment (individual, team or both) and its use (developmental, evaluative or both) depend on the configuration of membership and complexity of tasks.[20] Stable teams with routine tasks, such as service teams, are more suitable for team assessment whereas dynamic teams with non-routine, interdependent tasks, such as network teams, are more suitable for individual assessment. Similarly, teams with a hierarchical management structure and style require different assessment from self-directed teams. Generally, the more radical the change, the more is the need for employee participation and communication.

Following are some of the lessons learned from successful introduction of team appraisal:

- Team members are actively involved in deciding what and how to measure. Team members should clearly believe that they can truly influence the outcome on which they will be assessed. 'A truly empowered team must play the lead role in designing its own measurement system and the main objective of the system should be to help the team, rather than top managers, gauge its progress'.[24] Teams are 'typically trained to prepare and interpret their own performance data as part of continuous improvement efforts'.[20]

- While applying direct measures of quantity and quality, care should be taken to ensure that the measures are reliable, ascertainable, controllable and members are regularly updated on their achievement.

- Electronic methods of collecting multisource feedback are very useful. They are less expensive, quick to administer, and more flexible to collect and analyse.

- Team appraisal requires a gradual shift in culture. To facilitate the shift, initially team behaviour ratings should be used for developmental purposes only. As people get used to the system and internalize the desired behaviours and competencies over time by rating themselves and others and receiving feedback, it could be linked to rewards.

- Maintaining confidentiality of data is important. Members could be assured that only the aggregate data is presented.

Multisource Assessment

Multisource feedback includes feedback from

- self.
- individuals within the organization, i.e., those in positions above (superior), below (subordinates) and lateral (peers) in the organizational hierarchy, internal customers and subject matter experts.
- individuals outside the organization (external customers, vendors or suppliers and external subject matter experts).

The increasing popularity of multisource assessment or 360-degree feedback signifies the desire of organizations to be more customer centric in business processes and to be inclusive in dealings with employees. It also reflects the understanding that the best persons to assess individual or team performance are those who are most intimately connected with and/or affected by that performance. For example, leadership effectiveness is best assessed by subordinates in conjunction with peers and superiors, team skills by fellow team members, and customer focus by internal and external customers. Multisource assessment, thus, captures core, real and multi-dimensional aspects of performance that are deemed by the organization to be critical to the attainment of its goals and strategies.

While the justification for the introduction of multisource feedback (MSF) is sound, its implementation is challenging. First of all, it should fit the prevailing culture and overall HRM framework of the organization. Second, it should be tailor-made to suit the needs of different units and locations. The purpose of the scheme, whether for development or evaluation or both, should be well thought out. Considering that research is yet to throw light on the effects of MSF, it is advisable to proceed a step a time and learn from the experiences.

The proponents and practitioners of multisource assessment offer the following advice:

- Maintain anonymity of raters to reflect more accurate ratings. This is achieved by aggregating data.
- MSF instruments should be reliable (consistent) and valid (measure what they are supposed to measure). Validity includes content (task dimensions), criteria (outcome dimensions) and construct.[25]
- In MSF, agreement within source (e.g., between peers) is more important than between sources (e.g., between peers and customers).
- More accurate ratings are achieved when used for developmental purpose than evaluative purpose. The critical question to be answered at the planning stage is whether the data should be shared only with the ratee and used for evaluation. Research suggests that organizations should first start with sharing the data only with the ratee and use it only for developmental purpose and as the process matures and people develop confidence in using the MSF, it could be shared with the supervisor and used for evaluation.[26,27]
- Ratees should be given a say in who is best suited to measure their performance.
- It is to be ensured that raters have first-hand knowledge of ratee's work and performance. Instead of having all raters evaluate all employees in all areas, they should be asked to provide feedback only in those areas of work where they feel confident of giving feedback.
- A coach helps ratees sort out conflicting ratings from multiple sources, make sense of feedback information and develop an appropriate development plan.
- Let the raters write verbatim comments as a supplement to ratings in most MSF processes.

Thus, if designed and implemented well, MSF has the potential to be the best vehicle to communicate, promote and provide feedback on critical competencies identified by the organization.

Emerging Practices

A survey of new realities of performance management in best-practice organizations in the UK, conducted by the Institute of Personnel and Development (IPD) in 1997–98, revealed the following developments since 1991:

- From appraisal to joint review
- From outputs to inputs (behaviours)
- From focus on appraisal to development with less prominence to ratings
- From top-down appraisal to 360-degree feedback
- From a directive to supportive approach
- From monolithic to flexible
- From ownership by HR to ownership by the line.

The recent changes can be characterized as:

- Temporal changes: Conduct more frequent reviews.
- Source changes: Obtain appraisal data from multiple sources including external parties.
- Content changes: Appraisals based on input competencies rather than process outcomes.[28]

Typically, a successful performance management system has the following features:[29,30]

- Closely aligned with the organizational context and culture without being influenced by passing fads.
- Strategically linked to clearly defined and communicated organizational and unit-level goals. Ideally, the

process involves development of performance measures based on the critical success factors derived directly from the business strategy.[3]

- Clear identification of competencies and/or outcomes for each position and widely communicated to all employees.
- Involving employees through focus group interviews, surveys, etc. in all stages of the design, implementation and review process.
- Genuinely supported by top management.
- Closely linked to other HRM systems, particularly training and development, succession planning and career management. However, its link with remuneration and rewards remains a contentious issue. Many experts recommend separating appraisal for rewards from appraisal for development to avoid spill over of bitterness from the former to the latter. Further, to obtain a broader perspective, it is suggested that peer-level managers in each division, instead of just the immediate superior, should conduct the appraisals for rewards.[31]
- Seen as a continuous process of monitoring and feedback rather than an annual one-off event.
- Comprehensive training of managers to act as effective coaches.
- Perceived as fair, equitable and transparent.[31]
- Minimal bureaucracy in administering the system.
- Effective use of technology in conveying desired competencies and in monitoring, collecting and giving feedback.
- A dynamic system that is suitable for changing workplace realities, such as working in teams and alternative working arrangements (teleworking, job sharing, etc.).

In summary, trends in individual performance management suggest that organizations are trying to link performance with development and rewards and measure it in terms of output and behaviours/competencies. The range of behaviours considered has expanded to include soft skills, particularly in the services sector. However, the measurement errors and risk of bias continue to pose the biggest threat to objective performance measurement. In response, multisource feedback has been offered as a solution. The competency-based framework has found further application in the reward system, as discussed in the next chapter. However, as we will find out later, competency-based performance and reward management are 'more written about than practiced'.[32]

Agenda for Managerial Action

Points to Ponder . . .	. . . Steps to Consider
Without a sound performance management system, employees have no clue as to what is expected of them and how they measure up against management expectations. However, the appraisal system has been very unpopular and in some cases, counter-productive.	The central challenge in the appraisal process is how to secure agreement of all stakeholders on measuring behaviours or outcomes or both in an objective, situation-specific context. Here, the management has to be clear about what and how it wants to measure and the employees need to be convinced that the chosen process indeed does what it claims to do.
A holistic approach to performance assessment is needed to account for situational influence and secure employee acceptance.	A holistic approach • seeks the active involvement of all stakeholders in designing, implementing and reviewing the system, • to measure both the outcomes as well as behaviours (as a balanced scorecard), • by all those who are familiar with the performance, • to be done on a frequent basis, and • with equal emphasis on development as well as evaluation.

Coaching managers on how to provide negative feedback is crucial to the success of any appraisal system.	Managers as raters need to be trained to • gain the trust of ratees by being fair and transparent in everything that they do, • clarify what is expected, how it would be measured and for what purpose, • maintain records of critical incidents, • provide frequent feedback focusing on the job not the person, allow the employee to express freely and effectively manage negative emotions, • be aware of typical rater errors, and • be a genuine mentor and help improve performance by offering coaching and opportunities for improvement.
Teams pose a new challenge to the performance management process.	If organizations are serious about working in teams, they need to be clear on how to measure team performance accurately and fairly. It requires recognition of team-related competencies as well as differences in individual motivation, ability and performance. Different types of teams require different methods of performance measurement. Employee involvement in choosing the right method, multisource assessment and gradual cultural shift are some of the ingredients of successful team appraisal.
Today, most jobs are complex and ever-changing. Only multisource assessment can capture their multi-dimensional nature.	360-degree feedback schemes are yet to mature and require gradual transition and building on own experience. The value of self-rating has long been recognized. Ratees can suggest those best suited to rate them. Data needs to be used primarily for development purposes. Expert advice is required in meaningful interpretation of data.

Case Scenario: Perceived Fairness and the Performance Management Process

We have broken the performance management (PM) process into three stages related to system development, appraisal process, and feedback processes. We have also broken the fairness notion into three categories of fairness: procedural fairness, interpersonal fairness, and outcome fairness.

1. Promoting System Development Fairness at University of Arizona Intercollegiate Athletics

As part of HR decentralization, the Intercollegiate Athletics (ICA) department was asked to develop its own performance management system. The ICA department has approximately 150 administrative, coaching, support and clerical staff members occupying over a hundred different jobs. Even staff with the same job title often have very different duties. Therefore, the goals were to develop performance appraisal instruments that tapped the essential duties of each job, but to try to limit the number of different instruments to a manageable total.

Procedural fairness in this development process was managed by allowing all staff the opportunity to offer input during development. Initially, all staff members were interviewed, either individually or in groups. Interview questions addressed job duties and performance standards as well as comments on the existing PM process. Recommendations and concerns regarding the new system were also collected.

Interpersonal fairness was largely managed with written and oral communication. All staff members were sent a memo from the Director of ICA explaining why a new PM system was being developed. The steps in the development process were outlined during monthly staff meetings. A common fear among staff was that the new system was being developed because of the perception of impending downsizing and layoffs. Communication from the Director and feedback during the interviews from the consultants developing the system helped alleviate these unfounded fears.

2. Promoting Appraisal Process Fairness at FINOVA

FINOVA is a provider of corporate financial services. With over 2,000 employees around the world, a variety of separate business units, and a centralized PM system, fairness is somewhat difficult to ensure. A recently developed electronic PM system has allowed the central HR department to control the flow of performance-related information to and from employees and managers.

At the beginning of the PM period, all employees are sent performance objective forms via the company e-mail system. Across four performance areas, employees are required to set specific, challenging, objectively measurable performance objectives that are related to the company's strategic direction. Employees review these objectives with their supervisors and the completed form is sent back to HR. Having employees set their own performance objectives builds procedural fairness (through voice and job relevance) and outcome fairness (through the establishment of reasonable expectations). If something in the job or business climate changes, then employees are able to revise these objectives (with the approval of their supervisors).

At the end of the year, employees and their supervisors are sent the completed objectives form (again electronically) and together they decide the extent to which results met the objectives. Numerical evaluations indicate the extent to which results fell short of, met, or exceeded the stated objectives. Individual evaluations are reviewed by several layers of management and even include discussions between HR representatives and the CEO. This extensive review of individual performance evaluations helps minimize biases that may exist at the supervisory level. The annual incentive plan is tied directly to individual evaluations and is also based on the extent to which the employee's department and the company as a whole meet their respective objectives. These incentives are determined on strictly numeric bases, such that subjective judgements are minimized.

3. Continuous Feedback at Microsoft

A good example of a company building fairness principles into its performance feedback processes is Microsoft Corporation. Formal performance feedback sessions are conducted every six months, but informal feedback is provided continually. Every month each Microsoft employee participates in a one-on-one feedback session with his or her supervisor. In these sessions, the supervisor informally reviews the previous month's performance and offers advice or developmental counselling as necessary. The manager also allows the employee the opportunity to discuss any concerns.

In the formal performance feedback sessions, performance is assessed in terms of met objectives as well as specific job-related criteria. Given the frequency of informal performance discussions, employees recognize that supervisors are familiar with their performance and can offer job-related feedback. Employees know that they can challenge their performance evaluation if they disagree with it, but according to one HR representative, this rarely occurs. Employees trust the honesty of their supervisors, and they also know that every appraisal must be approved by a second line manager. All these provisions help enhance employees' perceptions that the appraisal and feedback processes are fair.

Outcome fairness also results from the attention given to procedural and interpersonal fairness. The continuous feedback allows employees to form realistic expectations of their performance. These expectations make it more likely that the outcome or evaluation communicated during formal feedback sessions will be perceived to be fair.

Source: Gilland, S.W. and Langdon, J.C. (1998) 'Creating performance management systems that promote perceptions of fairness'. In Smither, J.W. (Ed.) *Performance appraisal: State of the art in practice,*

References

1. **Smith, B., Hornsby, J.S.** and **Shirmeyer, R.** (1996) 'Current trends in performance appraisal: An examination of managerial practice'. *SAM Advanced Management Journal*, Summer 1996, pp. 10–15.
2. **Bernardin, H.J., Hagan, C.M., Kane, J.S.** and **Villanova, P.** (1998) 'Effective performance management: A focus on precision, customers and situational constraints'. In Smither, J.W. (Ed.) *Performance appraisal: State of the art in practice*, Jossey-Bass: SF.
3. **Schneier, C.E., Shaw, D.G.** and **Beatty, R.W.** (1991) 'Performance measurement and management: A tool for strategy execution'. *Human Resource Management*, Fall 1991.
4. **Deming, W.E.** (1986) *Out of the crisis*, Cambridge: Massachusetts Institute of Technology, Cambridge: MA.
5. **DeNisi, A.S.** and **Kluger, A.N.** (2000) 'Feedback effectiveness: Can 360-degree appraisals be improved?' *Academy of Management Executive*, Vol 14 No 1, pp. 129–39.
6. **Graber, J.M., Breisch, R.E.** and **Breisch, W.E.** (1992) 'Performance appraisals and Deming: A misunderstanding?' *Quality Progress*, June 1992.
7. **Levinson, H.** (1970) 'Management by whose objectives?' *Harvard Business Review*, January, 2003, pp. 107–16.
8. **Kozlowski, S., Chao, G.T.** and **Morrison, R.F.** (1998) 'Games raters play: Politics, strategies and impression management in performance appraisal'. In Smither, J.W. (Ed.) *Performance appraisal: State of the art in practice*, Jossey-Bass: SF.
9. **Bowles, M.L.** and **Coates, G.** (1993) 'Image and substance: The management of performance as rhetoric or reality?' *Personnel Review*, Vol 22 No 2, pp. 3–21.
10. **Malos, S.B.** (1998) 'Current legal issues in performance appraisal'. In Smither, J.W. (Ed.) *Performance appraisal: State of the art in practice*, Jossey-Bass: SF.
11. **McDonald, D.** and **Smith, A.** (1995) 'A proven connection: Performance management and business results'. *Compensation and Benefits Review*, Vol 27 No 1, p. 59.

12. **Murphy, K.R.** and **Cleveland, J.N.** (1995) *Understanding performance appraisal: Social, organisational and goal based perspectives*, Sage, Thousand Oaks: CA.
13. **Hartle, F.** (1995) *Transforming the performance management process*, Kogan Page: London.
14. **Kaplan, R.S.** and **Norton, D.P.** (1992) 'The Balanced Scorecard—Measures that drive performance'. *Harvard Business Review*, January–February.
15. **Kaplan, R.S.** and **Norton, D.P.** (1993) 'Putting the balance scorecard to work'. *Harvard Business Review*, January–February 1992.
16. **Gilliland, S.W.** and **Langdon, J.C.** (1998) 'Creating performance management systems that promote perceptions of fairness'. In Smither, J.W. (Ed.) *Performance appraisal: State of the art in practice*, Jossey-Bass: SF.
17. **Dogan, K.** and **Vecchio, R.P.** (2001) 'Managing envy and jealousy in the work place'. *Compensation and Benefits Review*, March–April.
18. **Evered, R.D.** and **Selman, J.C.** (1989) 'Coaching and the art of management'. *Organisational Dynamics*, Autumn 1989.
19. **Whitmore, J.** (1996) Coaching for performance. Nicolas Brealey: London.
20. **Scott, S.G.** and **Einstein, W.O.** (2001) 'Strategic performance appraisal in team-based organisations: One size does not fit all'. *Academy of Management Executive*, Vol 15 No 2.
21. **Reilly, R.R.** and **McGourty, J.** (1998) 'Performance appraisal in team settings'. In Smither, J.W. (Ed.) *Performance appraisal: State of the art in practice*, Jossey-Bass: SF.
22. **Stevens, M.J.** and **Campion, M.A.** (1994) 'The knowledge, skill and ability requirements for team work: Implications for human resource management'. *Journal of Management*, 20, pp. 503–30.
23. **Dominick, P.G., Reilly, R.R.** and **McGourty, J.W.** (1997) 'The effects of peer feedback on team member behaviour'. *Group and Organisation Management*, 22, pp. 508–20.
24. **Meyer, C.** (1994) 'How the right measures help teams excel'. *Harvard Business Review*, May–June.
25. **Guion, R.M.** (1998) 'Assessment, measurement and prediction for personnel decisions'. Erlbaum: Mahwah, NJ.
26. **Dalessio, A.T.** and **Vasilopoulos, N.L.** (2001) 'Multi-source feedback reports: content, formats and levels of analysis'. In D.W. Bracken, C.W. Timmerick and A.H. Church (Eds.)

The handbook of multisource feedback, Jossey–Bass, San Francisco: CA.

27. **Handy, L., Devine, M.** and **Heath, L.** (1996) *360-degree feedback: Unguided missile or powerful weapon?* Ashridge Management Group: Berkhemstead.

28. **Squires, P.** and **Adler, S.** (1998) 'Linking appraisals to individual development and training'. In Smither, J.W. (Ed.) *Performance appraisal: State of the art in practice*, Jossey-Bass: SF.

29. **Armstrong, M.** and **Baron, A.** (1998) *Performance management: The new realities*, Institute of Personnel and Development: London.

30. **Nelson, B.** (2000) 'Are performance appraisals obsolete?' *Compensation and Benefits Review*, May–June.

31. **Meyer, H.H.** (1991) 'A solution to the performance appraisal feedback enigma'. *Academy of Management Executive*, Vol 5 No 2, pp. 68–76.

32. **Thomson, M.** (2000) 'Salary progression systems'. In White, G. and Druker, J. (Eds.) *Reward management—A critical text*, Routledge: London.

8

Creating Reward Systems

If competencies are the wheels for managing knowledge work, rewards (both extrinsic and intrinsic) are the engine.

—Kochanski and Risher[1]

Rewards encompass everything that the organization has to offer, directly or indirectly, in return for employee contribution. They include extrinsic elements, such as pay, incentives and benefits, as well as intrinsic elements, such as pride in work, praise, social network and self-actualization. Rewards aim to achieve high commitment and high performance in the workforce by influencing employee attitudes, behaviours and motivation. Considering the high cost of personnel, reward strategies also aim to get strategic value out of investment in people.

Armstrong and Brown define rewards in relation to two dimensions—the nature of the reward (transactional or relational) and the basis of the reward (individual or communal).[2] Accordingly, their definition involves the following elements:

	Transactional	**Relational**
Individual	Pay	Learning and development opportunities
Communal	Benefits and perks	Working environment

Source: Armstrong, M. and Brown, D. (2000) *Paying for contribution*. Kogan Page: London.

Fig. 8.1: Reward Strategies

The holistic nature of reward highlights the fact that reward strategies by themselves cannot motivate people to perform better and their success is intimately connected with the overall HRM climate in the organization vis-à-vis market expectations for each occupational category. Hence, the best paymasters are not necessarily the best employers.

The analytical framework of reward management has been influenced by multidisciplinary viewpoints, such as organizational psychology (motivation, perceptions, attitudes and behaviours), economics (pay as a control mechanism, transactional cost), sociology (social and normative pressures) and politics (bargaining power). However, research studies on this topic often suffer from 'methodological myopia' through simplistic characterization.[3]

A wide spectrum of rewards is supposed to exert the maximum positive impact in a learning environment and together with measurement, rewards are 'the most powerful and visible management tools that can support changes'.[4] However, some studies also point out that rewards are no more than a trigger or a facilitating condition of an individual's attitude to knowledge sharing and what is more important is enhancing the positive mood state for social associations through feedback, social support and providing room for self-determination.[5]

Limitations of the Traditional Framework

In the context of wider economic and social change and redefinition of the very concept of 'work', the traditional framework of reward systems has become somewhat redundant.[6] In the traditional framework, jobs were mainly time based, and narrowly defined and categorized. Influenced by Taylor's scientific principles of management, organizations sought to define one best way of doing a task, setting clear boundaries of authority and accountability in order to achieve complete control over what workers do. The trade unions and the governments wielded enormous influence in determining wages and setting uniform standards across jobs, industry and the country. This attempt to 'standardize' work and pay suited the industrial economy, as it was less globalized, less competitive, and politically more socialist oriented.

However, since the last quarter of the 20th century, the global economy has changed dramatically. The organizations of today are being forced to substantially improve their performance standards so that they are comparable with the best in the world and consequently,

- focus on core capabilities, particularly intellectual capital
- remove excess fat through rightsizing
- promise employability in place of lifetime employment
- supplement full-time employment with part-time and casual work, particularly in service industries
- use information and communication technologies in redesigning work
- improve productivity through negotiations at the enterprise level rather than the industry or national level
- adopt team-based work methods
- delayer the management levels by broadening the scope of work through multi-tasking

◻ empower workers with a participative approach to management.

Many governments now believe that 'standardization' of employment terms and conditions has to make way for 'workplace flexibility' for economic survival and prosperity. Accordingly, governments are reducing their role in shaping employment relationship. Trade unions are helplessly witnessing a decline in their influence on collective bargaining. As a result of the above changes, the reward system is moving towards flexible job evaluation of both individuals and teams, enterprise bargaining, performance-based pay system and focus on non-monetary rewards from a holistic perspective.

In response to the limitation of the traditional framework with an administrative focus, the New Pay systems exhibit a strategic focus in that they highlight the person (instead of job), output or behaviours/competencies (instead of time) and are more inclusive, dynamic, and decentralized.[7] New Pay concepts include broad banding of base pay, skill/competency- or results-based variable pay, such as profit or gain sharing or employee stock options. Collectively, they aim to increase extrinsic satisfaction by linking rewards to performance and intrinsic satisfaction through employee empowerment.

Even though the number of organizations which have successfully adopted New Pay concepts is relatively low, the interest in them is growing rapidly across countries, industries and sectors (public and private). It will take some time for these trial-and-error experiments to become a way of life. Instead of treating the New Pay ideas as best practices, it is important for organizations to first ensure whether they fit in their current structure and culture. And also, instead of treating New Pay as a set of compensation practices, it is more useful to see them as a 'way of thinking' about the strategic design of reward systems.[8]

In the following sections we will examine the ideological underpinnings and the practical implications of some of the New Pay concepts.

Grading—Where is it Going?

The traditional job evaluation techniques define and grade jobs in terms of effort, skill and decision-making based on a limited set of skills and qualifications. They overemphasize technical skills and stress on narrow specialization. However, with the current emphasis on multi-skilling and role flexibility and in line with changing technology and work organization, job evaluation techniques have become more flexible, broader in coverage and tend to evaluate loosely defined, multi-skilled roles.[9]

A recent trend is towards skill-based or competency-based grading as defined by an objective standard that includes a wider range of skills and competencies, such as communication and IT skills. Broad competency bands are established so that employees can move up their career by acquiring additional qualifications. This approach suits both employers and employees as it provides retraining opportunities to existing employees without the need for additional labour. It is seen to encourage learning, reward acceptance of change, remove demarcation between jobs and support multi-skilling and teamworking.[10]

However, it entails massive investment in training and an equitable system that provides equal career opportunities to all employees.[9] Therefore, unless the organization is seriously committed to training and development, skill/competency-based grading and pay systems are likely to remain only on paper.

Historically, career progression through grades has been mainly based on seniority, particularly in white-collar jobs and public sector employment. It is being replaced by merit-based promotion. While this has posed adjustment problems to middle-level managers who spent significant part of their career believing in loyalty and tenure-based rewards, the younger generation is more open to meritocracy. However, the problem in totally abandoning the value of seniority is that it ignores the fact that a person matures with age and many of the emotional intelligence-related competencies are seen to increase with age. Moreover, by totally ignoring seniority in promotions, employers may indirectly encourage employee turnover and also discourage them from developing firm-specific competencies that are vital for sustainable competitive advantage.

It also needs to be emphasized that the number of years of experience does not necessarily correspond with quality of experience. As Mendenhall[11] points out, 'the idea of "non-proportionality of input to output" is a part of our daily experience and our common sense'. A manager with twenty years' experience cannot be assumed to be twice as productive as a manager with ten years' experience. Therefore, seniority as a basis for promotion has its merits and demerits. As we will see in the next chapter, in collectivist societies, seniority is indeed very important and seen as an equitable measure in the long run.

How Much to Pay?

Reward systems have to be internally consistent in measuring job worth and externally competitive. The pay competitiveness of an organization depends on its capacity to pay and the broader management philosophy of sharing profits with employees at all levels, and not just the top executives. Companies that treat people as costs to be controlled determine pay based on statutory requirements on minimum pay, tight bargaining with trade unions, and to ward off poaching of key personnel by competitors. Such companies clearly believe in the transactional mode of employment relationship. On the other hand, companies that treat labour costs as investment in people, would offer above than the market price, invest in training and development and establish fair, equitable and transparent reward system. Therefore, 'comparatively high compensation contingent on organizational performance' is one of the key practices of companies that produce profit through people.[12]

However, critics argue that the perceptions of inequity can never be fully eliminated and that focus on extrinsic rewards diminishes the impact of intrinsic rewards.[13] Salary surveys typically indicate that majority of employees feel that they are underpaid. Why? A survey on employee satisfaction with pay and other rewards concluded that 'while people are concerned about pay, they are more concerned about how they are paid. . . People want to know that the system for administering pay is effective, fair and inclusive'.[14] Studies reveal that more than the pay itself, distributive justice and to a lesser extent, procedural justice, play a far greater role in influencing pay satisfaction. Policies that are considered fair are typically 'free from bias, based on accurate information, consistent across persons and over time, correctable (open to appeals), and representative of employee concerns'.[14]

Thus, the answer to the question 'how much to pay' seems to lie in

- how fair, equitable and transparent the employees perceive the pay system to be, in terms of meeting their market value (expectations) and matching their contribution vis-à-vis other employees (equity)
- how holistic the reward system is in encompassing intrinsic incentives, such as pride in doing challenging work, appreciation for contribution, opportunities for advancement through training and a relaxed and enjoyable work atmosphere
- how effective and flexible the reward system is in aligning the organizational goals and individual needs

◻   how well the philosophy and the nature of the reward system are communicated.

Pfeffer points out that the cost of labour is relative to its productivity.[15] If a company pays its employees 10 per cent more than the market rate but its productivity is 50 per cent more than the market, it only stands to gain by paying more. Thus, how much money to pay depends on how productive the workforce is.

Pay for Performance—The Way to Go?

Variable pay, as an integral part of New Pay ideas, is intended to suit changing times and requirements. It becomes 'at risk' when part of the fixed pay is linked to performance but this is rarely the case. Variable pay is considered different from merit pay because the former is normally based on objective group measures whereas the latter is based on subjective evaluation of individual performance.[16] Thus, variable pay is supposed to overcome the problems associated with merit pay. Incentive payments have been in vogue since post-war years, particularly in manual jobs and in the manufacturing industry, and the results are disappointing. In many instances, trade unions have opposed the idea, arguing that any improvement in productivity is used by the management to raise the threshold of performance set to qualify for incentive payments in the next round of wage negotiations, thus depriving the workers of their legitimate share in extra gains. It is therefore not the concept per se but the management motivation that has often been questioned.

While there is general agreement amongst scholars and practitioners about the need for pay for performance, the main challenge relates to the way it is implemented. The operational difficulties include the difficulties in setting viable, meaningful and measurable targets, subjectivity in appraisal and lack of enough funds available to make a powerful impact.[3] The concept itself has been attacked on the grounds that it tends to encourage speed rather than quality, is problematic to define, and needs constant change, especially due to rapid technological improvements.[17]

Another dilemma associated with pay for performance schemes is that the proportion of variable pay to total pay should be big enough to make a real difference; however, if the fixed pay is too small, employees resent the fact that they cannot make lifestyle choices because of uncertainty of income. When people consider an employment offer, they are more likely to consider what is guaranteed and not what is subject to performance appraisal and other external factors, such as company profits. Further, while companies have no problem in identifying the top and bottom performers, they find it hard to discriminate among the remaining solid, everyday contributors, considered 'average' performers, with the result that the pay difference for them, based on performance, is negligible.[18]

Some companies limit the applicability of certain incentive payments to employees in short supply, such as IT personnel. The danger in such an approach is that it creates feelings of alienation in employees excluded from the scheme and can backfire when employment conditions change, upsetting the demand–supply equation.

Despite the difficulties surrounding its implementation, the pay for performance concept is intuitively compelling. It sends a strong message to the workforce that management is committed to continuous performance improvement for mutual benefit. Compared to merit pay based on individual performance, which is short-term oriented and subject to the supervisor's whims and fancies, the group- or organization-based pay for performance is relatively more objective with multisource feedback and reinforces the competencies that the organization really values, such as teamwork and customer focus. As for implementation, a participative and transparent approach with clear communication goes a long way in setting it on the right track.

The Benefit of 'Benefits'

Despite the constant tussle between governments and employers as to who should pick up the tab for social costs associated with old age, childcare, maternity, etc., employers appear to be shouldering an increasing proportion of the burden. Benefits include pensions, perquisites, such as company car, sick pay, health and life insurance, childcare, maternal and parental leave, paid holiday, subsidized meals, discounted company products and services, accommodation, low-interest loans and mortgages. With changes in lifestyles, employee well-being programmes, such as fitness programmes and counselling are gaining prominence. Benefits account for anywhere between 15 per cent and 50 per cent of normal pay, depending upon occupational level and category as well as industry practices.

Historically, white-collar employees have enjoyed more benefits than blue-collar employees. However, many companies have moved to harmonize the spread of benefits through uniform application to all employees, in order to be seen as fair and equitable, even though the principle of harmonization has not included, in most instances, part-time and casual labour. The advantage of benefits is subject to taxation laws and individual circumstances. Some organizations attempt to make the system flexible through flexi-benefit (cafeteria) schemes by giving the option of choosing a suite of available benefits depending on one's requirements.

Surprisingly, benefits are not scrutinized as vigorously as pay, particularly, in relation with performance.[19] They typically act as hygiene factors, i.e., their absence leads to demotivation but their presence does not necessarily increase motivation. This may be due to the weak 'line of sight' in that employees do not see a clear connection between behaviour and reward outcome. Therefore, many employers are not convinced about the rationale behind such schemes but are forced to continue providing benefits due to precedents, statutory obligations, or fear of backlash on withdrawal. Benefits by themselves may not trigger motivation in employees to perform better but in a harmonious HRM climate, certainly act as positive contributors.

One of the reasons why benefits are not well appreciated by employees is that not enough effort is made to communicate the benefit plans and explain their impact on their lives.[18] Benefits also need to be flexible enough to suit individual circumstances of employees. For instance, if many employees have young children, they would appreciate an on-site childcare service whereas if the majority of employees are young and unmarried, such as in an IT company, they might appreciate more take-home pay. The needs of singles, whose number is slowly increasing, would be different from those with families. Companies can also offer tax-effective benefits, such as concierge services, and flexi-time off or top-up benefits to cover tax liability. By increasing employee involvement in designing, implementing and reviewing benefits, employers can create better awareness and impact.

Team Rewards

In designing team rewards, one has to consider:

▫ The extent of involvement of team members in identifying and measuring performance. Generally, the more the involvement, the more the acceptance.

▫ Whether all team members will get the same reward or differently. This depends on the extent to which the tasks are interdependent. While uniform treatment may enhance team cohesiveness, differential treatment based on individual performance may appeal more to the high performers.[20]

The designing of team rewards should 'begin with the end in mind' and is best introduced when the team has matured.[21] Based on Motorola's experience in team pay,

Coli suggests that the suitability of team rewards depends on stages of team life cycle (forming, norming, inertia, storming, high performing and adjourning), type of teams (full-time department, project team, special teams, etc.), reward and recognition categories, public, private or not-for-profit sector, and culture of the team and organization.[22]

Teams are often motivated more by empowerment and socialization benefits than by mere monetary incentives. If team members enjoy a good rapport with each other, are passionate about the team goals, well resourced and are given sufficient freedom to operate, they are more likely to succeed. Given the importance of social fabric in teams, it is very important that they have a say in whether and how pay and other rewards are tied to their performance. The ability of a team to earn rewards depends on the quality of team members and since in the majority of cases, team members do not have a say in who joins or leaves the team, it may adversely affect their perception of equity.

Rewards are important in reinforcing desired behaviours in team members. Unless desired team-related competencies, such as mutual cooperation, mentoring, knowledge sharing, and openness to others' ideas, are specifically measured (preferably through peer ratings) and rewarded, the link between competency and pay will be lost.

Research on team rewards reveals that

- firms are more likely to use both individual and team rewards and allocate equally to all members,
- non-financial incentives (such as recognition, prizes, and non-cash gifts) are more common than financial incentives,
- team performance measures include productivity, financial performance, and quality, and
- the success of a team reward programme is measured on its effectiveness in tying pay to performance, encouraging co-operation, and job satisfaction.[23]

There is very little research evidence to determine the effects of different reward strategies on team motivation and performance. The difference in goals, composition and motivation of teams makes it difficult to generalize findings. 'Eventually, though, the right model emerges if commitment is sustained, the expertise is present, and the process is healthy'.[24]

Executive Compensation—Fat Cats?

Executive compensation has done the most damage to employer credibility in recent times, in terms of equity and fairness. Pay disparities between managerial and non-managerial cadres has increased at an alarming rate and as reported in Chapter 3, the gulf widened from 80 per cent in the 1980s to as much as 400 per cent in the 1990s. What is causing the most anguish is that while general employees are told to brace themselves for uncertain employment prospects and wage freezes, top executives in even loss-making companies have often walked away with hefty bonuses and severance packages. In many cases, executive compensation and incentives are tied to share market performance in the short term, which is often manipulated. The rhetoric on competency-based performance management and results-based pay gets obscured when employees perceive great inequity between executive and non-executive compensation.

Therefore, any organization that wants to set the right performance standards has to ensure that its executives walk the walk, as they talk the talk. In other words, they must apply the same principles in rewarding themselves as they do for others. Clearly, their performance standards have to go beyond short-term share market performance and include long-term measures such as employee satisfaction with the management style and a measurable improvement in productivity.

Organization-wide Rewards

These include organization-wide short-term incentives such as productivity gain-sharing programmes, profit sharing, annual bonus as well as long-term incentives and wealth-building plans like employee share ownership plans (ESOP). The objectives are to increase employee participation for mutual benefit, sense of affiliation, commitment, performance and retention. Some companies believe that by sharing productivity gains, profits and ownership, they can become an employer of choice for existing and prospective employees.

Short-term Incentives

Gain sharing, also called goal sharing, has been quite a popular and successful approach in recent years with the philosophy of sharing the benefits of productivity improvements based on an agreed-upon formula and performance measurements.[25] The measurements traditionally revolved around cost reduction but today many organizations look beyond cost and are including broader measurements, such as customer satisfaction and on-time delivery. The trend is also towards designing specific plans to suit different work groups.[26]

The success of gainsharing and profit sharing depends, amongst other things, on

- extent of employee involvement with the genuine belief that employees at all levels have the motivation and capacity to contribute to organizational improvements
- clarity of purpose, measurement (preferably a mixture of financial and non-financial measures), and feedback
- linkage with well-defined results having a clear line of sight; otherwise employees are likely to develop an entitlement mentality
- periodic review to suit changing market demands, and

□   considerable difference to employee earnings to create
     the desired impact.[27,28]

Further, when employees feel no sense of control on the
overall company performance, they are unlikely to factor such
schemes in their perception of organizational citizenship and
commitment.[3] In Japan, the effects of profit-sharing plans are
more positive in terms of job satisfaction and productivity because they form a significant portion of employees'
pay and are accompanied by other forms of employee
participation.[29]

Long-term Incentives

In the US, most of the ESOPs are linked to pensions and used
as a means of retirement benefit. The concept attracted
attention at a time of critical shortage of skills in a booming
economy and was actively encouraged by the governments
as a positive feature of privatization. ESOPs also received
statutory approval and tax incentives. However, with economic recession and consequent poor performance of companies in the share market, the enthusiasm for the concept has
significantly diminished in the eyes of employees.

Research in this area indicates that share allocations rep-
resent an average of hardly 4 per cent of remuneration and
are mainly regarded by employees as bonus.[30] ESOPs have
had negligible impact on share-ownership pattern as well as
on employee earnings. Thus, it is hardly surprising that the
majority of employees sell their shares at the first available
opportunity. Even studies that found employee-owned firms
(EOFs) performing generally better than non-EOFs concede
that 'there is clearly no automatic connection between employee ownership and performance'.[31]

One reason could be that in most cases, ESOPs do not make
a significant difference to employees' earnings. Significantly,

it is also argued that employees need to have higher relative levels of share ownership to have a high level of commitment and satisfaction.[32] Another potential difficulty with ESOPs is that when stock options are paid to all employees irrespective of individual performance, they fail to differentiate between a good and bad employee with the result that it can be a disincentive for a good employee and waste of money on a bad employee.

Obviously, no one variable pay plan is suitable for all categories of employees as the results expected of them vary significantly. Sullivan who studied incentive plans in American corporations and oversaw variable pay plans at DuPont, one of the largest corporations committed to using compensation to drive performance, recommends the following alternatives at different levels in the organization:[28]

Table 8.1: Pay-for-Performance Strategy

Group	Performance Measures	Basis for Rewards
Corporate leaders	Economic value added Balanced Scorecard Shareholder return	Stock ownership Economic value/Profit sharing
Business unit leaders	Business success of unit	Results sharing
Functional leaders	Contribution to corporate goals	Milestone awards
All other employees	Specific operational results measured periodically	Profit/Gain sharing Line of sight bonus awards

Source: Sullivan, E. (1999) 'Moving to a pay-for-performance strategy: Lessons from the trenches'. In Risher, H. (Ed.) *Aligning pay and results*, AMACOM, NY. Reprinted with permission. All rights reserved.

Recognition Rewards—Going Beyond Money

Money is important to people but they don't work only for money. As Senge puts it, breathing is vital but people do not live only to breathe. Companies that ignore the fact that people want to have fun while making money are 'essentially bribing their employees and will pay the price in lack of loyalty and commitment'.[15] No company has been able to attract and retain key people in the long run by throwing money at them. Joining bonuses may tempt a few people and golden handcuffs may retain a few others but those who are motivated by money alone will keep chasing a mirage and offer too little in return. Most people want to join a company that has a compelling vision and shares its passion and prospects with employees with due recognition of employee contribution. Yes, money is also recognition but recognition is more than money.

Recognition can take many different forms including formal events like monthly/quarterly/bi-annual/annual awards attended by senior managers, commendation letters on the conclusion of a project, cruise trips for star performers, as well as informal actions like simple thank-you letters and speeches, dinners for employees and their spouses, sponsoring for entertainment shows, cash amount, surprise party, time off and so on. 'Whether a company's climate is conservative or boisterous, recognition and celebration help the total pay accelerator pedal pump more gas'.[16]

Recognition rewards help recognize the contribution of those who are sandwiched between the top and bottom performers.[18] They also help recognize qualities that are not normally or adequately recognized by formal performance measurement systems, such as humour, enthusiasm in doing boring but important work like documentation, and natural desire to coach and mentor new members. Peer feedback will show that such people, even though considered average in their overall performance, are vital to the success of their team or department. Such people need recognition and a pat on their back; otherwise, their self-confidence and morale suffer and adversely affect the organizational performance.

Realizing this, some organizations have instituted monthly award schemes and designate each month to celebrate a particular quality or trait, such as humour, co-operation, and best teammate to work with. Every month, all employees are asked to nominate a person for the specified category and organizations not only reward the person who gets maximum votes but also send a congratulatory letter to everybody who receives a nomination. In many of these organizations, the scheme started off with low employee participation but gradually nominations started pouring in. Even simple measures, such as birthday greetings in salary slips or calling for nominations for best joke of the week (as long as it is not illegal, immoral or unethical) can add spice to the workplace.

Another reason why recognition rewards are important is that today, people are expected to take complete responsibility for their career and to do that, they need the back-up of frequent recognition awards to build the credibility of their technical, managerial and social skills and competencies. For instance, during recruitment, when candidates are asked to corroborate their claims on generic competencies, such as teamwork, customer service, and knowledge sharing, those candidates who produce such awards obviously make a better impression.

'Managers need to learn the art of what, when and how to praise'.[34] It should be genuine and generous and offered immediately after the event. Successful recognition programmes are timely, frequent, customized to suit different types of people and their preferences and circumstances, creative, sincere, fun-filled, widely publicized, refreshed periodically, and are designed and reviewed by people whom they affect.[16] Where possible, senior managers should attend recognition events and express their commitment and support.

Rituals and stories surrounding such programmes enrich their value and spread enthusiasm amongst employees. For instance, it is said that in one of the annual global meets of Microsoft employees, Bill Gates came forward to get his head shaved to honour the promise made by a project manager to his team members on the accomplishment of an ambitious target!

One of the limitations of the MBO approach is that it over-emphasizes company goals and ignores employee needs. The current literature on the New Pay systems seems to suffer from the same limitation and may prompt the question, 'pay for whose results?' No matter how much monetary and non-monetary incentives companies offer, if the performance expected by them is not aligned with individual career goals and personal needs, employees are likely to quit only to join an employer who can achieve such alignment. For instance, many star performers decide to quit well-paying jobs in highly respected companies because they want to start their own venture. In such cases, companies may be better off respecting their ambitions and offer them venture capital as business partners rather than expecting them to continue as employees. Similarly, a company that expects a star performer to continue to work on some imminently obsolete technology or work in a remote location to fulfil business needs against his/her will is most likely to lose that person despite generous incentives.

Therefore, pay and other reward strategies should revolve not only around business goals but also around the employee's needs and aspirations, such as the opportunity to work on challenging assignments, flexible work options, work transfer to take care of personal emergencies, and opportunities for training and higher studies. When employees make such requests, they do not always look for positive results from the management but in many instances are satisfied if the managers make a genuine effort. The cafeteria approach to benefits takes into account individual circumstances and gives the freedom of choice to employees. The same flexibility needs to be extended, within practical limits, to other forms of rewards. One-size-fits-all approach to reward management ignores increasing workforce diversity and 'runs a tremendous risk of giving individuals rewards that they do not value while failing to reward them with things that they value highly'.[35]

How do we manage rewards during troubled times? In answering this critical question, Poster points out that one common link between a healthy company and a troubled company is the need to retain top talent; however, reward strategies that work during good times seem awfully inappropriate during bad times and need to be overhauled.[36] According to Poster, the solutions depend on whether employees in a troubled company have confidence in the company's basic business proposition, perceive that the associated risks are manageable and feel committed to the company's future. Some of her recommendations include stay bonus (payable either as a lump sum at the end of restructuring or in instalments during the period), success bonus tied to an outcome, enhanced severance upon involuntary termination to provide more security and other short-term incentives to be chosen depending on company and employee circumstances.

Rewards at Crossroads

The government and trade unions still wield considerable influence in reward management particularly in the context of fairness and equity. The recent uproar on excessive CEO and top management compensation shows that organizations cannot ignore political and social pressures. With internationalization and outsourcing of work to developing countries for cost advantage, many political and trade union leaders are questioning the ruthless pursuit of profits at the cost of local employment and social stability. Thus, even in a rapidly globalizing world, organizations have to be mindful of their social and moral obligations.

The New Pay concepts discussed above raise many questions about equity in the workplace. The historical distinction between wage and salary earners (or blue-collar and white-collar employees), manufacturing and service industry, routine and non-routine jobs still exist[17] and the divide is set to be further entrenched with the increase in part-time and casual employment and the concept of knowledge workers. High commitment work practices cannot afford to ignore the feelings of alienation and discrimination in the minds of some employees.

As pay is linked more and more with performance, the responsibility for reward management is shifting from the HR department to individual managers. Earlier, it was typical of line managers to blame the HR for all problems related to rewards. Now they are expected to drive the system and navigate it around business strategies, competencies and results. They need to judge individual and group perfor-mances based on multisource feedback, offer effective coun-selling and coaching and provide developmental opportunities. Thus, as discussed in previous chapters, the image, quality and expertise of frontline managers are critical in successfully harnessing intellectual capital.

Many organizations adopt the 'New Pay' concept not because they are convinced of its merits, but because of the pressure that others are doing so and that consultants, aca-demics and professional bodies say so.[37] While the interest in the New Pay concept is on the rise, there is also evidence that nearly 40 per cent of organizations (particularly in the public sector) have changed or significantly modified their perfor-mance pay schemes between 1996 and 1998.[38] Frequent changes to performance measurement and reward systems are likely to potentially undermine psychological contracts that charac-terize commitment, motivation and trust—the very values that the New Pay concepts are supposed to reinforce.

'Pay should be the oil in the works of society, but some-times, very publicly, it is grit instead' when it fails to com-municate its purpose and relevance and win the commitment of people.[39] Finally, 'reward is a phrase, not a whole sen-tence'[40] unless it is tied to business and employee objectives and needs.

Agenda for Managerial Action

Points to Ponder . . .	*. . . Steps to Consider*
The New Pay concepts address strategic orientation of employee management by rewarding the ability to manage complexity and change in a fluid environment.	Successful adoption of New Pay concepts and practices requires fundamental changes in management mindset and an overhaul of HRM practices linking recruitment, training, performance and reward management to an empowered culture.
Money is as important as breathing but people don't live only to breathe.	There is no doubt that compensation has got be competitive; however, it also needs to be seen by employees as equitable, fair and supplemented by an intellectually stimulating and socially vibrant work environment.
Pay for performance is theoretically sound but practically challenging.	Incentive schemes have traditionally failed because of their subjectivity, lack of clarity on what is measured and how, and incremental value. Incentives should focus on the ultimate purpose, i.e., customer satisfaction; preferably be group based to encourage teamwork and designed with the active involvement of those whom they affect.
Benefits account for a considerable part of employee costs but are hardly scrutinized by employers and noticed by employees.	Harmonizing benefits across all employee levels is an effective symbol of inclusive culture. Improving awareness, line of sight between performance and reward, and customization help to increase the value and visibility of benefits.
With an increasing number of people working in teams, team rewards are essential to institutionalize the structure and the process.	The appropriateness of a team reward system depends on the type of organization and team, and the overall structure of performance and rewards. Intrinsic benefits and team cohesiveness are central to team rewards. The challenge is to balance individual and team motivation.

Profit-sharing and employee ownership schemes aim to reinforce employee involvement, empowerment and equity by directly linking employees' future to company's future.	Employees take organizational rewards seriously only when they are empowered to make a tangible contribution and rewards make a significant difference to their compensation package.
In line with increasing recognition of community spirit in knowledge-intensive organizations, reward management has shifted its attention from monetary rewards to recognition rewards.	Recognition programmes shower social attention and praise for a job well done. They are timely, frequent, creative and their benefits far outweigh the costs. They enhance employee self-esteem through social recognition of work-related achievements and assist in work-life balance through flexible work practices. They include any practice that gives an impression to employees that they are truly valued.

Case Scenario: Leading Change with Compensation at Newsday Corporation

During the 1980s, Newsday, a Long Island, USA based publisher of two daily newspapers, enjoyed great prosperity linked to a general prosperity in the local economy. However, the local economy began to slip in 1989 and the market became more competitive with the arrival of cable TV and the expansion of cheaper direct mail service. Profits fell and action was needed to stem the decline.

□ *Early attempts at change*: Attempts were made in 1990 and 1992 to change the compensation and incentive system for sales representatives to better service the needs of the advertisers, the dominant source of income, but the basic questions of how to align sales efforts to sales strategy and how to reward sales performance more effectively, remained unanswered. In January 1993, management retained a team of two consultants to help realign and refocus the sales incentive plans.

❑ *Designing the new scheme*: Through a profitability analysis, it was found that the profit margins on all Newsday products were not significantly different. It was therefore possible to adopt a non-differentiated selling strategy without significantly affecting profits. With that knowledge, it was agreed that the strategy would be confirmed as one of increasing sales revenue by focusing on the customers' needs and on building long-term relationships.

With a view to make the design process highly visible, participatory and acceptable, two groups generated recommendations on the design of the new plan. One, the Executive Task Force (ETF), consisted of 17 sales managers; the other, the Sales Compensation Task Force, mainly comprised sales reps of similar size. Although the groups were large, 'champions' emerged within each to form a core group of highly active members who withstood peer pressure, embraced the change process and ultimately directed the outcome.

Both groups' roles were defined as clearly advisory with the ultimate authority lying with the Executive board. Members were to review and consider facts, and then make recommendations on plan design. One of the early criteria was that the cost was to be no higher for the same performance as the previous year. Difficult discussions took place over issues such as:

1. The possible reduction of the sales reps' high base salary. While this provoked a strong reaction, severely testing trust in the organization, this highly emotional issue was the key that opened discussion and resolution of many operational issues.
2. The goal-setting process had been much criticized as it appeared to rely simply on the previous year's result plus some growth factor. A new process was proposed which was a collaborative enterprise between managers and reps to try to produce a more level playing field.
3. In the old scheme, a 'windfall' clause existed whereby if a sales rep brought in a great deal of revenue not

traceable to their direct efforts, then management would call it a 'windfall' and refuse to pay bonus on this sum. Under the new proposals, this would be abolished but goals would be updated each quarter.

4. A 'discretionary' fund existed previously which allowed managers to reward effort to sales reps who had worked hard but not met their goals. However, as fair as this seemed, there were no well-defined criteria for these awards and most sales reps viewed them as capricious and arbitrary. All bonus payments subsequently were made on clear and transparent objectives.

5. Previously, sales reps had their bonus reduced due to mistakes made by other departments. For example, when an advert appeared produced wrongly (i.e., a wrong telephone number or address) and the advertiser refused to pay. Under new proposals, only sales-related adjustments were charged against the rep.

6. The scheme would have no maximum payment.

□ *Gaining acceptance*: The latter four changes opened the door to the fundamental acceptance of the first proposal, a reduction of basic pay. Although this provoked a great deal of fear and uncertainty among the reps, their participation in the decision-making process assisted in convincing the group that the scheme was a viable one. A series of meetings took place to ensure everybody had a thorough understanding of the entire scheme and that all objections and doubts were addressed. Details of all the tests and dummy runs were given and nothing was held back. All the information was confirmed in an individually prepared package.

The final version was that the incentive target was roughly doubled, making it 40 per cent of the total targeted compensation for the job. The base salaries were reduced by $4500 (about ten per cent) and base rate increases were frozen for two years. The incentive scheme was relatively simple containing only four elements, rather than the eight or more in previous schemes. There were also additional team-based rewards which were a mix of cash and payments in kind. A special group was set up to consider the development and relevance of these rewards and the balance between team and individual payments. The performance management system was redesigned to support the incentive plan and provide better focused training and development for the reps, both those who met their targets and those who did not.

Source: Excerpts reprinted with permission from Stredwick, J. (1997) *Cases in Reward Management*, Kogan Page: London. Copyright © 1997 by Kogan Page: London. All rights reserved.

References

1. **Kochanski, J.T.** and **Risher, H.** (1999) 'Paying for competencies'. In Risher, H. (Ed.) *Aligning pay and results*, AMACOM: NY.
2. **Armstrong, M.** and **Brown, D.** (2000) *Paying for contribution*, Kogan Page: London.
3. **Kessler, I.** (2001) 'Reward system choices'. In Storey, J. (Ed.) *Human resource management—A critical text*, Thomson Learning: London.
4. **Thomsen, H.K.** and **Hoest, V.** (2001) 'Employees' perception of the learning organisation'. *Management Learning*, Vol 32 No 4, pp. 469–91.
5. **Gee Woo, B.** and **Young-Gul, K.** (2002) 'Breaking the myths of rewards: An exploratory study of attitudes about knowledge sharing'. *Information Resources Management Journal*, Vol 15 No 2, pp. 14–21.
6. **Druker, J.** and **White, G.** (2000) 'The context of reward management'. In White, G. and Druker, J. (Eds.) *Reward management—A critical text*, Routledge: London.
7. **Heneman, R.L., Ledford, G.E.** and **Gresham, M.T.** (2000) 'The changing nature of work and its effects on compensation design and delivery'. In Rynes, S.L. and Gerhart, B. (Eds.) *Compensation in organisations: Current research and practice*, Jossey-Bass: SF.
8. **Taylor, S.** (2000) 'Debates in reward management'. In Thorpe, R. and Homan, G. (Eds.) *Strategic reward systems*, Prentice-Hall: Harlow, England.

9. **Hastings, S.** (2000) 'Grading systems and estimating value'. In White, G. and Druker, J. (Eds.) *Reward management—A critical text*, Routledge: London.

10. **Cross, M.** (1992) 'Skill-based pay: A guide for practitioners'. In *Issues in people management, 3*, Institute of Personnel Management: London.

11. **Mendenhall, M.E.** (1999) 'On the need for paradigmatic integration in international human resource management'. *Management International Review*, Vol 39, Special Issue 1999/3, pp. 65–87.

12. **Pfeffer, J.** and **Veiga, J.F.** (1999) 'Putting people first for organisational success'. *Academy of Management Executive*, Vol 13 No 2, pp. 37–48.

13. **Risher, H.** (1999) 'Using pay as a tool to achieve organisational goals'. In Risher, H. (Ed.) *Aligning pay and results*, AMACOM: NY.

14. **Heneman, H.G.** and **Judge, T.A.** (2000) 'Compensation attitudes'. In Rynes, S.L. and Gerhart, B. (Eds.) *Compensation in organisations: Current research and practice*, Jossey-Bass: SF.

15. **Pfeffer, J.** (1998) 'Six dangerous myths about pay'. *Harvard Business Review*, Vol 76 No 3, pp. 108–19.

16. **Zingheim, P.K.** and **Schuster, J.R.** (2000) *Pay people right!* Jossey-Bass: SF.

17. **Druker, J.** (2000) 'Wages systems'. In White, G. and Druker, J. (Eds.) *Reward management—A critical text*, Routledge: London.

18. **Henderson, R.** (1997) *Compensation management in a knowledge-based world*, Prentice-Hall: NJ.

19. **Smith, I.** (2000) 'Benefits'. In White, G. and Druker, J. (Eds.) *Reward management—A critical text*, Routledge: London.

20. **Harrington, J.** (2000) 'Team-based pay'. In Thorpe, R. and Homan, G. (Eds.) *Strategic reward systems*, Prentice-Hall: Harlow, England.

21. **Cacioppe, R.** (1999) 'Using team–individual reward and recognition strategies to drive organisational success'. *Leadership and Organisation Development Journal*, Vol 20 No 6.

22. **Coli, M.** (1997) Strategic team reward and recognition strategies at Motorola. The best of team conference proceedings. Linkage Inc., SF.

23. **McClurg, L.N.** (2001) 'Team rewards: How far we have come'? *Human Resource Management*, Vol 40 No 1, pp. 73–86.

24. **Wilson, T.B.** (1999) 'Aligning pay to group results'. In Risher, H. (Ed.) *Aligning pay and results*. AMACOM: NY.

25. **Hattiangadi, A.** (1998) *Raising productivity and real wages: Through gainsharing*, Employment Policy Foundation: Washington, DC.

26. **Risher, H.** (1999) 'Aligning pay and group results'. In Risher, H. (Ed.) *Aligning pay and results*, AMACOM: NY.

27. **Bowey, A.** (2000) 'Gainsharing'. In Thorpe, R. and Homan, G. (Eds.) *Strategic reward systems*, Prentice-Hall: Harlow, England.

28. **Sullivan, E.** (1999) 'Moving to a pay-for-performance strategy: Lessons from the trenches'. In Risher, H. (Ed.) *Aligning pay and results*, AMACOM: NY.

29. **Jones, D.C., Kato, T.** and **Pliskin, J.** (1997) 'Profit-sharing and gainsharing: A review of theory, incidence and effects!' In D. Lewis, D. Mitchell and M. Zaidi (Eds.) The Human Resource Management Handbook, Part 1, JAI Press: Greenwich, CT.

30. **Hyman, J.** (2000) 'Financial participation schemes'. In White, G. and Druker, J. (Eds.) *Reward management—A critical text*, Routledge: London.

31. **Blasi, J., Conte, M.** and **Kruse, D.** (1996) 'Employee stock ownership and corporate performance among public companies'. *Industrial and Labour Relations Review*, Vol 50 No 1, pp. 60–79.

32. **Pendleton, A., Wilson, N.** and **Wright, M.** (1998) 'The perception and effects of share ownership: Empirical evidence from employee buy-outs'. *British Journal of Industrial Relations*, Vol 36 No 1, pp. 99–124.

33. **Horibe, F.** (1999) *Managing knowledge workers*, Wiley: Toronto.

34. **Lawler, E.E.** (2000) 'Pay strategy: New thinking for the new millennium'. *Compensation and Benefits Review*, January–February.

35. **Poster, C.Z.** (2002) 'Retaining key people in troubled companies'. *Compensation and Benefits Review*, January–February.

36. **Thomson, M.** (2000) 'Salary progression systems'. In White, G. and Druker, J. (Eds.) *Reward management—A critical text*, Routledge: London.

37. **Institute of Personnel and Development (IPD)** (1998) Performance pay: Summary report. IPD: London.

38. **Murlis, H.** (1997) 'Foreword'. In Stredwick, J., *Cases in reward management*, Kogan Page: London.

39. **Stredwick, J.** (1997) *Cases in reward management*, Kogan Page: London.

9

Managing People in a Multinational Context

Introduction

Declining protectionism, rapid strides in technology, collapse of communism, internationalization of capital markets, global mergers, acquisitions and takeovers have all added fuel to globalization. Historically, the US, the European Union and Japan have accounted for a lion's share of the top five hundred multinational enterprises (MNEs) and their dominance continues, despite the doubling of world trade in the last decade. However, the Asia-Pacific region that is home to two most populous countries (China and India) and dragon economies (Singapore, Taiwan, Malaysia, Korea, Thailand, Indonesia and Vietnam) is projected to account for 70 per cent of the future growth.

A few decades ago, the concept of globalization was mainly discussed in theory. There was no pressing economic need to understand and appreciate the history and culture of countries around the world. Today, the internationalization of business is a reality but what about internationalization of management? The rapid pace of globalization of markets is compelling management researchers to explore solutions to economic problems with universal applicability.

However, despite global production, global markets and global communications, the 'global culture' is still an elusive concept.

National culture has a powerful influence on almost all aspects of work and organization, such as strategy, goals, communication, negotiation, conflict resolution, structure, leadership, time orientation, social and interpersonal practices, decision-making style and managing people. For example, the contract-oriented style of the West clashes with the contract or relationship-oriented style of the East and requires Western managers to show patience, perseverance and long-term orientation in doing business with Asian partners. The Eastern ethic has a strong sense of duty-consciousness as against the rights-consciousness of the Western ethic. This realization has compelled many MNEs to adopt 'glocalization', that is, to think globally but act locally.

The following sections discuss the benefits and limitations of cross-cultural analysis, the convergence–divergence debate in international HRM and examine their implications on each of the core HRM functions, namely, recruitment, performance, rewards, training and development and industrial relations. The discussion uses certain terms, specific to international business/HRM that relate to

- Strategies: International, multinational, global, and transnational
- Employer attitude to staffing: Ethnocentric, polycentric, geocentric, and regiocentric
- Employee nationality: Parent-country, host-country, third-country nationals
- Employee type: Expatriate, inpatriate, repatriate

These terms have been defined in Table 9.1.

Table 9.1: Definitions of Specialist Terms in International Business/ HRM

Area	Term
International business strategies	The terms international, multinational, global and transnational refer to business strategy and structure based on pressure for cost reduction and local responsiveness.[1] • **International companies** centralize their operations and policies in the headquarters with very little pressure for cost reduction and localization. • **Multinational companies** (also called multidomestic) aim to achieve maximum local responsiveness through a highly decentralized structure. • **Global companies** aim for a maximum cost-reduction strategy through standardized products and operations. • **Transnational companies** aim to achieve both cost reduction and local responsiveness through a very high degree of local flexibility combined with global integration.
Employee nationality	• **Parent-country national** (PCN): Permanent resident of a country where the firm is headquartered. • **Host-country national** (HCN): Permanent resident of a country where the subsidiary of the firm is located. • **Third-country national** (TCN): Permanent resident of a country other than the parent country and the host country. Example: IBM, headquartered in the US, employs Australian citizens (HCNs) in its Australian operations, often sends US citizens (PCNs) to Asia-Pacific countries on assignments, and may send some of its Singaporean employees on an assignment to its Japanese operations (as TCNs).[2]
Employer attitude to staffing	• **Ethnocentric:** All key positions, in headquarters as well as subsidiaries, are staffed by parent-country nationals. • **Polycentric:** Key positions in subsidiaries staffed by host-country nationals and those in headquarters staffed by parent-country nationals. • **Regiocentric:** Key positions staffed by host-country nationals within particular geographical regions (such as North America, Europe and Asia). • **Geocentric:** Key positions in headquarters as well as subsidiaries staffed by people based on merit, irrespective of nationality.
Employee type	• **Expatriate:** A PCN sent on a long-term assignment to the host-country operation. • **Inpatriate:** HCNs or TCNs assigned to the home country of the MNE where it is headquartered. • **Repatriate:** An expatriate coming back to the home country at the end of a foreign assignment.

Structural Framework of Cross-cultural Analysis

The impact of national culture depends, amongst other things, on whether the country is in a high or low cultural context. Western countries generally have a low cultural context compared to Asian countries as they are mainly individualistic in their mindset with the result that their societies have a high tolerance for individuals and groups defining their own destiny, whereas in collectivistic cultures, society exerts considerable pressure on individuals and groups to conform to societal norms and values.

Cultural comparisons are usually made between Western and Eastern cultures. This may help very broad comparisons but it needs to be recognized that there are sub-cultures within Western and Eastern societies with major differences amongst them. One cannot treat the French culture in the same manner as British or German culture, even though all are in the same region and are considered as Western countries. Similarly, there is no typical 'Asian culture' as Asian countries, such as China, India, Japan, and Malaysia, differ quite markedly in their cultural norms and beliefs. In fact, some countries are so multi-cultural that there is little 'national culture'. Even in culturally homogeneous countries, such as Japan, the so-called 'three pillars of employment', namely, lifetime employment, seniority pay and promotion, and enterprise unions are seen as 'stylized, a caricature, partial and eroding'.[3]

The concept of time and space are different in different cultures. In low cultural context countries, there is a clear distinction between private space and public space. Similarly, in such countries, time is regarded as extremely valuable and strictly adhered to, whereas in others, social interactions and relationships are more important than adhering to schedules and hence, there is less difference between public and private space and time is conveniently stretched.[4] Thus, time and space act as an important means of communication and often cause misunderstandings in international business.

Culture also changes with time and therefore, any analysis of cultural impact on work values has limited validity in time. For instance, a survey of international HRM (IHRM) practices covering ten countries/regions in North America, Asia and Latin America revealed that collectivist countries such as Taiwan and China indicated more preference for pay incentives than the US and Canada. The Asian countries also showed reduced preference for seniority-based promotion 'indicating that some type of social change is occurring.[5]

Apart from culture, political, economic, institutional and other forces significantly influence people's attitudes to work. For example, employee preferences for various types of pay such as variable pay schemes, stock options and bonus might vary from one country to another, based on tax rates and incentives.[6] 'Some operations in China are incompatible with Confucian images and underlying beliefs as they are based on military discipline, unquestioning loyalty and authoritarianism in Chinese, Korean and Taiwanese management'.[3] Work values also change with changing economic conditions. For instance, countries like Singapore, Taiwan and Korea relied on cheap labour in their early stages of development but with increasing prosperity, the expectations of workers have changed and pushed labour costs upwards. These countries now face stiff competition from China and India and are forced to move up the value chain and require workers to be more knowledge oriented.

Therefore, national cultural comparisons are, in many ways, 'sophisticated stereotypes'. It is a natural human tendency to stereotype as a way of understanding a complex, unknown and vast phenomenon, such as national culture, even if it sometimes leads to 'ecological fallacy' by confusing an individual with a group/society and vice versa.[7] However, it is still useful to treat 'national models' as the basic unit of analysis, focusing on macro-institutional features as key dimensions, because 'national borders are synonymous with market scope, differences across states are more pronounced and salient than variations within, and certain national institutional arrangements are more effective than others at adapting to changing political-economic circumstances'.[3]

Thus, cross-cultural analysis is a complex and contingent phenomenon and needs to be treated with caution.

Dimensions of National Culture

Hofstede defines culture as 'collective programming of the mind' and argues that people carry mental programmes over their lifetime that contain a component of national culture and expressed in different values.[8] He conducted a survey in 1968 and 1972 on work values of more than 100,000 employees of IBM Corporation spread across more than 50 countries, and identified four (later extended to five) main dimensions of national culture. He analysed the data in terms of differences between countries, occupations, gender and age. In the second edition of his acclaimed book, *Culture's consequences*,[8] Hofstede demonstrates the empirical support to the following dimensions based on data from 140 other studies comparing from five to 39 countries.

- ▫ **Power distance:** This refers to the extent to which inequality in power is accepted. In a societal context, it refers to social status, prestige, wealth, power, laws, etc. The economic class system (aristocracy) in the UK and the caste system in India are manifestations of inequality in society. In an organizational context, it deals with the decision-making style of superiors and the perceptions of subordinates' fear of disagreeing with superiors. Hofstede points out that 'authority exists only where it is matched by obedience' and therefore, 'leadership can exist only as a complement to subordinateship'. Decision-making styles in countries with high power distance are likely to be autocratic or paternalistic compared to consultative or democratic styles prevalent in countries having low power distance.

□ **Uncertainty avoidance:** 'is the extent to which a culture programs its members to feel either uncomfortable or comfortable in unstructured situations.' It is different from risk avoidance.

□ **Individualism vs. collectivism:** 'is the degree to which individuals are supposed to look after themselves or remain integrated into groups.'

□ **Masculinity vs. femininity:** 'refers to the distribution of emotional roles between the genders as in "tough" masculine to "tender" feminine societies'. Almost universally, 'women attach more importance to social goals such as relationships, helping others and the physical environment, and men attach more importance to ego goals, such as careers and money.'

□ **Long term vs. short term:** 'refers to the extent to which a culture programs its members to accept delayed gratification of their material, social, and emotional needs.' This dimension was detected in Bond's Chinese values survey from values suggested by Chinese scholars. It refers to Confucius's values of the importance of thrift, persistence, personal stability and respect for tradition.

Hofstede draws detailed and useful implications of the above cultural dimensions on work organization, as presented in Table 9.2.

Table 9.2
Implications of Hofstede's Cultural Dimensions
on the Work Organization

	Low	High
Power distance	• Consultative/Participative decision-making	• Authoritative/Paternalistic decision-making
	• Freedom more important than equality	• Equality/Conformity more important than freedom
	• Authority based on rational arguments and consultation	• Authority based on traditions and rules
	• Top leaders younger	• Top leaders older
	• Stress on reward, legitimate and expert power	• Stress on coercive and referent power
	• Student-centred learning	• Teacher-centred learning
	• Subordinates expect to be consulted	• Subordinates expect to be told
	• Flat structure with few supervisory personnel	• Tall structure with large number of supervisory personnel
	• Subordinates influenced by bargaining and reasoning; MBO is feasible	• Subordinates influenced by authority; MBO cannot work
Uncertainty avoidance	• Innovations need good champions	• Innovations need good support from hierarchy
	• Managerial symbols and status symbols frowned upon	• Managerial symbols and status symbols expected and popular
	• Preference for tasks with uncertain outcomes, calculated risks and requiring problem-solving	• Preference for tasks with sure outcomes, no risks and following instructions
	• Preference for smaller organizations	• Preference for larger organizations
	• Competition amongst employees and preference for independent decision	• Avoid competition with peers and preference for group decisions
		• A pessimistic outlook on the motives guiding companies in spite of admiration for loyalty to companies
	Individualism	**Collectivism**
Individualism Vs. Collectivism	• More importance to freedom and challenging jobs	• More importance to training and use of skills in jobs
	• Employees responsible for themselves	• Company responsible for employees
	• Employees supposed to act as 'economic men'	• Employees act in the interest of their in-group, not necessarily of themselves
	• Family relationships seen as a disadvantage in hiring	• Relatives of employer and employees preferred in hiring

Individualism Vs. Collectivism

- Poor performance reason for dismissal
- Preferred reward allocation based on equity for all

- Innovation champions in organizations want to venture out on their own
- Greater social mobility across occupations
- Management is management of individuals
- Direct appraisal of performance improves productivity

- Poor performance reason for other tasks
- Preferred reward allocation based on equality for in-group, equity for out-group
- Innovation champions in organizations want to involve others
- Less social mobility across occupations
- Management is management of groups
- Direct appraisal of performance is a threat to harmony

Masculinity Vs. Femininity

Masculinity

- Challenge and recognition in jobs important
- Advancement and earnings important
- Achievement in terms of ego boosting, wealth and recognition
- Lower norms for emotional stability and ego control
- Ego orientation
- Live in order to work
- Stress on what you do
- Stress on equity, mutual competition and performance
- Big and fast are beautiful
- Managers expected to be decisive, firm, assertive, aggressive, competitive, just
- Job applicants oversell themselves
- Higher job stress

Femininity

- Co-operation at work and relationship with boss important
- Living area and employment security important
- Achievement in terms of quality of contacts and environment
- Higher norms for emotional stability and ego control
- Relationship orientation
- Work in order to live
- Stress on who you are
- Stress on equality, solidarity and quality of work life
- Small and slow are beautiful
- Managers expected to use intuition, deal with feelings and seek consensus
- Job applicants undersell themselves
- Lower job stress

Short term Vs. Long term

Short term

- Quick results expected
- Status not major issue in relationships
- Protection of one's 'face'

- Most important events in life occurred in past or occur in present
- Small share of additional income saved

Long term

- Persistence, perseverance
- Relationships ordered by status and this order observed
- Face considerations common but considered a weakness
- Most important events in life will occur in future

- Large share of additional income saved

Short term Vs. Long term	• In business, short-term results the bottomline		• In business, building of relationships and market position
	• Meritocracy: Economic and social life to be ordered by abilities		• People should live more equally
	• Analytical thinking and fuzzy problem-solving		• Synthetic thinking and structured problem-solving

Source: Adapted from Hofstede, G. (2001) *Culture's consequences: Comparing values, behaviours, institutions and organizations across nations.* Sage, Thousand Oaks, CA. Copyright © Geert Hofstede, with the author's permission.

Studies that have tried to link cultural characteristics with economic growth have yielded interesting results. One such recent study analysed the effect of national culture on economic growth in 51 nations and in two time periods, 1960–1980 and 1980–1998, controlling for national wealth at the beginning of each period.[9] All the above five cultural dimensions were included in the study and economic growth was measured in Gross Domestic Product (GNP) per capita. The study claims that 'national culture accounts for about 40 per cent of the variance in economic growth but the configuration of effects changes over time'. Between 1960 and 1980, individualism and long-term orientation had most significant effect on national growth, the former negatively and the latter positively. However, between 1980 and 1998, uncertainty avoidance becomes a significant negative factor in economic growth regression equation. The study explains that 'the difficulty of working collaboratively in high individualism countries versus the need for work in teams in large, complex organizations may provide one of the answers as to why individualism does not contribute to national economic growth'. As regards uncertainty avoidance assuming importance for the period 1980–1998, the study attributes it to the increasing need for ability to deal with uncertainty arising out of technological changes. The study claims that in the beginning of the new economy, those countries that score high on individualism, economic freedom and inventiveness and low on uncertainty avoidance stand to gain the most; however, once the new economy takes roots, high individualism may yet again lead to lower economic growth.

If we extrapolate the cultural dimensions on strategic HRM concepts in a knowledge economy, as discussed in Chapter 2, it appears that countries with low power distance, low uncertainty avoidance and long-term orientation, seem to have a better edge. As regards the individualism–collectivism dimension, the need for team structure and community orientation of knowledge workers seems to favour collectivism, provided there is less group thinking and social loafing that inhibit innovation and creativity. There is some evidence that social loafing is relatively less in collectivist cultures as members place group goals ahead of individual interests.[10]

However, whether the organizational culture can influence the national culture to get desired behaviours from employees is a moot point. Research suggests that some degree of convergence in HRM systems is evident in the Asia-Pacific region but to what extent this convergence will be sustained and strengthened remains to be seen.[3] The interplay between national and organizational culture is a significant factor in the success of global mergers, acquisitions and alliances. For example, cultural differences may increase the 'motivation' for learning-oriented alliances but restrict the 'ability' to learn from each other due to mistrust and communication barriers. However, 'ultimately, inter-firm cultural differences are the primary influence on the ability of firms to use alliances as mechanisms of knowledge transfer'.[11]

Cross-cultural Validity of Management Trends

The majority of today's management concepts originate from the US. However, the US-style management or manager hardly exists in Germany (where technical skills are more valued), in Japan (where the superior rises from the ranks and decides on group consensus), in France (where strict boundaries exist between the ruler and ruled) and amongst overseas

Chinese (where businesses revolve around small family networks controlled by one dominant family member).[12]

Rightsizing

Mroczkowski and Hanaoka argue that 'the downsizing programs of many American companies are poorly planned, badly managed and do not bring about expected improvements in company performance'.[13] They point out that despite overcapacity and poor profits, Japanese firms have resorted to limited layoffs because of their practice of 'koyochosei', a term referred to adjustment of employment levels, which coexists alongside the 'lifetime employment' concept. Under the koyochosei system, Japanese firms use compulsory redundancies as a last resort only after they have tried other measures, such as restricting overtime, redeployment, reducing work hours, stopping new recruitment, non-renewal of contracts, temporary leave, pay cuts, transfer to other companies including subsidiaries and suppliers on a temporary or permanent basis, and voluntary retirement with preferential conditions. Similarly, the French prefer to reduce work hours to cope with increasing unemployment.

Asians by nature dislike uncertainty in life. Since Asians are group centred, loss of job for one affects the morale of others. As Asian employees are generally loyal to their organizations and identify themselves very closely with their employers, retrenchments without a strong cause are likely to shake the foundations of their work ethic. So, hiring and firing at will is a culturally negative option in Asian countries. Termination of employment should be the last resort under extreme circumstances and when it becomes inevitable, the management needs to handle it as humanely as possible by consulting the employees so that the exercise is as painless as possible. Similarly, outsourcing may not work well in Asia because of the importance given by Asians to long-term security needs rather than short-term gains. Asians tend to trade off opportunity in favour of security.

Empowerment

The concept of empowerment is rooted in the belief that people are highly individualistic in nature; they value success and personal accomplishments highly (achievement oriented) and would like to define their own destiny. Empowerment is regarded as a key motivational tool but what is motivating to some may be demotivating to others. For example, 'in Spain, subordinates strongly prefer that their bosses supervise their work directly, and feel very uncomfortable making their own decisions or telling the boss what the decision should be'.[7]

While the concept of empowerment is laudable, extensive and time consuming, groundwork needs to be done in an Asian context. For a long time, Asians have been brought up in an environment where management sets the rules and employees follow. Some Japanese organizations have been successful in introducing total quality management concepts but in the context of 'limited autonomy' covering only the immediate work areas. In the absence of a congenial atmosphere, empowerment may lead to demotivation, quite the opposite of its purpose.

Flat and Flexible Organizational Structure

Weber's concept of 'bureaucracy' has negative connotations in today's context. But bureaucracy also brings order, discipline, security, which are highly valued by Asians. Asian societies are status driven. Authority, titles, official perks and benefits are highly valued. Promotions, even if small and incremental, are very important in terms of motivation. Therefore, in such cultures it is desirable to have many management levels. Fluid organizational structures have many negative connotations in the Asian context, such as uncertainty, imbalance in power equation, and unstable group cohesiveness.

Similarly, Table 9.2 illustrates how trends in performance appraisal and New Pay ideas (as discussed in Chapters 7 and 8) suffer from cross-cultural limitations.

Importance of Communication

In high-context cultures, most of the information is implicit as it is programmed in people's minds whereas in low-context cultures, it is explicit as people compartmentalize different aspects of their life, such as work and family, and need detailed background information each time they interact with others. Consequently, the information exchanged between the two may be seen as too little by low-context people (such as Americans) and too much by high-context people (such as Japanese).[4] Each culture has its own method of communication that is known to everybody in the culture but difficult for outsiders to identify. Culture influences the amount and speed of information, format of communication, definition of personal space, and time orientation that are vital for successful communication.

Drawing on his experience of managing the people aspect of MNEs, Holden emphasizes the importance of communication,[14] in terms of not just language, but mainly understanding. Even when everybody speaks the same language, the understanding may be different. For example, 'to the US manager, the drive for profit can mean an aggressive cost reduction plan whereas his/her European counterpart will instinctively look for top-line growth'.[14] In one instance, when a new CEO of a US-based MNE sent out an email on her first day addressed to everyone by their first name, managers in Germany, Italy and Spain considered that a first name communication was not appropriate for their people and modified it to a more formal style of address![14]

With reference to the dynamics of multi-cultural meetings, Holden points out that the very purpose of a 'meeting' can be different in different countries. 'In UK and USA, meetings are held to make decisions. In mainland Europe, they are held more for debate. In the Czech Republic, meetings are for communicating a decision that some higher authority has already made.' Similarly, an Indian IT company working for a Japanese customer was surprised when told that the Indian employees posted to Japan were good at their work but did not stay in office long enough. The Indians, in this case, used to leave the office at 8 p.m., which was considered too early by the Japanese!

HRM in an International Context

The very concept of HRM is seen by some as essentially an Anglo-Saxon construct[15] and 'institutionally restricted and culturally grounded in Western values'.[3] In Western countries, HRM has grown from a staff function looking after welfare and legal matters to a strategic function shared by line managers. In contrast, in Japan, rather than being regarded as a specialist function, it is considered a major responsibility of line managers. In a multinational context, the nature and influence of HRM depends on national culture, industry, proportion of foreign income to domestic income and the attitude of senior management. A key variable that differentiates international and domestic HRM is the 'complexity involved in operating in different countries and employing different national categories of employees, rather than any major differences between the HR activities performed'.[2]

The HRM system plays a key role in ensuring the success of international assignments. In fulfilling its role, the HR department has to answer the following questions:

How sophisticated is the expatriate selection system? How much lead-time is typically provided for expatriates to decide on an assignment? How extensive is the pre-departure training and orientation for the expatriate and family, and what type of relocation assistance is provided? How clear are the job responsibilities and the amount of authority inherent in the position? How will performance be measured and rewarded overseas? What is the compensation and the benefits package, and how is it tailored to the country of assignment? How tightly is the international assignment tied to career development, and what arrangements are made in advance for eventual repatriation?[16]

An integrated global human resource information system (HRIS) is critical to an MNE, particularly with a geocentric or regiocentric approach to staffing, where merit is the sole criterion to staff key positions, irrespective of nationality. It can store data on demographics of personnel, technical as well as multi-cultural skills of managers in every region, compensation and benefit practices, local HR policies and procedures and applicable labour laws and income tax.[17] It can also provide valuable information to an expatriate's family on issues such as schooling and healthcare and help HR to manage associated costs. An up-to-date and sophisticated global HRIS enables identification, grooming of and equitable career opportunities for high potential global managers. However, such systems face several challenges, such as uneven spread of technology and infrastructure and different interpretation of the same term amongst subsidiaries as well as the need for constant monitoring and update.

Many MNEs have very effectively leveraged information and communication technologies to spread global best practices throughout the organization to increase efficiency and offer better products and services. However, when it comes to transfer of tacit knowledge, they find it difficult to leverage HR practises because they are poorly defined and practised in an international context.

An additional challenge to IHRM is dealing with global terrorism, which has come to the forefront after the September 11 incident in the US, and violent opposition to globalization. For no fault of theirs, employees of an MNE may come under grave danger in facing the ire of protesters opposing the policies of a country where the MNE is head-quartered. McDonald restaurants are frequent targets for anti-US and anti-globalization demonstrators. MNEs have to ensure that their employees never compromise on safety to themselves and others by requiring them to strictly adhere to travel warnings issued by their country's foreign depart-ment and providing enough protection with the help of local police.

Research suggests that cultural incompatibility is one of the main reasons for the high rate of failure in international mergers and acquisitions. While the reference here is mainly to organizational culture, the influence of national culture plays an important role too, particularly when a company from a high-cultural context merges with or is acquired by a company from a low-cultural context or vice versa. In such situations, the corporate strategy and people managers at the headquarters need to centralize only essential operations and policies and decentralize the rest to provide maximum opera-tional flexibility. For example, American subsidiaries of Japa-nese companies typically follow compensation norms in the US and make no attempt to replicate the Japanese tradition of seniority wage or promotion system.[18]

Fit Between International Business Strategy and HRM Strategy

In choosing between standardized and customized HRM policies for their multinational operations, MNEs face com-peting pressures: the internal pressures for standardizing HRM practices with business strategy and external pressures to localize HRM practices with the environment.[19] The same dilemma is present in business strategy where the firm has to make a strategic choice to fit the business environment. It has to choose between

□ Cost-reduction strategy, followed by global operations in industries such as petroleum and commercial aircraft, where cost reduction is more important than customization and the need for parent–subsidiary integration is high,

□ Differentiation strategy, followed by multinational/multidomestic operations in industries such as soft drink, insurance and retailing, where customization is more important than cost reduction and the need for parent–subsidiary integration is low, or

□ A combination of both, followed by transnational operations in industries such as information and communication technologies, where a high degree of both cost reduction and differentiation are required and the need for parent–subsidiary integration is optimum.

As illustrated in Figure 9.1, Bird and Beechler recommend a choice of following HRM strategies to suit business strategy:[19]

□ **Utilizer strategy:** Where the firm deploys human resources as efficiently and flexibly as possible through hire and fire of personnel to suit short-term business needs and matching employee skills to tasks. This HRM strategy suits global operations with cost-reduction strategy. It helps organizations to maintain a lean workforce that has been handpicked to suit immediate task requirements.

□ **Accumulator strategy:** Where the firm acquires as well as develops human resources with the potential to service the needs of the organization over a longer period of time. It 'emphasizes the accumulation of resources and possesses more organizational slack and latent human resources potential'. This HRM strategy suits multinational operations with differentiation strategy.

□ **Facilitator strategy:** Where the firm 'seeks to develop the human resources of the firm as effectively as possible through the acquisition of self-motivated personnel and the encouragement and support of personnel to develop, on their own, the skills and knowledge which, they, the employees, believe are important. Thus, it is focused on new knowledge and its creation and calls for an evolutionary, learning orientation.' This HRM strategy suits transnational operations which face strong pressures for both cost reduction and differentiation.

Type of Operation	Cost-reduction Strategy	Differentiation Strategy	Need for Parent–Subsidiary Integration	Structure	HRM Strategy	Staffing Strategy
Global	High	Low	High	Centralized	Utilizer	Ethnocentric
Multinational / Multi-domestic	Low	High	Low	Decentralized	Accumulator	Polycentric/ Regiocentric
Transnational	High	High	Optimum	Both centralized and decentralized	Facilitator	Geocentric

Source: Adapted from Bird, A. and Beechler, S. (2000) 'The link between business strategy and international human resource management practices'. In Mendenhall, M. and Oddou, G. (Eds.) *Readings and cases in international human resource management*, South-Western College Publishing, Ontario.

Figure 9.1: International Business Strategy and HRM Strategy

Convergence or Divergence?

Jackson argues that 'across cultures, people are valued differently as human beings within work organizations'.[20] He distinguishes between Western-oriented instrumental view of people as a means to an end and Eastern-oriented humanistic view of people as an end in itself. He also recognizes the possibility of 'cross-vergence' or the intermixing of cultural systems and gives the example of Australia as an individualistic Western culture but with a humanistic orientation. This distinction resonates with the hard and soft approach to HRM as well as with the individualist–collectivist dimension of culture.

A survey of IHRM practices covering engineers/managers in ten countries/regions in North America, Asia and Latin America identified the following HRM trends that appear to have universal applicability, either now (as is) or in the future (should be):

◻ Compensation: Pay should be based on individual performance; benefits (and not pay incentives) should comprise an important part of a compensation package.
◻ Selection: 'Getting along with others' and 'fit with the corporate values' signals a shift in selection from 'West meets East'. In Western countries, job interview, technical skills and work experience are the most important selection criteria with a desire to replace work experience with person–organizational value fit in the future. Asian countries generally deemphasize work experience and focus on the person's potential.
◻ Performance appraisal: There was universal agreement in all countries that the stated purposes of appraisal are not being met, which highlights the need for thorough overhaul of the system. All countries indicated that a greater emphasis be placed on developmental orientation of the appraisal system.
◻ Training and development (T&D): In most countries, T&D practices are used to improve employees' technical skills with a growing trend to use them for soft skills such as team building (Von Glinow: 2001).[5]

A study of HRM practices across the Asia-Pacific region concludes that 'despite some change, HRM often continues to be, on one hand, diverse and dynamic while on the other, locationally-specific and contradictory'. 'Political/structural and cultural/societal configurations in countries produce different HRM systems'.[3] Any possible convergence is further challenged by differences in industry, occupation, gender, etc. The convergence–divergence debate in international HRM needs to be mindful of fundamental influences at the macro level as well as influences at the micro level, such as organizational size, ownership pattern, culture, management style and strategies. Therefore, IHRM research in 'contextual isolation is misleading' and 'needs to use multiple levels of analysis: the external social, political, cultural and economic environment; the industry, the firm, the sub-unit, the group, and the individual'.[21]

Social Responsibility and HRM

Ethical behaviour is something that is not defined by law but expected by society. In an international context, ethical responsibilities pose a special challenge as ethics is defined and understood differently in different countries. Even though it is understood that cross-cultural studies aim to understand not 'evaluate' culture, sometimes a particular cultural practice may clash with universally accepted human values, such as compassion and dignity.

Can an MNE tolerate child labour in a country because it is an accepted local practice or that the children will remain hungry without employment? Many MNEs, such as Nike, have come under fire for indirectly encouraging child labour in countries such as China and Indonesia by subcontracting work to local vendors. Many other MNEs have been accused of exploiting the lax laws in developing countries on product standards, labour, environment and safety. In countries where women are not allowed or actively discouraged to work or where recruitment quotas are in place that favour a particular community (e.g., native Malays in Malaysia) or religion (e.g., Muslims in Saudi Arabia) or practice of employing relatives (e.g., Indonesia), how does an equal employment opportunity MNE's equal employment opportunity (EEO) policy fit in?

Here MNEs have to take a cautious approach. If a particular practice is a law, it has to be obeyed. Where a practice is widely prevalent but clearly unethical from the MNE's point of view, the pros and cons have to be weighed. In certain cases, an accepted practice in one country may be illegal in the home country. For example, US law prohibits offering bribes in foreign operations. Even otherwise, certain practices such as offering bribes and meddling in local politics are counterproductive and even destructive in the long run. Where doubts arise, it is preferable to collect all the facts instead of relying on unsubstantiated assertions and do the best for all involved stakeholders 'by fulfilling obligations, observing laws and contracts, avoiding deception and knowingly causing harm'.[7]

There are many socially responsible behaviours that any country would welcome—sourcing raw materials locally, hiring local personnel, offering apprenticeships and traineeships to local youth, donation for worthy causes, and helping to develop local schools, hospitals and community groups. By going beyond statutory obligations with respect to safety, environment protection and community development, an MNE can develop a positive image as a responsible corporate citizen.

While the corporate citizenship behaviour of an organization is under scrutiny even in domestic operations, it is more so in international operations due to unfamiliarity of cultures, practices and regulations. An MNE is under constant pressure to develop trust and a harmonious relationship with the government, political parties and the community at large. In this regard, trust-enhancing strategies include alignment of interests, focusing on procedural and outcome justice in conflict resolution, partner accommodation and flexibility in negotiations, and judicious use of power. In terms of cross-cultural communication, factors such as discreetness, openness and receptivity play an important role.[22] While being direct in negotiations may be appropriate for individualistic cultures, it is considered rude in collectivist cultures. Thus, parties have to invest considerable effort and time in understanding subtle cultural clues. Interestingly, available research evidence suggests that 'people from individualistic cultures have a higher predisposition to trust than people from collectivist cultures, irrespective of whether the trust referent is people in general, family members, people from the same country, or in-group or out-group members'.[22]

Functional Implications of International HRM

Recruitment and Retention

International staffing has to be considered in a strategic perspective of exposing managers to international education in conducting business and managing people globally rather than treating it as an ad-hoc mechanism to fill key overseas positions with PCNs. No classroom training, no matter how well designed and implemented, can ever prepare managers to come face to face with the complexity of global business. MNEs need to provide training and development opportunities through global job rotation to develop global managers who have a 'state of mind' that 'perceives global competition as an opportunity, has a hands-on understanding of global business and an ability to work across organizational, functional, and cross-cultural boundaries; and is able to balance the simultaneous demands of global integration and local responsiveness'.[23]

A survey revealed that nearly 50 per cent of companies surveyed believed in geocentric attitude to staffing, i.e., to choose the best in the entire organization, regardless of country of origin. Nearly 35 per cent of companies followed an ethnocentric approach by sending PCNs for foreign assignments. The average length of assignment was two-three years for 45 per cent of expatriates and more than three years for another 35 per cent.[24] The cost of an expatriate varies from two to five times his/her salary. The cost of expatriate failure is too high in terms of money, replacement, time and adverse effects on the assignment.

Naturally, MNEs are concerned about the high rate of expatriate failure as well as low retention rate for repatriates. The reasons are not far to seek. Research suggests that MNEs overemphasize the importance of technical skills in expatriate selection and ignore the importance of cross-cultural competencies such as 'cultural empathy, adaptability, diplomacy, language ability, positive attitude, emotional stability, and maturity'.[2] It is then hardly surprising that the main reason for expatriate failure is the inability of the expatriate and his/her family to adjust to foreign culture.

International assignments involve family and emotions more than economic considerations. The MNE has to consider the implications of a foreign assignment on the employee's family, such as spouse's employment in a dual-career situation, children's education, care of elderly, and financial impact (e.g., sale of home). Considering these difficulties and the expenses, some MNEs turn their attention to possible alternatives, such as 'virtually' managing the international assignment through communication link-ups and frequent short trips, hiring HCNs and exposing them to organizational culture through inpatriation, hiring fresh college graduates of host-country origin studying in Western universities, and employees of host-country ethnic origin.

Expatriates of host-country ethnic origin are a potentially rich source of addressing international staffing difficulties. For example, an American MNE that operates in India may approach its employees of Indian origin who are US citizens or permanent residents and working permanently in its headquarters to fill up certain key positions in India. Most MNEs in the IT industry that have set up shop in India to harness the potential of the vast pool of cost-effective and high-quality English-speaking engineers and scientists, have sent expatriates of Indian origin to fill up key positions in their Indian operations. The author's current research on them indicates that it is a win-win situation for both expatriates and MNEs. These expatriates are willing to temporarily or permanently relocate from their adopted country to their country of origin with which they still have family and emotional links. Their familiarity with Indian culture places less stress on them and enables them to often do better than Western expatriates.

However, this may not always be the case. A study that looked at overseas Chinese from Hong Kong and Western business expatriates currently working on Chinese mainland concluded that the former were unwilling to adjust to mainland environment and tended to use symptom-focused strategies, such as resorting to parent-country escapism, whereas the latter were more open and used problem-focused coping strategies, such as showing tolerance and patience.[25]

Women managers are very much underrepresented in international staffing. Many organizations worry about the special problems they might face in posting a woman for foreign assignments, such as safety, dual-career and work-life balance issues. They also, sometimes falsely, believe that women managers are not keen on expatriate postings (without even checking it with them) or that they are not suitable for countries with male-dominant attitudes, such as the Middle East. A study revealed that in fact women managers are far more successful negotiators in the Middle East and are preferred by Middle Eastern businesses over Western men because they believe that women are better in empathy and listening.

Therefore, MNEs, particularly those that believe in geocentric attitude to international staffing, should strategize about ways and means of getting more women into their global managerial pool. These strategies could include wider communication about staffing opportunities and measures in place for affirmative action and diversity programmes, clarifying misconceptions amongst women managers about working abroad, showcasing the achievements of successful women expatriates and using them as ambassadors to enlist more women, etc.

Not much thought is given to retaining and utilizing the international experience gained by expatriates and inpatriates. Repatriation is shown to be as stressful an adjustment process as expatriation. The reasons include lack of preparation and clarity on assignments on return, unclear impact on career development, lack of value on overseas experience, reduced job discretion, and adjustment difficulties for self and family.[26] Research shows that the retention rate for repatriates (expatriates who come back from overseas assignments) is considerably low[27] and one of the reasons given by employees during exit interviews is that the organization did not have a proper repatriation plan in place and that their new experience was neither adequately appreciated nor utilized. Expectation management is the key to manage smooth repatriation. Expatriates accept foreign assignments amidst immense personal odds to boost their career prospects and they need to be clear about what they can expect in return.

Performance Management

Our previous discussion on cultural dimensions clearly points out the limitations of the US-style performance management system, such as MBO, and is likely to cause the most damage if it ignores important cultural differences. These differences affect the choice, measurement and administration of a performance system. The validity of the concept of collaborative and consultative approach to agreeing on objectives and joint review has been questioned in Western countries where it originates. It is even less likely to work in Eastern cultures, where 'open responses to seniors are discouraged, where challenging the boss's expectations of what is possible would be seen as insubordination, where admitting faults amounts to a loss of face and where, for example, the idea of criticizing the boss's work in front of that boss would be seen as some sort of organizational suicide'.[28]

A survey on current purposes of performance appraisals in ten different countries and regions in Asia, North America and Latin America revealed that 'the potential of appraisal (e.g., documentation, development, subordinate expression, etc.) is not fully realized in current practice, not only (as widely believed) in the US, but also in most other countries'.[29] The survey noted that even in the US, appraisal discussion typically lasts about one hour or less and clearly, there is a need for organizations to substantially change or improve the process and devote more time and effort to implement it if they are serious about the process.

The performance of expatriates is assessed by the superiors in the host country or parent country or both. The expatriate is likely to run into problems on both fronts. They are psychologically distant from the host country and physically distant from the home country. HCNs 'typically evaluate the expatriate's performance from their own cultural frame of reference and set of expectations' whereas PCNs, who are geographically distanced from the expatriate and hardly have international experience themselves, are not fully aware of what is happening overseas and do not really understand their experience—'neither its difficulty nor its value'.[30]

Apart from the problems relating to the 'perception' of performance, expatriates face daunting challenges in their 'actual' performance. While their technical skills might have mainly contributed to their success in their domestic assignments, they quickly learn that more than technical skills, they need to have cultural adjustment skills to succeed in foreign assignments. One of the main reasons for the high rate of expatriate failure is the cultural adjustment problem faced by the expatriate as well as the spouse. Furthermore, the expatriate's performance can be adversely affected by reasons beyond the control of the expatriate and sometimes 'invisible' to the headquarters, such as 'strikes, devaluation of currency, political instability and runaway inflation'.[30]

Some of the suggested solutions to improve the effectiveness of expatriate performance management are: recognizing and formally incorporating the 'difficulty level' of operating in different countries (e.g., an American would find a Japanese posting more difficult than a British posting), relying on assessment by the present or former on-site manager of the expatriate's nationality, requiring the foreign on-site manager to consult the home-site manager before finalizing evaluation, involving the expatriate in deciding on performance criteria and making them more appropriate to the expatriate's position and circumstances.[30]

Training and Development

Despite the obvious importance of pre-departure training, MNEs, particularly from North America, have a poor record of adequately preparing the expatriate and his/her family for international assignments. In many cases, MNEs are content to provide just-in-time, superficial training without really addressing the issues uppermost in the minds of the expatriate families. The depth and breadth of pre-departure training can vary from a simple information-giving approach (films/books) to affective approach (culture and language training) to immersion approach (field experience) depending on the length of stay and nature of the position.[31]

It is essential for an MNE to develop a global pool of international managers and rotate them across foreign locations to facilitate transfer of best practices and mentoring of future global managers. As learning is culture bound, the global managers should be sensitive to cultural differences and adept at managing them.

Training HCNs can be very expensive and a long-drawn process. The return on this investment depends on the ability of the MNE to retain them with appropriate reward mechanisms. Information and communication technologies now provide a cost-effective alternative to train a large number of multinational workforces.

Rewards

There are two commonly used approaches in international compensation systems—the going-rate approach where pay is tied to host-country norms and the balance-sheet approach which ties pay to home-country norms. In both approaches, additional expenses, such as housing and extra taxes, are reimbursed with top-up allowances. The going-rate approach aims at equity between people working in the same location but can have devastating effects in a financially unattractive location. The balance-sheet approach is more practical in recognizing that an employee's current home pay and emoluments need to be protected and augmented to compensate for hardship and additional expenses. The objective is to keep the employee financially 'whole' with no loss from present emoluments. However, the company and the employee can interpret the concept of 'whole' differently.[32] For instance, an employee who lives in a spacious home in the US may not consider an apartment in Tokyo as a way of maintaining the whole in housing despite being aware of the high cost of real estate in Japan.

A modified balance-sheet approach features many variations, 'encompassing common salary structures, fixed-percentage tax withholding, or the blending of certain local elements, such as housing or spendable income, with home country benefits or taxes'.[24] Some of the new approaches to international compensation are using a variety of stock ownership schemes as equity compensation; pegging compensation for all foreign assignments to uniform US dollar structure irrespective of location; and a regional approach to compensation.[24]

In comparison with domestic compensation, the issues of equity and fairness are far more complicated in international compensation and are more emotional than rational. MNEs must 'balance local country taxation and social welfare structures, indigenous pay delivery mechanisms and social and cultural expectations against organizational needs for cross-country equity and fairness'.[33]

More importantly, the MNEs need to address the basic motivation of an expatriate in accepting foreign assignments, i.e., how the assignment is going to boost the employee's career prospects. While expatriates realize that no company can guarantee what will happen after two-three years, they look for signals, such as how much the international experience is valued in promotions and what happened to those who went on such assignments in the past. It is more of a psychological contract where the terms are implied. 'It would add weight if the career path of other employees who were peers prior to the expatriate employee accepting an international assignment could also be tracked and compared in terms of advancement and promotion over a set period of time. In this way, companies could do more than promise that international assignments will result in career enhancement; they could prove it'.[32] Such an approach takes the emphasis away from contentious issues in compensation. Thus, international compensation and rewards have to be seen in a holistic perspective and address broader issues of career management.

With regard to convergence–divergence in international compensation practices, a ten-country international survey revealed that the current state of practice is relatively low with regard to pay incentives and high with regard to benefits. While, as expected, collectivistic countries emphasized pay based on long-term results and individualistic countries emphasized short-term results, surprisingly, seniority-based pay decisions did not figure prominently in any culture.[34] With regard to pay-for-performance and pay incentives, many trends are visible.[35] Some MNEs (such as Unilever) have made pay-for-performance and incentives part of their global pay philosophy whereas some others (such as Motorola) have limited them to global managers. 'The evidence suggests that the alignment of pay and results on a global basis is still in the early stages'.[35]

Industrial Relations

Depending on the history, legal framework, power relations, and ideologies of management and trade unions in each country, collective bargaining takes place at different levels, such as enterprise, industry, craft and conglomerate (more than one industry) levels. Therefore, MNEs have to adopt specific employment relations strategies to suit local conditions. However, they also face pressure for standardization in terms of productivity and equity, at least within regions and industries, if not internationally. In MNEs where one unit is interdependent on another for raw materials, a coordinated labour relations policy becomes vital for global production strategy.[2]

American MNEs are said to exercise more centralized control, are averse to trade unions and prefer to deal with labour issues at the enterprise level than European MNEs. Japanese MNEs believe in informal centralized coordination of their foreign operations through an international network of Japanese expatriate managers but the coordination is not to impose policies from the top but to facilitate local adaptation.[36] Thus, 'nationality of ownership is a significant determinant of MNE behaviour'.[36] Realizing that they need sufficient freedom to determine employment level, pay and productivity to maintain their global competitiveness, MNEs today increasingly scrutinize local labour laws and political and social attitude before bringing in direct foreign investment.

Accordingly, they negotiate and lobby with governments and trade unions to get a better deal. They also try to minimize the fallout of any possible adverse employee relations situation, such as strikes, by setting up production facilities in different countries / regions and making arrangements for alternative sources of supply.

In response, trade unions around the world have attempted to form international coalitions and alliances with some success. The International Labour Organization (ILO) has established certain voluntary guidelines in employment relationships to be respected by all nations, within the framework of local laws: 'freedom of association, the right to organize and collectively bargain, abolition of forced labour, and non-discrimination in employment'.[2] The European Union has established its own social charter that is legally binding on all EU nations and aims to improve health and safety in the workplace through employee consultation and provide equality of opportunity for men and women; however, it excludes matters of pay, the right of association, and the right to strike or to lock out.[2] Further, according to the European Work Councils (EWC) directive, multinationals with at least 1,000 employees, having 100 or more employees each in two member states, should establish EWCs to 'enhance employee's rights to information and consultation in general, and provide rights to information regarding international corporate decisions that would significantly affect workers' interests'.[2]

Managing Diversity

People have different degrees of tolerance towards others from different cultural / ethnic / religious backgrounds. Their tolerance level depends on the breadth and depth of their exposure to and experience with cultural diversity as a society, community group and as individuals. The concept of multi-culturalism goes hand in hand with globalization;

however, those who welcome globalization for economic benefits do not necessarily and wholeheartedly accept the benefits and challenges associated with a multi-cultural society. The increased acceptance of migrants and foreign labour in developed countries is attributable to a variety of reasons, such as falling birth rate, ageing population, shortage of skilled labour, social responsibility towards refugees and sometimes, a genuine desire to be an inclusive society. However, all multi-cultural societies experience in-built tensions.

While governments, political parties and community groups play their role in managing the challenges of a multi-cultural society, organizations, whether local or international, need to find their own solutions in managing diversity. Diversity encompasses a wide range of differences based on gender, age, disability, marital status, sexual orientation, ethnicity, religion etc. While many developed countries have separate EEO laws to prohibit employment discrimination and offer incentives to promote affirmative action for upliftment of women, minorities and other disadvantaged groups, it is the organizational culture and management philosophy that underpin the success of any diversity management initiative.

Today, most CEOs recognize that management of diversity is one of the most important challenges of the 21st century. At the root of any complex, potentially volatile issue 'we are likely to find communication failures and cultural misunderstandings that prevent the parties from framing the problem in a common way, and thus, make it impossible to deal with the problem constructively'.[37] In an international context, global managers need to develop a deep and genuine belief in understanding and empathizing with cultural differences and consciously attempt not to let their managerial decisions be influenced by stereotypes, prejudices and ethnocentric attitudes. 'Success in building cross-border networks of relationships which are the core veins of effective global organizations is dependent on understanding and valuing cultural diversity'.[23] Any superficial approach to managing diversity will only breed racism in hidden forms and deprive the organization of the benefit of a diverse workforce.

Conclusion

The evidence that 'cultural differences can influence work values, motivation and job attitudes' is now so irrefutable that no management theory can ignore the role played by culture as an important variable and no MNE can underplay its importance in corporate decision-making.[38] However, in understanding the nature and influence of national culture, most studies resort to convenience sampling and focus on US-based themes by trying to translate concepts that, in some cases, have no conceptually equivalent meaning in other cultures. They continue to ignore themes that are important in some cultures but have not been recognized, appreciated and understood in Western cultures.[32] For example, very few studies focus on why team orientation is in-built in the Japanese psyche or saving face is so important in Chinese societies or how Buddhist values, such as karma and rebirth, induce people to focus on the long-term returns and reduce the attraction of material rewards.

Those who tend to believe that globalization of economies would ultimately lead to convergence of different cultures, ignore the deep impact of culture, particularly in high-context societies. An important lesson from Eastern culture is the need to maintain harmony between family and work life since both are inseparable. An individualistic culture may produce dramatic, short-term results but eventually upset the balance in the family, society and the environment. However, the experience of Western countries proves that low power distance, freedom to think and act independently and the ability to explore uncertainty with confidence lead to economic success. While wholesale import of work values and practices of another culture is bound to fail, a balanced approach calls for understanding and appreciating different cultures and deriving the best from all within the tolerable limits of one's own culture.

Agenda for Managerial Action

Points to Ponder . . .	. . . Steps to Consider
Despite the rapid pace of globalization, sensitivity and adaptability to differences in national culture are crucial to the success of any MNE.	The complexity of people management is greater in an MNE as it deals with different types of international business strategies, employee staffing and work ethics. Standardizing organizational culture and HRM policies across countries leads to misunderstanding in cross-cultural communication and dilutes the effectiveness of HRM. However, national culture does not operate in a vacuum and its analysis needs to be grounded in the specific context in which it is applied.
Cross-cultural research throws light on different dimensions of national culture in the context of a work organization.	Cultural dimensions clearly indicate that many of the strategic HRM concepts, such as empowerment, self-management, flat organizational structure, flexible employment options, individual performance-based rewards and incentives, de-emphasizing seniority and status symbols in favour of meritocracy may lead to demotivation in collectivist cultures, if introduced suddenly without time for acclimatization.
IHRM is more complex and contingent than domestic HRM.	Too many divergent factors influence IHRM at the macro and micro levels. Yet, HR needs to resolve the conflict between standardizing HR practices to drive a common organizational

	culture and at the same time, be responsive to local laws, customs, and employee and community expectations.
In IHRM, the international dimensions and implications of each practice area need to be carefully considered.	Some best practices in IHRM include: • Considering international staffing as a strategic learning and development initiative in exposing managers to global operations • Expatriate selection, performance assessment and rewards are based on the 'whole', i.e., to take into account soft skills as much as technical skills, family considerations, situational impact on performance and maintaining overall financial status • Repatriate retention based on demonstrable career opportunities
Diversity management is more a matter of conviction, spirit and values than legal considerations.	Diversity management initiatives need to be strategically driven by the management and aim at changing the mindset of people and not just surface-level changes. They need to systematically search and eliminate stereotypes and prejudices hidden within policies and processes.

Case Scenario: Suji–INS KK

Mike Flynn, president of the international division of Information Network Services Corporation (INS), was undecided as to how he could best approach several delicate issues with his Japanese joint venture partner, during his first trip to Japan after taking over as president. INS was a major provider of value-added network (VAN) services in the USA. International operations accounted for roughly 25 per cent of the company's total sales, and the company's top management felt that international markets represented a major field for future growth.

The company had a joint venture in Japan with Suji Corporation, a leading Japanese telecommunications equipment manufacturer, since 1987. Suji owned two-thirds of the joint venture and INS one-third of its equity, as Japanese law limited foreign ownership in telecom services vendors to one-third equity partnership. The agreement also stipulated that both companies would have equal representation on the board of directors, with four people each, and that Suji would provide the entire personnel for the joint venture from top management down to production workers. The companies also agreed that the Japanese partner would nominate the president of the joint venture, subject to approval of the board, and the US company would nominate a person for the position of executive vice-president. INS also agreed to supply, for the time being, a technical director on a full-time basis.

In the fall of 1988, the Japanese president of the joint venture company died suddenly and Suji, in accordance with the agreement, nominated Kenzo Satoh as the new president. Flynn, when he heard Satoh's qualifications, concluded that he was not suitable for the presidency of the joint venture. Satoh had joined Suji 40 years ago upon graduation and during the previous 15 years, had served almost exclusively in staff functions. Flynn was concerned that Satoh had virtually no line experience. He became even more disturbed when he received the following letter from Jack Rose, the executive vice-president of the joint venture company, about how Satoh was selected:

> I have learned the manner in which Mr Satoh was chosen for the position. I must point out at the outset that what I am going to describe, though shocking by our standards, is quite commonplace among Japanese corporations: in fact, it is well-accepted.
>
> As you are well aware, a Japanese corporation is well known for its paternalistic practices in return for lifetime service, and they do assume obligations, particularly for those in middle management or above, even after they reach their

compulsory retirement age (which is typically around 57), not just during their working careers. Appropriate positions are generally found for them in the company's subsidiaries, related firms, or major suppliers where they can occupy positions commensurate to their last position in the parent corporation for several more years.

A similar practice applies to the board members. Directorships being highly coveted positions, there must be regular turnover to allow others to be promoted to board membership. As a result, all but a fortunate few who are earmarked as heir apparent to the chair, presidency or executive vice-presidency must be 'retired'. Since most of these executives are in their late fifties or early sixties, they do not yet wish to retire. Thus, it is common practice among Japanese corporations to transfer senior executives of the parent company to the chair or presidency of the company subsidiaries or affiliated companies. Typically, these people will serve in these positions for several years before they retire. Suji had a dozen subsidiaries, and you might be interested in knowing that every top management position is held by those who have retired from the parent corporation. Such a system is well routinized.

Our friend Mr Satoh is clearly not the calibre that would qualify for further advancement in the parent company, and his position must be vacated for another person. Suji's top management must have decided that the presidency of the joint venture was the appropriate position for him to 'retire' into. These are the circumstances under which Mr Satoh has been nominated for our consideration.

When he read this letter, Flynn instructed Rose to indicate to the Suji management that Satoh was not acceptable. In his response to Rose, Flynn suggested as president, Takao Toray, marketing manager of the joint venture. Flynn was much impressed by Toray when he visited the INS headquarters in the US, some time ago. Flynn was aware that Toray, at fifty years, was a little too young to be acceptable to Suji. In pressing Toray's nomination, Flynn was trying to question the wisdom of adopting Japanese managerial practices blindly in the joint venture. Flynn had also noticed in the past that the joint venture had been consistently slow in making decisions because it engaged in a typical Japanese group-oriented and consensus-based process. He also learned that control and reporting systems were virtually non-existent. Flynn felt that INS's sophisticated planning and control system should be introduced in the joint venture. He recalled from his Canadian experience that US management practices, if judiciously applied, could give US subsidiaries abroad a significant competitive advantage over local firms. Flynn also felt that by pushing Toray's nomination, it would help INS gain stronger influence over the management of the joint venture.

Suji's reaction to Flynn's proposal was swift; they rejected it totally. Suji management was polite, but made it clear that they considered Flynn unfair in judging Mr Satoh's suitability for the presidency without even having met him. Suji management also told Flynn, through Rose, that the selection of Toray was totally unacceptable because in the Japanese corporate system such a promotion was unheard of and would be detrimental not only to the joint venture but to Toray himself, who was believed to have a promising future in the company.

Flynn was surprised at the tone of Suji's response. He wondered whether it would be possible to establish an effective relationship with the Japanese company. Flynn felt that Suji seemed determined to run the venture on their own terms. He was left wondering how best to approach and organize his meetings and discussions with Mr Ohtomo, executive vice-president of Suji Corporation, during his forthcoming visit to Japan. While practising with chopsticks, he returned to reading *Theory Z*, a popular book on Japanese management, in the hope of gaining insight for the days ahead.

Source: Excerpts reprinted with permission from Davidson, W.H., *Suji-INS KK*. Copyright © Davidson, W.H. All rights reserved.

References

1. **Hill, C.** (1998) *International business: Competing in the global marketplace,* Irwin/McGraw-Hill: Boston.
2. **Dowling, P.J., Welch, D.E.** and **Schuler, R.S.** (1999) *International Human Resource Management: Managing people in a multinational context,* South-Western: Cincinnati, OH.
3. **Rowley, C.** (1998) 'Introduction: Comparisons and perspectives on HRM in the Asia Pacific'. In Rowley, C. (Ed.) *Human Resource Management in the Asia Pacific Region: Convergence questioned,* Frank Cass: London.
4. **Hall, E.T.** and **Hall, M.R.** (2001) 'Key concepts: Underlying structures of culture'. In Albrecht, M.H. (Ed.) *International HRM: Managing diversity in the workplace,* Cornwall: Blackwell Publishers.
5. **Von Glinow, M.A., Drost, E.A.** and **Teagarden, M.B.** (2002) 'Converging on IHRM best practices: Lessons learned from a globally distributed consortium on theory and practice'. *Asia Pacific Journal of Human Resources,* Vol 40 No 1, pp. 146–66.
6. **Milkovich, G.T.** and **Bloom, M.** (1998) 'Rethinking international compensation'. *Compensation and Benefits Review,* January–February.
7. **Lane, H.W., DiStefano, J.J.** and **Maznevski, M.L.** (2000) *International management behaviour,* Blackwell: Oxford, UK.
8. **Hofstede, G.** (2001) *Culture's consequences: Comparing values, behaviours, institutions and organizations across nations,* Sage: Thousand Oaks, CA.
9. **Franke, R.H., Hofstede, G.** and **Bond, M.H.** (2002) 'National culture and economic growth'. In Gannon, M.J. and Newman, K.L. (Eds.) *The Blackwell handbook of cross-cultural management,* Blackwell: Oxford.
10. **Earley, P.C.** (1989) 'Social loafing and collectivism: A comparison of the United States and the People's Republic of China'. *Administrative Science Quarterly,* Vol 34 No 4, pp. 565–81.
11. **Almeida, P., Grant, R.** and **Phene, A.** (2002) 'Knowledge acquisition through alliances: Opportunities and challenges'. In Gannon, M.J. and Newman, K.L. (Eds.) *The Blackwell handbook of cross-cultural management,* Blackwell: Oxford.

12. **Hofstede, G.** (1993) 'Cultural constraints in management theories'. *Academy of Management Executive*, Vol 7 No 1, pp. 81–94.
13. **Mroczkowski, T.** and **Hanaoka, M.** (1997) 'Effective rightsizing strategies in Japan and America: Is there a convergence of employment practices?' *Academy of Management Executive*, Vol 11 No 2.
14. **Holden, R.** (2001) 'Managing people's values and perceptions in multi-cultural organisations'. *Employee Relations*, Vol 23 No 6, pp. 614–26.
15. **Lawrence, P.** (1992) 'Management development in Germany'. In Tyson, S., Lawrence, P., Poirson, P., Manzolini, L. and Vincente, C.S. (Eds.) *Human resource management in Europe: Strategic issues and cases*, Kogan Page: London.
16. **McEvoy, G.M.** and **Parker, B.** (2000) 'The contemporary international assignment: A look at the options'. In Mendenhall, M. and Oddou, G. (Eds.) *Readings and cases in international human resource management*, South-Western: Ontario.
17. **Stroh, L.K., Grasshoff, S., Rude, A.** and **Carter, N.** (2001) 'Integrated HR systems help develop global leaders'. In Albrecht, M.H. (Ed.) *International HRM: Managing diversity in the workplace*, Cornwall: Blackwell Publishers.
18. **Pil, F.K.** and **Mac Duffie, J.P.** (1999) 'What makes transplants thrive: Managing the transfer of "best practice" at Japanese auto plants in North America'. *Journal of World Business*, Vol 34 No 4, pp. 372–92.
19. **Bird, A.** and **Beechler, S.** (2000) 'The link between business strategy and international human resource management practices'. In Mendenhall, M. and Oddou, G. (Eds.) *Readings and cases in international human resource management*, South-Western: Ontario.
20. **Jackson, T.** (2002) 'The management of people across cultures: Valuing people differently'. *Human Resource Management*, Vol 41 No 4, pp. 455–75.
21. **Schuler, R.S., Budhwar, P.S.** and **Florkowski, G.W.** (2002) 'International human resource management: Review and critique.' *International Journal of Management Reviews*, Vol 4 No 1, pp. 41–70.
22. **Johnson, J.L.** and **Cullen, J.B.** (2002) 'Trust in cross-cultural relationships'. In Gannon, M.J. and Newman, K.L. (Eds.)

The Blackwell handbook of cross-cultural management, Blackwell: Oxford.

23. **Pucik, V.** (1997) 'Human resources in the future: An obstacle or a champion of globalisation?' *Human Resource Management*, Vol 36 No 1, pp. 163–67.

24. **Dwyer, T.D.** (1999) 'Trends in global compensation'. *Compensation and Benefits Review*, July / August, 1999.

25. **Selmer, J.** (2002) 'Coping strategies applied by western vs overseas Chinese business expatriates in China'. *International Journal of Human Resource Management*, Vol 13 No 1, pp. 19–34.

26. **Mendenhall, M.E., Kuhlmann, T.M., Stahl, G.K.** and **Osland, J.S.** (2002) 'Employee development and expatriate assignments'. In Gannon, M.J. and Newman, K.L. (Eds.) *The Blackwell handbook of cross-cultural management*, Blackwell: Oxford.

27. **Solomon, C.M.** (1995) 'Repatriation: Up, down or out?' *Personnel Journal*, Vol 74 No 1, pp. 28–37.

28. **Brewster, C.** (2002) 'Human resource practices in multinational companies'. In Gannon, M.J. and Newman K.L. (Eds.) *The Blackwell handbook of cross-cultural management*, Blackwell: Oxford.

29. **Milliman, J., Nason, S., Zhu, C.** and **De Ceri, H.** (2002) 'An exploratory assessment of the purposes of performance appraisals in North and Central America and the Pacific Rim'. *Asia Pacific Journal of Human Resources*, Vol 40 No 1, pp.105–22.

30. **Oddou, G.** and **Mendenhall, M.** (2000) 'Expatriate performance appraisal: Problems and solutions'. In Mendenhall, M. and Oddou, G. (Eds.) *Readings and cases in international human resource management*, South-Western: Ontario.

31. **Mendenhall, M.E., Dunbar, E.** and **Oddou, G.R.** (1987) 'Expatriate selection, training and career pathing: A review and critique'. *Human Resource Management*, Vol 2b No 3.

32. **Oemig, D.R.** (1999) 'When you say, "we'll keep you whole", do you mean it?' *Compensation and Benefits Review*, Vol 31 No 4, pp. 40–47.

33. **Thompson, M.A.** and **Yurkutat, J.** (1999) 'Rewards in a global context'. *Compensation and Benefits Review*, July / August, 1999.

34. **Lowe, K.B., Milliman, J., De Ceri, H.** and **Dowling, P.J.** (2002) 'International compensation practices: A ten-country

comparative analysis'. *Asia Pacific Journal of Human Resources*, Vol 40 No 1, pp. 55–80.

35. **Coleman, N.K.** (1999) 'Global pay and results'. In Risher, H. (Ed.) *Aligning pay and results*, AMACOM: NY.
36. **Ferner, A.** (1997) 'Country of origin effects and HRM in multinational companies'. *Human Resource Management Journal*, Vol 7 No 1, pp. 19–37.
37. **Schein, E.H.** (1993) 'On dialogue, culture and organisational learning'. *Organisational Dynamics*, Vol 22 No 2, pp. 40–51.
38. **Steers, R.M.** and **Sanchez-Runde, C.J.** (2002) 'Culture, motivation and work behaviour'. In Gannon, M.J. and Newman, K.L. (Eds.) *The Blackwell handbook of cross-cultural management*, Blackwell: Oxford.

10

Lessons from Learning Organizations

This concluding chapter brings together the lessons learned from learning organizations in harnessing people's intellectual power for the benefit of the individuals, groups, organizations and the wider community. To reiterate, the main objective of the book is to strategically position the practice of HRM in the knowledge economy. The knowledge management body of literature and practice appear to be skewed in favour of exploiting explicit knowledge through information technologies. The fuzzy nature of people management and its uncertain outcome make it a daunting task for most organizations to tap the tacit knowledge in people. However, sooner or later organizations have to accept the challenge because technology, no matter how brilliant it is, can only provide partial protection from hyper-competition and that too only for some time before competitors catch up with it. Further, technology does not like ambiguity, uncertainty and paradoxes. It needs a black and white picture. However, today's workplaces are anything other than black and white.

Managing Paradoxes

The introductory chapter began by saying that management is a balancing act. The subsequent chapters have raised more questions than answers in their quest to find a better way to manage the various aspects of employment relationship. It is because there is no one right way to manage people. Even those organizations that apply the same set of management principles differ remarkably in their understanding, practice and outcome of those principles. That is why managing people is a competitive advantage that is difficult to imitate.

Managers are faced with an endless array of conflicting choices in managing people and their work:

□ The difficulty in defining and measuring knowledge work and knowledge workers, such as acquiring knowledge as an end in itself or acquiring it for commercial exploitation, and the danger of creating and glorifying a new class of knowledge workers.

□ 'Paradoxes inherent in multiple HR roles', i.e., strategic partner vs. employee champion (when strategic focus may lead to HR taking its eyes and ears off the employee concerns on the ground) and change agents vs. administrative experts (in trying to balance stability and change).[1]

□ The difficulty in measuring the effectiveness of HR in a learning organization, particularly in areas that are crucial but are very hard to account for, such as the social architecture or the communities of practices, informal learning, and mentoring.

□ The conflict between acquiring speed and agility by being lean and mean in a globally competitive and uncertain environment and the necessity of a long-term relationship with knowledge workers to build trust and passion for organizational goals for a common future.

□ The tension between autonomy and structure: freedom induces creativity that may evaporate without a structure but a rigid structure may become a stumbling block in generating new ideas.

- The need to create an organizational culture with shared beliefs, values and competencies without encouraging a herd mentality and trampling on the uniqueness of individual personality and creativity.

- The need for different teams and projects to be best in whatever they do by being both competitive and collaborative at the same time. Organizations that choose team structure but measure and reward individual performance will go nowhere.

- The competing pressure on MNEs in dealing with IHRM issues: the internal pressure for standardizing HRM practices with business strategy and the external pressure to localize HRM practices with the environment.

Thus, the book raises more questions than it answers. In so doing, it highlights the complexity of managing people and the futility of searching for universal solutions in the new economy that is inherently complex, uncertain and full of paradoxes. There is no use in wishing away paradoxes in the new economy. They are here to stay and grow. 'Chaos, complexity and contradictions are the new corporate reality'.[2] We have no alternative but to accept them as a fact of life and learn to deal with them.

The challenge is how each organization finds its own balance in managing conflicting challenges. Successful learning organizations face this challenge by adopting the principles of holographic design, i.e., to build the whole into parts, deploying a variety of functions, skills and design, matching internal complexity to that of the environment, defining no more than is absolutely necessary and endlessly scanning and adapting to the environment.[3]

The principles of managing paradox include stability in the fundamental aspects of the organization (such as culture, community, vision, strategy and core competencies), building a global organization around individual employees, focusing on culture (that is driven by leadership, vision, performance, structure and people), purposeful leadership, and tearing down to build anew so that less is more.[2]

Roadmap for Managing People in the New Economy

With the realization that 'change has changed' and that change is the only constant phenomenon in the 21st-century economy, let us revisit the key themes from the preceding chapters.

Navigating the Contours of Knowledge Management

- □ Create a dedicated cell in the organization that is well supported and well resourced to advocate and advance the cause of knowledge management initiatives at the macro and micro levels.
- □ Define and drive knowledge management primarily in terms of people and their social context—their cultural values, attitudes, competencies, commitment and community spirit.
- □ Enlist the support of employees at all levels as champions of the cause of knowledge management.
- □ Comprehensively and collaboratively leverage both IT and HR interventions to tap explicit and tacit knowledge.
- □ Successfully deal with the dual nature of 'knowledge as knowing' and 'knowledge as commodity'.

Embedding Strategic HR into Managerial Ethos and Practice

- □ Top management should give the HR function appropriate recognition and status in strategic decision-making and implementation.

- Ensure that HR functionaries are competent enough to discharge their varied and often, conflicting roles of becoming a strategic partner, administrative expert, employee champion and change agent.[1]
- Treat people management as one of the core responsibilities and accountabilities of all the managers in the organization and incorporate people management competency as a key success factor in their recruitment, performance assessment, training and reward determination.
- Make managers realize that employee satisfaction leads to customer and shareholder satisfaction and therefore, are held responsible for employee morale.
- One of the key contributions of HR to knowledge management is to nurture and harness the social energy of knowledge workers in the form of communities of practices within and across organizational boundaries.
- HR policies address the unique contribution and needs of different types of workers (such as core, contract and casual) in active collaboration with external partners.
- Diversity management is one of the key responsibilities of the HR function in the new economy, aimed at tapping the largely hidden potential of older workers, women and migrants.

Building People-centric Culture

- The management is committed to building enduring relationship with employees, customers and shareholders based on trust, fairness and ethics.
- The management demonstrates its trustworthiness, fairness and commitment to ethics through
    - longer-term outlook and philosophy on management in general,
    - treating people management as a long-term investment and not as costs to be reduced or assets to be controlled,

- transparent flow of information,
- reasonable parity between executive and non-executive compensation and other employment matters,
- charting a common future with employees through employee involvement, equitable sharing of wealth and instilling a sense of stability in employment and work organization, and
- managing stakeholder expectations by under-promising and overdelivering.

Institutionalizing Learning to Learn

- At the heart of a learning organization lies the constant endeavour to shape and reshape mental models to suit the changing environment.
- There is no standard way to become a learning organization. Each organization has to experiment, learn from failures and chart its own path.
- Creative ideas need space to grow, support to flourish and rewards to be reinforced. Cynicism and bureaucracy kill creativity. Creative people need a community where there is an intense passion to achieve a clear, common goal; diversity is valued and celebrated; sharing and mentoring are natural; and experimentation is a way of life.
- The systems thinking approach requires that each part of the organization should reflect the whole. While engaged in a specific activity, each part should not take its eye off the main and common goal. Together, the parts should detect and act on early warning signals.
- A learning organization values productive failure more than unproductive success.
- Learning is mostly informal and on the job. Therefore, more than formal training activities, it thrives in a culture of natural curiosity, sharing and mentoring. It

needs to be navigated by committed leaders and nurtured in a conducive organizational environment.

Attracting Talent

□ The competency framework is grounded in the realization that today's world of work is radically different from that in the industrial economy and so is the profile of the workforce needed. The focus is on the behaviours and characteristics that distinguish a superior performer than the rest. The challenge is how to measure desired competencies and attract those who have them.

□ Actions speak louder than policy in creating the image of a compelling place to work. A company that genuinely embraces diversity, is socially responsible, provides learning and development opportunities, treats potential employees like customers and drives the recruitment process with seriousness and commitment, races ahead of competitors in attracting talent.

□ Selecting the right talent is a painstaking process with uncertain outcome as no standard formula exists. Selection managers need to develop their intuitive skills based on distilled experience.

Retaining Talent

□ The critical success factor in retaining employees is the alignment between organizational and individual goals. 'Help us but help yourself' attitude to career management erodes trust and confidence in employees.

□ The key expectation of knowledge workers today is to attain 'employability' by working on challenging assignments that give them the much-sought-after skills, knowledge and competencies.

□ Holding managers responsible and accountable for employee morale, sculpting the job to suit individual personality, nurturing social communities in the workplace and honouring the psychological contract are some of the ways to retain key people.

Creating a Performance Enhancement System

□ Instead of becoming a catalyst to improve performance, the appraisal system has degenerated into a malignant tumour and is in urgent need of a radical surgery. Selection of wrong measures that ignore situational factors has led to the job driving the person. Emphasis on evaluation over development has turned it into a fire-fighting exercise stifling creativity and innovation.

□ A good system displays a balanced approach that takes into account both input and output and is frequently measured by all the key stakeholders; involves employees in its design, execution and review; and trains managers to be effective coaches in giving feedback and providing developmental opportunities.

Creating a Holistic Reward System

□ The New Pay concepts reflect the need for workplace flexibility required in the new economy. From broadening the base pay to linking pay-for-performance, the focus is on empowerment and gain sharing.

□ Distributive justice is at the heart of pay satisfaction.

□ Pay-for-performance can succeed only when performance measures are clearly understood, measured and accepted. It also needs to resolve the tension between individual performance and teamwork.

□ Recognition rewards play a key role in boosting the morale and motivation of knowledge workers. Combined with competitive and equitable remuneration, rewards can be a powerful engine of motivation.

Glocalizing People Management

◻ Management concepts and practices are culture bound. HRM should therefore be grounded in local realities of the environment and organization.

◻ Strong organizational culture may lead to some convergence in international HRM practices facilitating transfer of best practices but lack of sensitivity to cross-cultural differences can be counter-productive.

◻ The ethical standing of an MNE is under more scrutiny in a foreign land and any compromise will have long-lasting impact on its future prospects.

Nature—The Best Teacher

Human beings coexisted with nature for thousands of years before trying to break apart to control and exploit nature, particularly during the agricultural and industrial economies. Now as they stand at the doorstep of 21st century, they find themselves at a crossroads. As Senge (1994) explains,

> We have learned how to influence our environment, to the extent that our very survival as a species is now at risk. We have evolved our ego, to the extent that our personal happiness is somehow separate from the happiness of those around us. We have separated ourselves from nature, to the extent that we have lost our sense of awe at the mystery of life, and our sense of belonging to something larger than ourselves.[4]

Organizations are living organisms. The issues and challenges they face in the new economy appear to be trivial compared to those faced by different species of plants and animals in their natural habitat over thousands of years. Documentaries on how penguins face freezing cold and gusty winds in Antarctica or how plants grow on sand-covered land in Fraser Island, Australia make fascinating stories of how organisms adopt and adapt to their environment. It is inconceivable to think of any animal or plant in isolation of the environment in which they live. Therein lie the key lessons for a learning organization, i.e., the 'primacy of the whole' (and not parts) and the 'community nature of the self'.[5]

Ancient civilizations, such as India, have long stressed the need for learning from natural elements, such as earth, water, air, fire and sky, in facing human challenges, conflicts and paradoxes. Organization theory can also be compared to biology 'in which the distinctions and relations among molecules, cells, complex organisms, species and ecology are paralleled in those between individuals, groups, organizations, populations (species) of organizations, and their social ecology'.[3] However, organizations have the strategic choice to influence the environment by either transforming themselves or creating 'resource niches that never existed before'. However, in trying to gain an upper hand over the environment, they should not disturb and destroy its very essence.

Thus, as Kenneth Boulding has put it, evolution involves the 'survival of the fitting' not just the survival of the fittest, particularly when competition between organizations is often accompanied by collaboration.[3] Kiuchi and Shireman demonstrate how by gleaning information from nature—the very system it once sought to conquer—business can learn to be ecologically responsible and economically profitable. 'They highlight the lessons from nature, such as overcoming limits, creating a niche, coexistence, waste management, and doing more with less.

Senge concludes:

There is a ferment in management worldwide. It is being driven not just by global competitiveness, but by the growing awareness that the keys to success in the twenty-first century may be quite different from the keys to success in the nineteenth and twentieth centuries.

. . . The management ferment is also driven by an even deeper realization: there must be an antidote to fragmentation. The politics, games playing, and internal competition that characterize modern organizations sap people's energy and commitment, and can never be a foundation for a great enterprise or a sustainable society.[4]

Closing the Curtain

People management is complex and more so in the new economy. But the fact is that it is the key to survive and prosper in the 21st century. Despite the realization that people are central to a service-driven knowledge economy, many organizations have done little, if anything at all, to harness their people's potential. As Bartlett and Ghoshal (2002) describe,

. . . a decade of organizational delayering, destaffing, restructuring and reengineering has produced employees who are more exhausted than empowered, more cynical than self-renewing. Worse still, in many companies only marginal managerial attention—if that—is focused on the problems of employee capability and motivation. Somewhere between theory and practice, precious human capital is being misused, wasted or lost. . . Very few top executives have been able to transform themselves from being analytically driven strategy directors to people-oriented strategy framers. Yet for a traditional company to make the transition into the New Economy, that transformation is vital.[7]

The transformation requires that the management pays utmost attention to development of people by moving away from its obsession with capital-based criteria, in judging the success of business. The traditional focus on management by strict measurement, particularly the conventional accounting principles that focus on the short term, can be harmful to the intellectual health of the organization.

As discussed in the previous chapters, successful people management requires that the organization practice a sound management philosophy that respects human dignity and diversity, is committed to the growth of people, believes in the value of people's contribution and involves them in decision-making, and shares its wealth equitably and fairly. Only such a philosophy can truly transform the nature and quality of key such HR functions, as recruitment, learning, performance management and development, remuneration and rewards, industrial relations, and career management. Without the strong foundation of people management philosophy that is practised as a way of life, no HR management concept can ever have an enduring impact on the bottomline.

In their book, Hidden value—*How great companies achieve extraordinary results with ordinary people*, O'Reilly and Pfeffer describe how successful companies, such as Southwest Airlines, Cisco Systems, and SAS Institute, practise values-based view of strategy where strategy formulation begins with defining the fundamental values and beliefs of and about their people and used to design management practices, build core capabilities and invent a strategy that is consistent with the values.[8] Their people-centred practices express their core values and their managers ensure that values remain alive and kicking all the time, every time, no matter whether the business is in boom or bust cycle.

The strategic focus on people in the knowledge economy dramatically increases the expectations of HR managers. They have long been used to a 'operationally reactive' role and now find it challenging to shift to a 'strategically proactive' role of nurturing an intellectually stimulating environment in the workplace.[9] Today's employment relationship is as much decided by the knowledge workers as by the company's HR policies, if not more. Instead of asking, 'tell us, why we should recruit, train or reward you', HR managers need to answer 'how we can offer mutually satisfying employment terms and conditions so that you find it worthwhile to stay and grow with us'.

HR managers also need to overhaul the tools of their trade: HR planning and recruitment based on narrowly defined job analysis, description and specifications that ignore the changing world of work; performance assessment based on skills and seniority rather than competencies and customer satisfaction; training for immediate needs at scheduled intervals rather than lifelong learning on the job with the help of mentors; remuneration based on monetary incentives with little emphasis on the larger work environment; and career management that suited organizational culture and convenience more than employee needs and expectations.

Thus, as the industrial economy transforms itself into a knowledge economy, the people management function needs a similar transformation to be able to fulfil its critical role in leveraging intellectual capital as a sustainable competitive advantage. The success of this endeavour depends on the commitment of all managers in the company—from the frontline to the top—in forging endurable collaboration with people—within and outside of organizational boundaries.

References

1. **Ulrich, D.** (1997) *Human resource champions: The next agendas for adding value and delivering results*, Harvard Business School Press: Cambridge, MA.
2. **The Price Waterhouse Change Integration Team** (1996) *The paradox principles*, Irwin: Chicago.
3. **Morgan, G.** (1997) *Images of Organization*, Sage: Thousand Oaks, CA.
4. **Senge, P.** (1994) 'From the foreword to the Chinese edition of *The Fifth Discipline*', In Senge, P., Kleiner, A., Ross, R.B. and Smith, B.J., *The fifth discipline fieldbook: Strategies and tools for building a learning organization*, New York: Doubleday.
5. **Senge, P., Kleiner, A., Ross, R.B.** and **Smith, B.J.** (1994) *The fifth discipline fieldbook: Strategies and tools for building a learning organization*.
6. **Kiuchi, T.** and **Shireman, B.** (2002) *What we learned in the rainforest: Business lessons from nature*, Global Futures: San Francisco, CA.

7. **Bartlett, C.A.** and **Ghoshal, S.** (2002) 'Building competitive advantage through people'. *MIT Sloan Management Review*, Vol 43 No 2, pp. 34–41.
8. **O'Reilly, C.A.** and **Pfeffer, J.** (2000) *Hidden value—How great companies achieve extraordinary results with ordinary people*, Harvard Business School Press: Boston, MA.
9. **Brockbank, W.** (1999) 'If HR were strategically proactive: Present and future directions in HR's contribution to competitive advantage'. *Human Resource Management*, Vol 38 No 4, pp. 337–52.

Recommended Reading

The following is a selection of books that reflect the state of the art in people management. This book has been greatly influenced by the ideas and experiences of the authors mentioned below; however, readers would be able to fully understand and appreciate their contribution by directly referring to these books.

On Images of New Economy

- Hesselbein, F., Goldsmith, M., and Beckhard, R. (Eds.) (1997) *The Organisation of the Future*. Jossey-Bass: SF, CA.
- Magretta, J. (Ed.) (1999) 'Managing in the New Economy'. Harvard Business School Press: Boston, MA.
- Morgan, G. (1997) *Images of organization*. Sage: Thousand Oaks, CA.

On HRM

- Becker, B.E., Huselid, M.A. and Ulrich, D. (2001) *The HR Scorecard: Linking People, Strategy and Performance*. Harvard Business School Press: Boston, MA.
- Pfeffer, J. (1998) *The human equation*. Harvard Business School Press: Boston, MA.

- Ulrich, D. (1997) *Human resource champions: The next agendas for adding value and delivering results.* Harvard Business School Press: Cambridge, MA.
- Russ-Eft, D., Preskill, H. and Sleezer, C. (Eds.) (1997) *Human resource development review: Research and implications.* Sage: Thousand Oaks, CA.
- Storey, J. (Ed.) (2001) *Human Resource Management: A critical text.* 2nd Edition. Thomson Learning: London.
- O'Reilly, C.A. and Pfeffer, J. (2000) *Hidden value: How great companies achieve extraordinary results with ordinary people.* Harvard Business School Press: Boston, MA.
- *Harvard Business Review on Managing People* (1999). Harvard Business School Press: Boston, MA.

On HRM, Learning Organization and Knowledge Management

- Krogh, G. Ichiyo, K. and Nonaka, I. (2002) *Enabling Knowledge Creation.* Oxford University Press. New York.
- Horibe, F. (1999) *Managing knowledge workers.* Wiley: Toronto.
- Newell, S., Robertson, M., Scarbrough, H. and Swan, J. (2002) *Managing knowledge work.* Palgrave: UK.
- Pedler, M., Burgoyne, J. and Boydel, T. (1997) *The learning company.* McGraw-Hill: London.
- Argyris, C. (1999) *On organisational learning.* Blackwell: Oxford, UK.
- Senge, P., Kleiner, A., Ross, R.B. and Smith, B.J. (1994) *The fifth discipline fieldbook: Strategies and tools for building a learning organization.* Nicholas Brearley: London.
- Senge, P.M. (1990) *The Fifth Discipline: The art and practice of the learning organization.* Random House: New York, NY.
- *Harvard Business Review on Knowledge Management* (1998). Harvard Business School Press: Boston, MA.
- *Harvard Business Review on Organizational Learning* (2001). Harvard Business School Press: Boston, MA.

On Recruitment

- Harris, J. and Brannick J. (1999) *Finding and keeping great employees.* AMACOM: NY.
- Woodruffe, C. (1999) *Winning the talent war:* A strategic approach to attracting, developing and retaining the best people. Wiley: Chichester.
- *Harvard Business Review on Finding and Keeping the Best People* (2001). Harvard Business School Press: Boston, MA.
- Wood, R. and Payne, T. (1998) *Competency-based recruitment and selection.* Wiley: West Sussex, England.

On Performance Management

- Smither, J.W. (Ed.) (1998) *Performance appraisal: State of the art in practice.* Jossey-Bass: SF.

On Reward Management

- White, G. and Drucker, J. (2000) *Reward management: A critical text.* Routledge: London.
- Risher, H. (1999) *Aligning pay and results.* AMACOM: NY.
- Zingheim, P.K. and Schuster, J.R. (2000) *Pay people right!* Jossey-Bass: SF.
- Rynes, S.L. and Gerhart, B. (Eds.) (2000) *Compensation in organizations: Current research and practice.* Jossey-Bass: SF.
- Thorpe R. and Homan G. (Eds.) (2000) *Strategic reward systems.* Prentice-Hall: Harlow, England.

On International HRM

- Hofstede, G. (2001) *Culture's consequences.* 2nd Edition. Sage: Thousand Oaks, CA.
- Mendenhall, M. and Oddou, G. (Eds.) (2000) *Readings and cases in international human resource management.* South-Western: Ontario.

◻ Gannon, M.J. and Newman, K.L. (Eds.) (2002) *The Blackwell handbook of cross-cultural management*. Blackwell: Oxford.

◻ Dowling, P.J., Welch, D.E. and Schuler, R.S. (1999) *International human resource management: Managing people in a multinational context*. South-Western: Cincinnati, OH.

Index